Phonics Teacher's Book

Teaching *Jolly Phonics* with *Phonics Pupil Books 1, 2* and *3*.

Written by

Sara Wernham and Sue Lloyd

Edited by Louise Van-Pottelsberghe

Contents

PART 1

Introduction

For ease of use, the *Phonics Teacher's Book* has been divided into two distinct parts. The first part (with yellow page borders) gives a comprehensive introduction to *Jolly Phonics* and explains the *Jolly Phonics* teaching method in detail. It is a good idea to read the first part of this book before using the *Phonics Pupil and Teacher's Books* in the classroom. The second part of this book provides a thorough and structured lesson plan for each day of phonics teaching. The lesson plans in this part of the book are designed specifically for use with the corresponding pages in *Phonics Pupil Books 1, 2* and *3*.

The *Phonics Pupil and Teacher's Books* provide a programme for teaching the skills of reading and writing in English. The focus of the programme is on the teaching of the English alphabetic code; this includes teaching the ways in which the code knowledge is put into practice. The phonics teaching, covered in Part 2 of this book, is not intended to take up all the time allocated for English lessons. This means that teachers are free to teach the other aspects of literacy, such as comprehension and poetry, in the remaining time.

The *Jolly Phonics* programme is multi-sensory, active and specifically designed for young children. There are activities in the *Phonics Pupil Books* and corresponding guidance in the *Phonics Teacher's Book* for each day. Useful supplementary materials are also mentioned in this book, although all of the teaching can be carried out without the support of these extra materials. For instance, whiteboard software, called *Phonics for the Whiteboard*, is available for those teachers who have interactive whiteboards in their classrooms. This product includes printable worksheets, which support the phonics teaching. The *Phonics Pupil Books* and the *Phonics for the Whiteboard* software cover the same teaching and can be used together in the classroom. The *Phonics Pupil Books* are designed so that each book follows the same teaching as the corresponding step in the whiteboard software.

With the *Phonics Pupil Books*, the children are not just taught the alphabet sounds, but all the 42 main letter sounds and how they are written. With this knowledge, they are taken through stages of blending sounds together to form words and then on to reading. At the same time the children are taught to write by listening for the sounds in spoken words and identifying the letters corresponding to those sounds. This skill is also referred to as 'segmenting'.

The main 42 letter sounds are introduced at a rate of one a day. Most children are very capable of coping with this fast and stimulating pace. However, the rate of introduction can be adjusted according to the number and duration of lessons available and the age of the children.

The *Phonics Teacher's Book* offers step-by-step lesson plans, which bring a better understanding of the *Jolly Phonics* programme and the activities in the accompanying *Phonics Pupil Books*. Teachers using the *Phonics Pupil and Teacher's Books* can be assured that their children will read and write independently at an earlier-than-average age.

In this introduction, the teaching programme has been divided into the following five basic skills, each of which has its own section:

1. Learning the Letter Sounds
2. Learning Letter Formation
3. Reading (Blending)
4. Identifying the Sounds in Words
5. Tricky Words

Although in this introduction the teaching has been separated into these five basic skills, in the *Phonics Pupil Books* the first four skills are taught simultaneously from the beginning and the fifth skill, learning the tricky words, is taught after the first few weeks.

Learning to read and write fluently is vital for children. All parents know this and want their children to master these skills. The majority of parents are keen to help, but are not sure how to go about it. It is a good idea to invite new parents to a meeting, where it is explained to them how reading and writing is taught in the school. These meetings provide an opportunity to introduce the *Phonics Pupil Books* and to explain how the parents can support their children.

The *Jolly Phonics* method of teaching was developed and tested over a period of time at Woods Loke Primary School in Lowestoft, England. Before 1975, reading was taught at this school using an essentially visual, whole-word approach. Most children read well. However, there was always a group of children who had problems remembering words and who could not cope satisfactorily with reading or writing. These children did not pick up letter sounds easily or relate them to words. It was, therefore, decided to teach the letter sounds first, to see if early letter knowledge would help them. This approach proved to be much more successful for the children as a group, and those children who had problems were much fewer in number.

This outcome reflects the findings of several research studies, which found that knowing the letters was the best predictor of success in learning to read.

Later, in the early 1980s, Woods Loke Primary School introduced some structured blending, in addition to the letter-sound work. The school then took part in an external research experiment. The children were first taught to listen carefully for the sounds in words, to identify them, and to relate them to the letters (phonemic awareness). This teaching method made it much easier for the children to learn to read and write. They became fluent readers much earlier than before, and best of all, the group of children with reading problems was almost non-existent. It was rare to have a child in the school scoring below 90 on the Young's Reading Test, and the average was between 110 and 116. (The Young's Reading Test is designed so that a score of 100 is the average. It is also designed so that half of all children will fall in the range 90-110). The children learnt to read much faster when they knew the letter sounds and could work out words for themselves. Independent writing started much earlier than usual and accurate spelling developed more quickly.

These results also reflect the findings of independent research studies, which show that both blending skills and phonemic awareness are strong predictors of reading success.

The key advantages of *Jolly Phonics* are that it teaches children to recognise all the main letter sounds early on, and that it shows them how to relate the sounds to the symbols, and so, to understand the alphabetic code used for reading and writing. At an early stage, the children have a way of writing every letter sound and this means that they are soon able to write whatever they wish. With *Jolly Phonics*, children can be taught to read at a young age, even at a pre-school age.

The effectiveness of *Jolly Phonics* has been highlighted by numerous research studies, in which the achievements of children taught with *Jolly Phonics* have been much greater than those of children taught with other methods. A number of research studies can be viewed on the Jolly Learning website:

www.jollylearning.com

The letter sounds of the English language:

a	ant, sand, caravan	
ai	**ai**m, **ai**d, dr**ai**n	(long /a/)
b	**b**at, **b**end, cra**b**	
c	**c**at, **c**ot, du**ck**	
d	**d**og, **d**ip, su**dd**en	
e	**e**gg, **e**nd, sh**e**d	
ee	**ee**l, cr**ee**p, tr**ee**	(long /e/)
f	**f**og, li**f**t, **fl**u**ff**	
g	**g**oat, **g**ap, di**gg**er	
h	**h**op, **h**it, **h**ill	
i	**i**nk, **i**nstant, dr**i**nk	
ie	p**ie**, t**ie**, d**ie**	(long /i/)
j	**j**elly, **j**et, **j**umper	
k	**k**ing, **k**ind, **k**ettle	
l	**l**eg, **l**ost, she**ll**	
m	**m**an, **m**ill, shri**m**p	
n	**n**ut, **n**ip, spi**n**	
o	**o**strich, **o**n, sp**o**t	
oa	**oa**k, **oa**ts, b**oa**t	(long /o/)
p	**p**lug, **p**et, ste**p**	
qu	**qu**een, **qu**ick, **qu**ack	
r	**r**un, **r**abbit, ba**rr**el	
s	**s**and, **s**un, twi**s**t	
t	**t**op, **t**ug, ma**t**	
u	**u**p, **u**nder, lu**n**g	
ue	val**ue**, arg**ue**, c**ue**	(long /u/)
v	**v**an, **v**et, gi**v**e	
w	**w**ind, **w**ent, s**w**im	
x	bo**x**, o**x**, fle**x**	
y	**y**ell, **y**es, **y**ellow	
z	**z**oo, **z**ebra, bu**zz**	
sh	**sh**ip, **sh**op, wi**sh**	
ch	**ch**op, **ch**ick, mu**ch**	
th	**th**is, **th**en, wi**th**	(voiced /th/)
th	**th**in, **th**ick, **th**imble	(unvoiced /th/)
ng	so**ng**, ba**ng**, stri**ng**	
oo	l**oo**k, b**oo**k, f**oo**t,	(little /oo/)
oo	m**oo**n, sp**oo**n, sh**oo**t	(long /oo/)
ar	**ar**t, **ar**m, st**ar**t	
er	h**er**b, st**er**n, sist**er**	
or	**or**der, c**or**n, st**or**m	
oi	**oi**l, **oi**ntment, sp**oi**l	
ou	**ou**t, cl**ou**d, f**ou**nd	

These letter sounds can be heard at: www.jollylearning.com

1. Learning the Letter Sounds

All words are made up of sounds. There are at least 42 sounds in English, but only 26 letters are used to represent these sounds. For reading and writing, the children need to be fluent at saying the sounds that go with the letters.

Initially, only one way of representing each sound is taught. Afterwards, the main alternatives are covered. For example, at first, the /ai/ sound is taught with the ‹ai› spelling, as in *rain*. Later on, the alternatives ‹ay›, as in *day,* and ‹a_e›, as in *came,* are taught.

All of the main 42 letter sounds are introduced in *Phonics Pupil Book 1* (43 letter sounds are listed, but ‹c› and ‹k› make the same sound). One page is devoted to each letter sound, with a number of activities designed to teach the basic skills. Each letter sound is introduced through a story, which is provided in the *Phonics Teacher's Book*. Pictures, linked to the story and the action, are provided in the *Phonics Pupil Books* for the children to colour.

Young children learn particularly quickly when there is a physical activity involved. By doing an action for each letter sound, the children use movement, sight, hearing and speech to help them remember. This multi-sensory approach is a very effective way of teaching, as well as being fun for the children. The action boxes are provided in *Phonics Pupil Book 1* as a guide for the parents and as a reminder for the children.

Merely introducing the letter sounds will not ensure that the children have learnt them; the letter sounds must be revised regularly. The revision is usually carried out with flash cards showing the letter sounds. Teachers can either make these flash cards, or purchase the *Jolly Phonics Cards*.

Every day, flash cards showing the letter sounds that have been taught should be held up for the children to say the sound and do the action. Alternatively, letter sounds can be written on the board for this purpose. The aim of the revision is to develop fluency and an automatic response to the letters.

Occasionally, the children should be encouraged to say the letter sounds without doing the action. On these occasions, you could tell the children to sit on their hands; this amuses them, and helps them to avoid doing the actions.

Rate of introduction

The first letter sound can be introduced on the children's first day. Their enthusiasm for learning is high and this provides a meaningful start for the children.

Where possible, it is recommended that the letter sounds be introduced at the rate of one letter sound a day. Although this may seem a great deal at first, children are able to cope with it and look forward to their new letter sound every day. All the 42 letter sounds are introduced at this rate, so that they can be covered in about nine weeks. The result is that children become competent readers much sooner, and can use all these letter sounds to produce more expressive independent writing at a much earlier stage than is usual.

If the children are younger than four or five, if they do not have a lesson every day, or if there are other special factors, then the rate of introduction of the letter sounds is likely to be slower. The teacher will need to decide on the appropriate pace for his or her own class. If a slower pace is adopted, then it is important to avoid asking the children to read books that contain letter sounds that they have not yet been taught. Children will not be able to decode (work out) words if the relevant letter sounds have not yet been taught.

Introducing each letter sound

In the first lesson, the /s/ sound is introduced. Start the lesson by telling a story about the /s/ sound, or by reading the story from the *Phonics Teacher's Book*. The sound and the action are incorporated into each story. In this case, the snake makes the /ssss/ sound, and the movement of the snake provides the action; the children weave their arm like a snake saying /ssss/. The children are told that /s/ is one of the letter sounds.

If the *Finger Phonics Books* are available, they can be used at this stage to help illustrate the stories. These books also have grooved letters, which allow the children to see and feel the shape of the letters. A *Jolly Phonics Wall Frieze* is also useful in the classroom. This can be used to make a cheerful wall display, which acts as a visual reminder of each letter sound. Young children may also enjoy singing the songs linked to each letter sound, which are available as *Jolly Songs* and *Jolly Jingles*.

Once the /s/ sound has been introduced with the story, the children should look at the letter ‹s› in their *Phonics Pupil Books*. The children can then be shown the letter ‹s› on a flash card, on the *Wall Frieze*, or in the *Finger Phonics Books* before being shown how to form the letter correctly. The teaching of correct letter formation is covered in Section 2: Learning Letter Formation. The children then look at the picture of the snake, and the action box in their *Phonics Pupil Books*. The picture on the page can then be coloured in. In the first few lessons, the children can play 'hunt the letter sound' by searching for it in books, or around the classroom. This helps the children to understand the link between the letter sounds and the words in books.

In *Phonics Pupil Book 1*, the emphasis should be on the lower case letters. The capital letters, although shown in the book, need only be referred to incidentally. Capital letters are dealt with in more depth in *Phonics Pupil Books 2* and *3*. In the very early stages, it is important that all letters are introduced by their sounds and not by their names. In this case, say /sssss/ and not /ess/ when introducing the /s/ letter sound.

The other letters are introduced in a similar fashion. When /a/, /e/, /i/, /o/ and /u/ are taught, the children need to know that they are 'special letters', and are called vowels. Later, they will be told useful rules that relate to the vowels, which will help them with reading and spelling. The children can then be taught that the other letters are called consonants.

Reinforcement of the letter sounds is very important. Flash cards showing the letters that have been taught should be held up during every lesson for the children to call out the sounds. It is important that the cards are shown in a random order so that the children truly recognise the letters and do not simply recite the sounds in order. The faster children are at recognising the letters and saying the sounds, the easier it is for them to read and write.

Learning to read and write in English is complicated because there are more than 42 sounds, but only 26 letters with which to write them. This means that sometimes two letters are put together to make a new sound, as with /sh/, /ee/, /ou/ and /ng/. These are called digraphs, and they are different from blends. A digraph has just one sound, for example, the /sh/ in *ship*, whereas a blend has two or more sounds, for example, the /s-t/ in *stop*. This is an important difference, as will be seen in Section 4: Identifying the Sounds in Words.

The ‹oo› and ‹th› digraphs are initially introduced in two sizes. This helps the children to understand that they each make two sounds, as in *book* and *moon*, and *this* and *thin*.

oo	(little /oo/ in *book*)
oo	(long /oo/ in *moon*)
th	(voiced /th/ in *this*)
th	(unvoiced /th/ in *thin*)

When preparing the children for cursive writing, a helpful start is to show them how the two letters in digraphs join. This also develops the understanding that sometimes two letters are needed to make one sound. Forming the letters in the air enables the children to feel how they go together.

Order of the letter-sound groups

The letter sounds are arranged in groups of six. They have been ordered carefully, so as to aid learning. For instance, the first six letters can be used to make many simple words, such as *pin*, *tip*, *pan*, *sat*. This means that it is possible for the children to make words at an early stage in their learning. Furthermore, the letters that are often confused, such as ‹b› and ‹d›, are in separate groups. The ‹c› is introduced early on, because it forms a template for writing the letters ‹a›, ‹d›, ‹o›, ‹g›, ‹q›. The letter-sound groups, listed below, are used throughout the *Jolly Phonics* materials.

The letter-sound groups

1. s, a, t, i, p, n
2. c k, e, h, r, m, d
3. g, o, u, l, f, b
4. ai, j, oa, ie, ee, or
5. z, w, ng, v, little oo, long oo
6. y, x, ch, sh, voiced th, unvoiced th
7. qu, ou, oi, ue, er, ar.

Revision of the letter sounds

As well as holding up flash cards, there are lots of activities that will help the children to learn the letter sounds. Large letters could be placed in the corners of the room and the children told to run to the correct corner when they see or hear one of the letter sounds.

By taking part in a number of activities, all of which aim to achieve the same goal (learning the letter sounds), the children are stimulated and become more enthusiastic.

Letter names

Initially, it is helpful to use only the letter sounds when teaching children to read and write. When letter names are introduced at the same time as the letter sounds, many children become confused. For this reason, it is recommended that the teaching of letter names is left until *Phonics Pupil Books 2* and *3*. A good way of introducing the letter names is through the alphabet.

The alphabet is introduced in four colour-coded sets in *Phonics Pupil Book 2*. This helps to prepare the children for using a dictionary, as each set of letters corresponds to roughly a quarter of the words in a dictionary. Once the letter names have been taught, you could ask the children to say letter names when flash cards are held up.

Alternative spellings of vowels

Once children have learnt the 42 letter sounds taught in *Phonics Pupil Book 1*, they need to be aware of the alternative ways in which some of the vowel sounds can be written. The table opposite details the alternative vowel spellings, most of which are taught in *Phonics Pupil Books 2* and *3*.

Alternative vowel spellings

Long /a/	**ai** a_e ay	rain, waist, drain date, plate, flame day, stay, play
Long /e/	**ee** e_e ea	seed, bleed, street these, theme, seat, cream, read
Long /i/	**ie** i_e y igh	pie, tie, lie pipe, line, shine my, fly, cry night, fight, bright
Long /o/	**oa** o_e ow	boat, float, goat bone, close, smoke snow, slow, pillow
Long /u/	**ue** u_e ew	value, argue, cue cube, fuse, mule few, pew
Little /oo/	**oo** u	book, foot, shook put, push, pudding
Long /oo/	**oo** ue ew u_e	moon, fool, shoot glue, blue, true blew, flew, brew rude, flute, rule
/er/	**er** ir ur	supper, sister, blister bird, shirt, third turn, burn, purse
/or/	**or** au aw al	fork, port, storm fault, pause, taunt claw, saw, shawl talk, walk, chalk
/oi/	**oi** oy	oil, coin, spoil boy, toy, enjoy
/ou/	**ou** ow	loud, mouse, cloud cow, clown, brown

Supplementary work

In most classes, there will be a few children who are not learning the sounds fast enough to keep up with the other children. This could be for any number of the following reasons:

1. The child may have a poor memory for letter sounds and words.
2. The child's attendance is, for some reason, limited.
3. The child's concentration is poor.
4. There is little individual help given at home.

Whatever the reason, the problem must be overcome. Extra individual or group teaching in class may be necessary.

Sometimes, a child who knows the letter sounds well is able to listen to a struggling child go through the letter sounds and help the struggling child to learn them.

The cooperation of parents is also invaluable. At the parents' meeting, it helps to inform parents that approximately 20% of children have some problems with learning to read and write, not because they are unintelligent, but because they have a poor memory for symbols and words. If their child is not managing to learn a letter sound a day, it is likely that they are amongst this 20% and will benefit from some extra help.

Parents need to know when their child is struggling, so they can understand their child's problem, and give their time to helping him or her. Young children are keen and enjoy the attention of their parents. One idea would be to write out the 42 letter sounds on small pieces of card or paper. The known letter sounds could be put in a box or envelope for the child to take home and revise. The remaining letter sounds should be added to the box gradually, at a pace with which the child can cope. The aim of this exercise is to reinforce knowledge and develop fluency.

Once the main aspects of the alphabetic code are mastered, and reading and writing are relatively fluent, the children will generally manage well in school and keep up with the others.

Conclusions

It is vital that the children know the letter sounds; they need to be able to say the sound as soon as they see the letter(s).

However, learning the letter sounds is not enough. The children need to know how to apply their letter knowledge. From the beginning the children should be taught to blend the sounds and hear the words for reading. This is a technique that can be taught and is explained in Section 3: Reading. For writing, the children need to be taught to hear the sounds in words and know which letter(s) are needed for those sounds; this is explained in Section 4: Identifying the Sounds in Words.

2. Learning Letter Formation

For young children to learn fluent, neat handwriting they need to be taught how to hold their pencil and form their letters correctly. Early mastery is well worth the extra effort involved. Anyone who has tried to correct an older child's bad pencil hold, or incorrect formation, knows how difficult, if not impossible, it can be. It is far better to teach it correctly from the start.

Pencil hold

The pencil rests between the thumb and the first finger. The next finger prevents the pencil falling down; the last two fingers are tucked away. The hand rests on the table and the movement of the pencil is through the thumb and first finger. It is important that the knuckles point outwards. Young children are amused if their fingers are likened to 'froggy legs'. They move the pencil forwards and backwards with their 'froggy legs'!

Letter formation

A multi-sensory approach to teaching helps the children to learn more easily. For this reason, the children are introduced to the formation of each letter in the following ways:

1. The teacher shows the formation on the board.

2. The teacher shows the formation in the air, taking care when facing the children that the letter is formed the correct way round for the children (in mirror writing, from the teacher's own point of view). The children hold up their fingers and follow the movement,

saying the sound at the same time. They do this several times.

3. In the *Phonics Pupil Books*, a line of dotted letters is provided for the pupils to write on. Arrows guide the pupils in the correct direction. The teacher, if possible, watches them write and tries to check that they are forming the letters correctly. The dotted line helps the children to understand that all the letters are the same size, except for the tall sticks and the tails.

4. The children feel the formation in the cutout letter grooves in the *Finger Phonics Books*.

5. The children can watch the formation of the letters on the *Phonics for the Whiteboard* software, *Jolly Phonics DVD*, or the *Phonics Games CD*. The *Phonics Games CD* also gives the children a chance to form the letters themselves.

The following list covers the basic letter knowledge needed for good handwriting:

1. All the letters are the same size except the seven letters that have sticks above the body of the letter: ‹b›, ‹d›, ‹f›, ‹h›, ‹k›, ‹l› and ‹t›, (note that the ‹t› is not quite as tall as the other tall letters), and the six letters that have tails that go below the line: ‹f›, ‹g›, ‹j›, ‹p›, ‹q› and ‹y›.

2. Most letters go down towards the line first: ‹b›, ‹h›, ‹i›, ‹j›, ‹k›, ‹l›, ‹m›, ‹n›, ‹p›, ‹r›, ‹t›, ‹u›, ‹v›, ‹w›, ‹x›, ‹y› and ‹f›. (Note that ‹f› has a little arch backwards before it goes down.)

3. The following letters start like a ‹c›: ‹a›, ‹d›, ‹o›, ‹g›, ‹q›. In *Jolly Phonics*, these are referred to as the 'caterpillar c' letters.

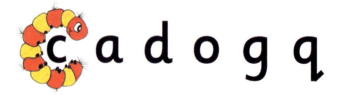

4. ‹z› and ‹e› start by going towards the end of the page. Note that ‹e› starts lower than the other letters and comes back over like a 'caterpillar c'.

Parents can be invaluable here. They are in a good position to encourage correct formation and a good pencil hold. This can be explained at the parents' meeting.

The children are told that the letters in a word are written close together, but without bumping. They are also told to leave a space between words. It is important to revise the formation of each letter regularly. When the children are writing, especially during dictation, it is a good idea to check the pencil hold and make sure the letter formation is correct.

Capital letters

Phonics Pupil Book 1 concentrates on the formation of lower-case letters. Later, in *Phonics Pupil Book 2*, the formation of the capital letters is taught. Capital letters are the same size as tall letters. They all go down to the line first, apart from: ‹C›, ‹G›, ‹O› and ‹Q›, which go round anticlockwise first. Capital letters do not join.

Joined-up writing

In *Jolly Phonics*, the children are encouraged to use joined handwriting at an early stage. This is recommended because the children develop greater fluency in their writing and because joined-up writing encourages better spelling. The children feel how the letters go together by writing the word in one continuous movement, which reminds them to put the letters in the correct order. It is for this reason that *Jolly Phonics* uses the Sassoon Infant typeface. Many of the letters in this font, such as ‹m›, ‹h› and ‹a›, have a joining tail at the end (an 'exit' stroke). By first learning to form letters with the joining tails, children progress more naturally to joined-up writing.

The ideal time for introducing joined letters is when the digraphs are being taught. The children are shown how letters join together and are reminded that sometimes two letters are needed to make one sound. Once again, if the children form and join the letters in the air with their hands they find it much easier when it comes to putting it down on paper.

Supplementary work

Some children have poor motor control. They need more practice if they are to form letters correctly and neatly. Colouring the pictures, and tracing the letters and patterns in their books can help the children to develop this skill. In addition, using lined paper encourages the children to limit the size of their letters, and allows for greater accuracy when it comes to their letter formation.

Conclusions

By concentrating on correct letter formation and pencil hold from the beginning, bad habits can be prevented. It also makes it easier for the children to develop neat, fluent, joined handwriting, and to take pride in their work.

3. Reading (Blending)

When reading, children need to understand the meaning of the words. Before they can do this, they have to be able to work out what the words say. The phonic skill for this is to look at the letters, say the sounds and hear the word. This is called blending. Blending is sometimes referred to as synthesising, which is why *Jolly Phonics* is known as a synthetic phonics programme.

In the beginning most children are not able to blend, and need to be taught how. With the ability to blend, the children are able to read unknown regular words. They are also in a far better position to attempt the so-called irregular words, as no words are completely irregular.

The pages of the *Phonics Pupil Books* are a good starting place for teaching blending. Take the /s/ page; the teacher should ask the children if they can see a picture of a /s-u-n/. Only a few children in the class will hear the word *sun*, after it has been split into its individual sounds. After a few more examples, such as /s-p-ie-d-er/, /s-n-ai-l/ and /f-l-ow-er/, one or two more children might be tuned in to hear the words. The following day, after teaching the next letter sound, a few examples from the /a/ page could be called out, such as /a-n-t/ and /a-rr-ow/. Any object on the page could be used, although short words are preferable. Each day, a few more children will be able to hear the words. Some children have a natural ability for blending, but success comes to all in the end.

Once the children can hear the word when an adult says the letter sounds, they are ready to try saying the sounds for themselves and try listening for the word. Blending needs practice, and should be started as soon as possible. On most days, teachers should try to write short regular words, using the letters that have been taught, on the board or on flash cards. Examples of such words are: *tap*, *pan*, *pit*, *sit* and *pin*. The children then say the sounds and listen for the word. The daily Word Bank in the *Phonics Teacher's Book* is useful for this activity. In addition to the Word Bank, there are words to blend each day on the letter sound pages in *Phonics Pupil Book 1* (although the pages for /s/ and /a/ show only the sounds). Children should not use any actions when blending words.

The children who can hear the words understand how the alphabetic code works for reading. They realise that it is something they can work out for themselves. This knowledge fascinates them and their confidence grows.

For most children, blending is relatively easy. However, some children find it difficult and need to be taught exactly what to do. There are two main reasons for children not being able to hear the word when they have said the sounds:

1. **They do not know the letter sounds well enough.**
   As soon as the child sees a letter, the sound should come automatically to them. If they have to pause to think, they lose track of the word. To correct this, it is necessary to revise the

sounds regularly with flash cards, actions and other letter-sound activities.

2. **The letter sounds are emphasised wrongly.**

The emphasis should be on the first letter sound, for example, on the /d/ of /d-o-g/. If the children put the emphasis on the last letter sound, they may try to start the word with that sound and fail to hear the word.

There are two types of sound in English. One sort makes a pure, continuous sound; examples are the sounds, /sssss/, /ffffffff/, /rrrrr/, /mmmm/, /nnnnn/, /vvvvvv/. The other sort has a 'schwa' on the end. The schwa is like an /uh/ sound on the end of the letter sounds. For example, /b/ cannot be said without a schwa: /buh/. The continuous sounds can be said with, or without, the schwa. Sounds should be said with as little schwa as possible.

With blending, the first sound needs to be louder than the others. This helps the children to remember the sound the word starts with. The sounds that follow in the word need to be spoken softly and quickly, and the schwa should be avoided where possible. This technique has been found to be effective and about three quarters of the children master it quite quickly. Although blending is more difficult for the other quarter of the group, all they need is more practice. Frequently, in a whole-class situation, the children who are good at blending call out the answer too quickly and the less able copy them, as they do with letter sounds on flash cards. To remedy this situation, teachers can provide an extra blending session for the weaker children.

Blending skills can be improved if the children practise saying initial consonant blends on their own. Examples of common consonant blends are: /cr/, /fl/ and /str/. It is important to make sure that the children have been taught the individual letter sounds and are just learning to blend separate sounds together. For example, if the /w/ letter sound has not yet been introduced, then avoid using the /sw/ blend. Saying the blend makes it easier to read the words that have initial consonant blends. The children are encouraged to work the word out by saying the blend, followed by the individual sounds, for example, /pl-a-n/, and not /p-l-a-n/. In *Phonics Pupil Book 1*, words with initial consonant blends are introduced from page 17 onwards.

When blending words with digraphs, the children have to remember to look at the two letters and say one sound. This more complicated skill is mastered when regular words, using the digraphs, are blended. For example, flash cards can be made showing regular /ai/ words, like *pain*, *rain*, *train*, *Spain*, *hail* and *snail* so that, when the /ai/ sound has been taught, they can be held up for the children to sound out aloud and blend. Alternatively, the words could be written on the board for the class or for a group to blend.

Another way to develop speedy blending is to snap together the initial consonant(s) and the short vowel. Teachers can, on a regular basis, write a few of these consonant-vowel combinations on the board, and encourage those pupils who are weaker at blending to read them.

Consonant-vowel combinations

pa	pe	pi	po	pu
na	ne	ni	no	nu
ra	re	ri	ro	ru
fra	fre	fri	fro	fru
sta	ste	sti	sto	stu
gra	gre	gri	gro	gru

Initially, the children blend words by calling out the sounds aloud, but gradually, they should be encouraged to blend silently in their head. This promotes fluency for reading.

One activity for developing this skill involves the teacher doing the actions for a word without saying the sounds. For example, with the word *pin*, the teacher does the actions for the letter sounds, in this case puffing on the finger for the /p/, wiggling fingers on the nose for the /i/ and the arms out for the /n/ sound. The children try and work out the word and either write it down or call it out. Alternatively, a child could mime the actions for the sounds in a word, or three children could do one letter-sound action each. Another simple way to help children learn to blend sounds in their heads is as follows; the teacher writes letters randomly on the board and then points to one letter after another, spelling out a word. The children watch this and try to put the sounds together in their head to identify the word.

Once the children have started to blend simple words, it is important to provide many words for them to read, using their newly acquired blending skills. This will develop the essential fluency that is needed. Eventually blending should become an automatic response from the children every time they are confronted with a word that they have not seen or read before. Many words are provided in the *Phonics Teacher's Book*. More words are available in the *Jolly Phonics Cards*, the *Jolly Phonics Wordbook* and in the Word Bank, which can be printed from the *Jolly Phonics Resources CD*. Other blending activities are available on the *Phonics Games CD* and in the *Jolly Phonics Workbooks*.

Introducing decodable storybooks

During the first nine weeks, the aim is to prepare the pupils for reading books. Stories and poems can be read to the pupils, but the children should not be expected to try to read books for themselves until they have learnt the 42 letter sounds and the twelve tricky words that are introduced in *Phonics Pupil Book 1*.

Teachers and parents may find it difficult not to give the children books to read for themselves in the first few weeks. However, spending this extra time devoted to letter work at the beginning means that the benefits of following this programme can be greater, with higher reading abilities gained and much lower levels of remedial help needed. The children gain confidence and can enjoy storybooks independently at an earlier stage.

Storybooks intended for children to read themselves are best introduced once the child can work out simple regular words independently, and after *Phonics Pupil Book 1* has been completed. Ideally, decodable readers, such as the *Jolly Phonics Readers*, should be used initially. There are a number of progressively difficult levels in the *Jolly Phonics Readers*. In addition, there are two sets of *Jolly Phonics Read and See* books for any children who have not yet mastered the necessary skills and who need extra blending practice and letter-sound knowledge.

Jolly Phonics Readers: Red Level (first level)
The words in these books are spelt regularly and can be read using knowledge of the 42 letter sounds and the 12 tricky words taught in *Phonics Pupil Book 1*. The children will also need to recognise the tricky word *of*, which is introduced in the *Jolly Phonics Readers*.

Jolly Phonics Readers: Yellow Level (second level)
These books follow on from the Red Level and can be read when the new sound for ‹y›, which occurs in the words *funny*, *happy* and *floppy*, has been introduced, and the next ten tricky words have been learnt. This teaching is covered at the beginning of *Phonics Pupil Book 2*.

Jolly Phonics Readers: Green Level (third level)
These books follow on from the Yellow Level and can be read when the 'magic ‹e›' or 'hop-over ‹e›' words, such as *late*, *these*, *fine*, *hope* and *cube*, have been introduced and the next twenty tricky words have been learnt. This teaching is covered in *Phonics Pupil Book 2*.

Jolly Phonics Readers: Blue Level (fourth level)
These books follow on from the Green Level and can be read when the remaining tricky words have been learnt, and when the following alternative vowel spellings have been taught: ‹ay›, ‹ea›, ‹igh›, ‹ow›, ‹ew›, ‹ir› and ‹oy›. These are common spellings found in words such as: *day*, *seat*, *light*, *snow*, *brown*, *stew*, *bird* and *boy*. This teaching is covered in *Phonics Pupil Books 2* and *3*.

Note that the amount of text increases with each level, and light type is used for those few letters that should not be sounded out, such as the silent ‹b› in *lamb*.

When pupils can read the Blue Level Readers fluently and have completed *Phonics Pupil Books 1*, *2* and *3*, they are able to read any material that is appropriate for their intellectual age and knowledge of vocabulary.

Reading schemes

If it is not possible to use decodable readers, then the next most effective books are those linked to a reading scheme. Reading scheme books should use a controlled vocabulary, which is initially limited as much as is possible to regular words, and gradually increases to include words that have alternative or irregular spellings. Most pupils, who have been taught with *Jolly Phonics*, are able to cope well with this limited structure. However, the weaker children can struggle.

Great care should be taken to match the structure of the books to the reading ability of the pupil. When children are given books that use words that they cannot work out, they lose confidence in blending and start trying to remember the words by their shape, or simply to guess. This frequently leads to serious reading problems. Good readers are good at blending and they use this technique every time they meet an unknown word. Conversely, poor readers are poor at blending and rarely use this technique. It is important that teachers do not cause their children problems by failing to develop their blending skills sufficiently well, or by giving them the wrong type of books too early.

Once there is fluency in the reading and in the working out of unknown words, the children have the ability to read anything that is appropriate for their intellectual age. If they understand text when it is spoken to them, they will understand it when they read it themselves. It is at this stage that the children start reading to learn instead of learning to read. They also begin to read for pleasure, which encourages them to read more books. This, in turn, further improves their literacy skills and increases their vocabulary.

Helpful hints for blending

The following hints enable the children to blend more words. The extra knowledge helps to develop their understanding and confidence.

1. **When two vowels go walking, the first does the talking**
   When two vowel letters appear together in a word, the sound made is often the long vowel sound of the first letter. The second vowel says nothing. The following type of words can be worked out with this understanding: *dream* and *people*. The saying, 'When two vowels go walking, the first does the talking,' amuses the children and helps to remind them that usually the first vowel is spoken and the second vowel is silent. Occasionally, it is the second vowel that gives the sound, as in the words *young* and *field*, and the children delight in finding the 'naughty' second vowel!

2. **If the short vowel doesn't work, try the long one**
   This saying is a good hint to know for blending. It helps with words like *he, be, blind, mind, acorn, union, able, emu* and *item*. The saying also helps the children cope with the split digraphs, introduced in *Phonics Pupil Book 2*, which are often called 'magic ‹e›', or 'hop-over ‹e›', words. The following words have a 'magic ‹e›'

in them: *late*, *theme*, *pipe*, *home*, *cube*. The ‹e› on the end of the word does not say a sound itself, but the so-called 'magic' hops back over the consonant and changes the first vowel from a short vowel to a long one.

3. Shy ‹i› and toughy ‹y›

The letter ‹i› is very 'shy' and 'toughy y' takes its place. The words *day* and *boy* are not written *dai* or *boi*, because ‹i› is too 'shy' to go on the end, so 'toughy y' takes its place. The letter ‹i› is replaced by ‹y› in words like *funny*, *system* and *toy*. For young children, it is enough for them to know that when a ‹y› is not the first letter, it often takes the place of the ‹i›, and it is then a vowel. When blending a ‹y›, which is not the first letter, the children should first try the short ‹i› and, if that doesn't work, try the long ‹i›. With some accents, ‹y› can make an /ee/ sound when it comes at the end of words such as *happy*, *merry* and *holly*.

4. Soft ‹c› and soft ‹g›

If the letter ‹c› is followed by the vowels ‹e›, ‹i› or ‹y›, the sound is usually softened to a /s/, as in the words *ice*, *race*, *city*, *circle* and *cycle*. Similarly, when a letter ‹g› is followed by an ‹e›, ‹i› or ‹y›, the /g/ sound usually changes to /j/, as in *gently*, *giant* and *gymnastics*. This teaching is covered in *Phonics Pupil Book 3*. Flash cards showing these types of words help to reinforce the pattern.

5. Alternative vowel spellings

Lastly, the seven alternative ways of writing the vowels, listed in the table below, cannot be worked out using the above helpful hints, and will need to be learnt as alternative spellings.

/igh/	/ew/	/ir/	/ur/	/au/	/aw/	/al/
night	few	bird	turn	fault	saw	ball
light	stew	girl	nurse	haunt	draw	talk
high	flew	shirt	curl	taunt	straw	small

Supplementary work

Children need to have plenty of blending practice. In Part 2 of this book, lists of words and sentences are provided for blending practice in an exercise entitled: Further Blending Practice. For this exercise, the teacher writes the words and sentences on the board for the children to read as a class. The children should be encouraged to spot any tricky words, and to blend any unknown words. Once the children have read the sentences with their teacher, they can discuss them and the teacher can explain the meanings of any words that the children do not understand.

A few children seem to have great difficulty learning to blend. It is easy to think that they may never achieve this skill. However, with extra support and practice, they will succeed. These children tend to be those who have a poor visual memory. The ability to blend will be even more essential for these children, as they will always have difficulty memorising words.

The Word Banks and Further Blending Practice in Part 2 of this book provide words for this extra practice. When the children have developed the necessary skills and are ready to read books for themselves, it is important that they are given decodable books. The decodable books used should contain only the letter sounds and tricky words that have been taught and learnt. Once the children use their blending skills automatically, know the letter sounds and read fluently, they are able to read any books that are suitable for their age and intellect.

Conclusions

Children who can blend words fluently have few problems with reading. Once the fluency is there, reading extension and comprehension become the more important aspects. Early phonic teaching with *Jolly Phonics* makes reading and writing easier for all children. For those children with a poor memory for words, it is absolutely essential.

4. Identifying the Sounds in Words

Hearing the sounds in words is one of the main skills needed for writing. For example, when children can hear each sound in a simple word, and know how to write the letters for those sounds, they can write hundreds of words by themselves, such as *mat*, *pen*, *hop*, *lid*, *fun*, *run* and *sunset*.

From the beginning, the children are taught how to write the letter sounds as they are introduced to them. This was covered in Section 2: Letter Formation. At the same time, the children are taught to identify the sounds in words. The first step is to encourage them to listen for the sound that is being taught. There is an example of this kind of activity for every lesson in *Phonics Pupil Book 1*. For example, the first letter sound is /s/, so the pupils have to look at the pictures of a *sun*, *snail*, *spider* and *flower* and decide which word does not have a /s/ sound in it. Initially, only a few children will have the ability to hear this. Gradually, all the children listen more carefully and start to answer correctly. They may even be able to say whether the sound comes at the beginning, in the middle, or at the end of the word.

The second step, which starts after the first few pages of *Phonics Pupil Book 1*, is to ask the pupils to listen and identify all the sounds in a word, and to hold up a finger for each sound. For example, *pan*, *sit* and *rain* each have three sounds: /p-a-n/, /s-i-t/ and /r-ai-n/. Identifying sounds is a skill known as phonemic awareness. A few examples should be done every day. At the beginning, you should use the letter sounds that have been taught. For example, the word *pat* could be used when the /p/ letter sound has been taught. Ask the children what sound comes at the beginning of *pat*. When a child identifies the /p/, hold up a finger (usually the thumb), and ask the children to do the same. Then ask for the next sound in *pat*, placing a strong emphasis on the /a/. When the /a/ is identified, hold up the second finger (usually the index finger), and ask for the last sound. Hold up the next finger when the /t/ sound is called out. Then do the same with other words, such as *sit*, *at* and *sat*. Call the word out and encourage the children to say the sounds with you, holding up a finger for each sound. In the beginning, the children are guided by their teacher, but after a short while the children hold up their fingers and call out all the sounds by themselves.

Teachers could also demonstrate the skill of writing by asking for the sounds in the words and writing the letters on the board as the children call them out. The word can then be blended and read. This allows the children to see the significance of encoding to write and decoding to read. It is this understanding that makes the children confident and the programme so successful. Later on, the children learn that the English language is not quite so simple. There are several alternative ways of writing the letter sounds, and sometimes there are quite bizarre spelling patterns. However, by going from simple skills and gradually introducing the more complex ones, virtually all the children become successful readers and writers.

When most of the children can call out the sounds in three-letter words, longer words can be tackled. This often involves hearing the single sounds in consonant blends. Frequently, the children fail to hear one of the consonants, and might write 'fog' instead of *frog*, or 'wet' instead of *went*.

Initial consonant blends

bl-	cl-	fl-	pl-	sl-	br-	cr-	dr-	fr-	gr-	pr-
tr-	st-	sc-	sm-	sn-	tw-	shr-	thr-	scr-	spr-	str-

Final consonant blends

-lb	-ld	-lf	-lk	-lm	-ln	-lp	-lt	-ct	-ft	-nt
-pt	-st	-xt	-mp	-nd	-sp	-sk	-nk			

In order to help the children hear all the sounds in initial and final consonant blends, call out the blends and ask the children to say the sounds, holding up a finger for each sound. For example, say /cr/ and ask the children to respond with the sounds /c/ (holding up the thumb) and /r/ (holding up the index finger). Repeat with a few other consonant blends. Take care that these letter sounds have already been taught. Then, on a regular basis, call out a few words with consonant blends, so that the children can count the sounds. Any of the following examples could be used for this exercise.

Examples of words with initial consonant blends

bran	clap	clip	club	flag	flat	flap	flip	glad
plan	plug	plum	plot	slap	slim	slug	crab	crop
drag	drip	drop	drug	drum	frog	from	grab	grim
grip	print	prop	trim	trap	trip	smog	snap	snip
snug	swam	swim	swum	twig	twin	spin	span	stop

Examples of words with final consonant blends

bulb	held	golf	milk	silk	film	help	gulp	belt
melt	quilt	gift	lift	soft	ant	pant	bent	went
tent	mint	hunt	kept	next	camp	damp	lamp	bend
mend	wind	pond	felt	desk	risk	best	nest	lost
must	sank	west	ramp	plump	slept	frost	grand	crisp

When the digraphs are being taught, the children need to understand that sometimes they have to write two letters for one sound. The first digraph taught is the /ai/ sound. The children listen for the sounds in a word, such as *nail*, and call out /n-ai-l/, holding up a finger for each of the three sounds. Then other /ai/ words can be called out for the children to identify the sounds in them, such as *rain, paint, sail, fail, pain, drain*.

Once the children can hear the sounds in these words, it is relatively easy for them to write similar words during dictation, in their *Phonics Pupil Books*. There are also games on the *Phonics Games CD*, which encourage children to identify the sounds in words, providing them with the practice they need.

Letter board

This can be made from a large piece of card. Three smaller strips of card are stapled across the first sheet, so that letters can be slotted into the strips. The vowels are placed on the top row and some consonants, needed for making words, are placed on the bottom row.

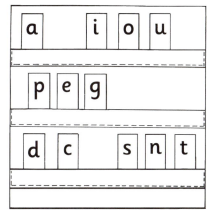

The teacher asks a child to make a word by putting the letters in the middle strip. For example, with the word *peg*, the children listen for the sounds and a child is chosen to pick out the letters and place them in the correct left to right order. Then the rest of the class can indicate if

they think the word is correct or not (thumbs up for 'yes', and thumbs down for 'no'). Then, all the children blend the word to check if it is correct. If it is wrong, the child might like to have another go. After that, the teacher could ask, 'Who can change it from *peg* to *pen*?' and then, 'Who can change *pen* to *spend*?'

Regular word building with the letter board shows the children, in a practical way, how regular words are built up. Alternatively, a similar activity could be carried out with magnetic letters.

Dictation

Dictating letters, words and sentences is important for developing writing skills. Dictation begins almost immediately in *Phonics Pupil Book 1*, with the teacher calling out letter sounds that have been taught. All the children attempt to write the letter sounds. Then the teacher can write the letter sounds on the board and the children look to see if they have written them correctly. The number of letters dictated increases as confidence grows. In the beginning the standard of achievement will probably range from very good to hardly legible.

Word dictation starts at the time the letter sound /c k/ is taught. First of all, a few letter sounds are dictated and then the words *it* and *at*. Each child has to try and identify the sounds and write the letters for the sounds. Encourage the children to write the letters in a word close together, but with no bumping. When the first word has been attempted, ask the children to call out the sounds and watch you write the letters on the board. Then the children can see if they have written their word correctly. Some teachers encourage the children to put a little tick next to the word if they are correct. At this stage, not all children will be able to write the words; they may only get the first letter sound. However, it is not long before they start to tune in to the sounds and realise what is expected of them. Some children may need extra support at home or at school.

Dictation of regular words with consonant blends and digraphs should follow on from the dictation of simple CVC words (consonant-vowel-consonant words). The digraphs can be written in joined-up handwriting, as mentioned in Section 1: Learning the Letter Sounds.

Once the children are familiar with some tricky words, and know how to spell a few of them, sentences can be dictated. The sentences should be made up of regular words, which can be written by listening for the sounds, and can include those tricky words that have been taught. Sentence writing begins in *Phonics Pupil Book 2* and is the start of independent writing. The exercises in *Phonics Pupil Book 2* not only provide the opportunity for practice writing words, but also give the children a feeling for what a sentence is and that a capital letter and full stop are needed. Additional sentences suitable for this exercise are available on the *Jolly Phonics Resources CD*.

The dictation of capital letters, once they have been taught, is needed to make sure that the children know how to write them. This is also covered in *Phonics Pupil Book 2*. Frequently, young children have the ability to recognise the capital letters, but this does not necessarily mean they know how to write them.

In the beginning, only one way of writing a digraph is used; for example the long /a/ sound is taught as ‹ai›. So words used for dictation should be restricted to those with the ‹ai› spelling, such as *rain*, *drain*, *tail*, *Spain*, *pain*.

Independent writing

Independent writing is the desired outcome. When the children have learnt the letter sounds, can identify the sounds in words and have done some dictation, they are well on their way to being able to write independently.

As soon as children can hear the sounds in words and know one way of writing each sound, they can write anything they want to write. In the early stages, children might not use conventional spelling, but their work will still be readable: for example, 'mie mum poot mie book in mie scool bag'. Accurate spelling comes through reading many books, knowing the alternative letter sounds and following a systematic spelling programme.

This is an example of a child's writing after just over half a year (reduced to half of its original size).

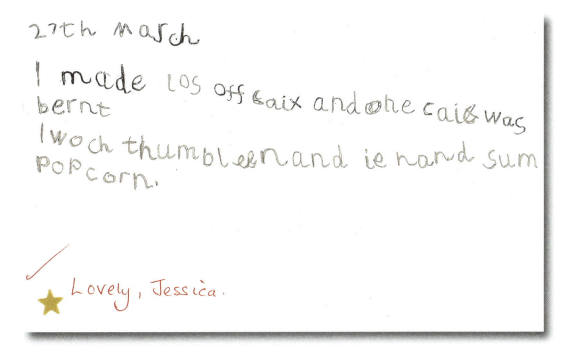

27th March

I made los off caix and ohe caig was bernt Iwoch thumbleen and ie nand sum popcorn.

Lovely, Jessica.

Notice how this child has joined up some of the digraphs: ‹ch›, ‹ee›. However, she needs to listen more carefully to some words, so that she can hear the ‹t› in *lots*, and that *had* does not have a ‹n› in it.

Developing independent writing

Independent writing starts in *Phonics Pupil Book 2*. At this stage, the children are used to word building, listening for the sounds and writing the appropriate letters. In *Phonics Pupil Book 2*, a themed picture is provided and the pupils are asked to say sentences about the picture and make up a little story about it. The children are then given a model sentence to copy into their books.

In *Phonics Pupil Book 3*, the children are provided with a theme only; they have to draw their own picture and write about it. Some of the words, those that are difficult to spell accurately through listening for the sounds, can be written on the board. Teaching tips for each independent writing exercise are provided in the *Phonics Teacher's Book*.

Initially, the teacher reads out the model sentence that is provided in the notes, and the children, with help from the teacher, work out how to write it. The sentence has a controlled vocabulary so that it uses only those tricky words that have been taught, and regular words using the 42 letter sounds. This enables the children to work out the sentence for themselves by calling out the letters for the tricky words and identifying the sounds in the regular words, which the teacher writes on the board. The children are then encouraged to copy this sentence under their picture.

When those children who are good at writing words from dictation finish copying their sentence, they can be encouraged to write some more sentences by themselves. Naturally, at a young age, it is impossible to spell all the words correctly and close attempts are acceptable.

Marking policy

Children's earliest efforts at independent writing do not need rigorous marking. Missing sounds can be pointed out and any tricky words already taught can be corrected.

It is impossible for young children to have the freedom to write exactly what they want to say and spell all the words correctly. If everything is corrected it is demoralising, and discourages the children from writing freely. Generally speaking, it is best to restrict the errors marked to about four words. These words can be learnt with the 'Look, Copy, Cover, Write and Check' method, referred to in Section 5, once the work has been marked.

By the end of the second year at school the majority of words are written correctly. If the error is one that the child should have known not to make, it should be marked. However, if the error is not due to carelessness, and the word is out of the ordinary, a dot can be placed underneath it. This tells the child that the word is spelt wrongly, but that their attempt was a good one and the correct spelling will be taught later. Teachers should select four words, which the child has spelt wrongly, for them to revise underneath.

Those children who have a good visual memory and a certain amount of maturity, but have been careless, need more rigorous marking than those children who are less able. In the end, it comes down to judgement. It is not encouraging to have too many red pen marks over a piece of work, but as they get a bit older the children need to know when they are wrong, and to learn from their mistakes. The use of dictionaries is encouraged once the skill of looking up words has been mastered. This skill is taught in the *Grammar 1* and *2 Pupil and Teacher's Books*.

Supplementary work

Most children will learn to hear the sounds in words during class lessons. The few who are finding it difficult may need to be taught in the same manner, but in a smaller group, or if necessary individually.

The Further Blending Practice words, provided in the Daily Lesson Plans, are ideal for improving the children's blending skills, but they can also be used to encourage the children to hear the sounds in words. The teacher copies the list of words onto the board and blends them with the children. Then the teacher reads each word again, more slowly this time, and asks the children to identify the individual sounds, holding up a finger for each sound. In the Daily Lesson Plans for *Phonics Pupil Books 2* and *3*, the Further Blending Practice words often contain some of the alternative letter-sound spellings that the children have learnt. For example, after the children have been introduced to the soft ‹c› and soft ‹g› in *Phonics Pupil Book 3*, words like *space* and *fragile* are included in the Further Blending Practice section. Teachers can ask the children to spot the alternative letter-sound spellings when the list of words is written on the board.

Conclusions

The aim of this teaching is to enable the pupils to hear the sounds in regular words and to write the letters that relate to those sounds. A different technique is needed for coping with words that are spelt irregularly. This is covered next, in Section 5: Tricky Words.

In every class, there will be a few children who find it difficult to memorise the letter sounds and who struggle to blend and segment words. These children tend to have a weak visual memory and poor auditory skills. However, this does not mean that they need different teaching from the more able children; they simply need the same teaching, but more of it.

It is necessary to identify any struggling children at an early stage. It is a good idea to provide some extra teaching for these children if possible. Not all of the children who are struggling will be at the same stage; there will be a range of abilities. Some children will only need extra support for a few weeks before they begin to make steady progress. Other children may have more significant difficulties. Despite their differences, all the children should receive the same type of teaching. With regular blending and writing practice and by revising the letter sounds, teachers can ensure that the children master these skills.

5. Tricky Words

Tricky words are either irregular, such as *to*, *your*, *one* and *said*, or are frequently used words that can only be read with phonic knowledge that has not yet been taught, for example the words *made*, *like*, *my* and *here*. The children like to think of the awkward bits as being out to trick them! Despite this, some part of a tricky word will be regular. For example, in the word *come*, the ‹c› and ‹m› are regular. The children might find it helpful to underline the tricky part(s) of each tricky word in their *Phonics Pupil Books*.

Children are more able to read tricky words when they have knowledge of letter sounds and can relate those sounds to symbols. They should, initially, blend the letter sounds and then learn the correct pronunciation. The children find it interesting to look carefully for the 'tricky' part in the words; by doing this they start to analyse words. The children's extra attention to the details helps to store the word in their memories. For example, if the children recognise that the letter ‹a› in the word *was* has an /o/ sound, they are more likely to remember the correct spelling.

The first set of tricky words is introduced towards the end of *Phonics Pupil Book 1*. It is important that tricky words are taught in a systematic way and with plenty of revision.

Learning to spell tricky words

The children should learn how to spell the tricky words after they have been taught to read them. Some fortunate children have a sufficiently good visual memory to master the spelling of the tricky words just by reading them, but most children have to be taught. The following six techniques for teaching spelling, listed below, are all useful.

1. Look, copy, cover, write, check

This is the principal method for teaching the spelling of tricky words in the *Phonics Pupil Books*. The children first look at the word and identify the tricky part(s). For instance, the word *said* has an /e/ sound in the middle, but it is spelt with an ‹ai›. The ‹s› and ‹d› are regular. Then the children say the letter names (not the letter sounds) several times. The reason for saying the names rather than the sounds is that the letter names trot off the tongue more easily and these particular words do not sound out reliably. After that, the children trace the word in the air or on the table, saying the letter names as they do so. Following that, they copy the word by going over the dots in their *Phonics Pupil Book*, saying the letter names again. Then they cover up the dotted word, and write it on their own in the next column, looking back to see if it is correct. This is repeated in the last column. Encourage the children to continue saying the letter names as they write the word. Regular revision and dictation ensure that the spelling of these words is mastered.

2. Word wall

In *Jolly Phonics*, the tricky words are divided into six colour-coded groups, of twelve tricky words each. The blue group comes first, then yellow, and so on. The coloured groups correspond to the colours suggested for the tricky word flowers in the *Phonics Pupil Book*s and on the *Phonics for the Whiteboard* software. These colours are also used on the *Tricky Word Wall Flowers*, which are designed to be used as a wall display. The flowers can be pinned to a wall once the tricky word they contain has been taught; in this way, the wall display builds up week-by-week. Alternatively, you could make your own display by writing each tricky word onto card shapes and pinning these to the wall as you teach the words.

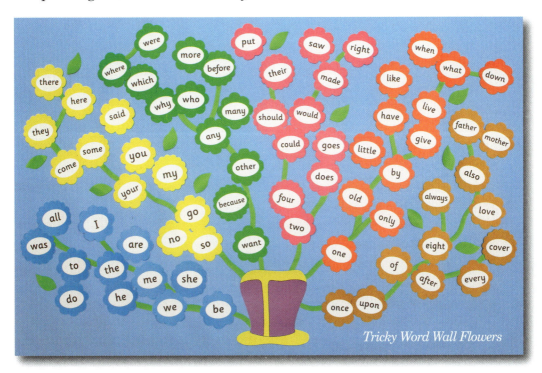

Tricky Word Wall Flowers

3. Say it as it sounds

This spelling method is useful for words, though not necessarily high-frequency ones, which have one element that makes the word difficult to spell. Take, for example, the word *Monday*. The difficult part is the ‹o›, because instead of having an /o/ sound, it has an /u/ sound. It helps the children to remember this awkward spelling if they say the word as it should be spoken, so that *Monday* starts like the word *monster*. Frequently, these odd spellings have other words that follow the same pattern, in this case words like *monk*, *monkey*, *month* and *money*. Sometimes it helps to introduce the other words at the same time, depending on how useful you think it will be for the children at this stage, and how capable they are.

Another awkward aspect of spelling is the fact that we often swallow the pronunciation of the vowels, particularly in words with more than one syllable. For example, the ‹e› in *children* has an /uh/ sound, which is known as a schwa. It often helps the children to spell these words if they 'say it as it sounds', in this case by emphasising the /e/.

Silent letters can also be taught in this way. By pronouncing the ‹w› at the beginning of words like *write, wrong, wrap* and *wring*, the children find it much easier to spell the words correctly. Teachers can make a list of these words as they occur and then, in odd moments, call out the words so that the children can say them as they are spelt, pronouncing the silent letters and the swallowed vowels.

Teacher says	Children respond
mother	'**mo**ther' (to rhyme with *bother*)
doctor	'doct**or**' (emphasising the /or/)
Wednesday	'**Wed**-**nes**-day'
front	'fr**o**nt' (with an /o/ sound and not an /u/)
knock	'***k***-nock'
island	'***is***-land'

4. Word families or patterns

When one word is taught, it is helpful to show others with the same spelling pattern. For example, the word *like* could be linked to *bike, trike, hike, pike,* and other words ending in ‹ike›. Each word family can then be linked to a wider group, in this case, ‹i_e› words, such as *hive, pine, pipe, shine, line, mine, time* and *rice*.

Later, more awkward patterns can be taught, including the worst letter combination of all, the ‹ough›, found in words like *rough, ought, plough, doughnut* and *through*. Note that in each of these words the ‹ough› has a different sound. Fortunately, there are not too many of this type of word.

5. Does it look right?

When children are uncertain about how to spell a word, they can write it down on some scrap paper, trying different ways of writing it. This is particularly useful for working out the vowels, which often have more than one way of being written. For instance, *brown* could be written 'broun' or 'brown' and *bird* could be 'berd', 'burd' or 'bird'. The children choose the one that looks right. At a later stage, the children should be encouraged to look up the correct spelling in a dictionary, especially when their dictionary skills are good enough.

By dictating the tricky words regularly, teachers can check how well the children are learning to spell them. Similarly, frequent use of tricky word flash cards will help the children to read these words. On the *Phonics Games CD* the children can revise reading and spelling the tricky words by playing the relevant games.

Vowels and helpful hints for spelling

The way vowels work is probably the least understood aspect of phonic teaching. Many of the vowels have more than one way of being written. In addition, vowels often have irregular spellings. Some knowledge about vowels is useful, but it is important that you do not get too bogged down in rules.

Generally, the early rules relate to the short vowels /a/, /e/, /i/, /o/ and /u/. When the children have been taught to listen for the short vowel and can easily identify it in words, they can understand the following rules:

1. A short word with a short vowel, followed by a /ck/ sound, is written with a ‹ck›, as in *black, neck, tick, tock, duck*. If the word does not have a short vowel, then only the ‹k› is required, as in *look, dark, jerk* and *leek*.

2. In a short word with a short vowel, ending in ‹f›, ‹l›, ‹s› or ‹z›, the final consonant needs to be doubled, as in *cliff, spill, miss, buzz*. The few exceptions include the very short words *if, is* and *of*.

3. If the suffixes ‹ing›, ‹ed›, ‹er› or ‹y› are added to a short word with a short vowel, there must be at least two consonants before the suffix. If the short word has only one consonant at the end, then this consonant is usually doubled before the suffix is added. This means that in *running, stopped, thinner* and *funny*, the final consonants of the original words, *run, stop, thin* and *fun* have been doubled. If there are already two consonants at the end of the word, no such doubling is needed. Furthermore, if the word does not have a short vowel, it is not necessary to have two consonants before the suffix, so *looking, heated, lighter* and *dreamy* have only one consonant.

Conclusions

The tricky words in English always cause problems. Learning to read these words is easier than learning to spell them. By teaching the children to observe the irregularities, and by giving them techniques and simple rules, you are enabling them to be more accurate in their spelling. A certain amount of rigour is needed when teaching the awkward spellings, particularly when teaching children who do not have a good visual memory.

PART 2

Teaching with Phonics Pupil Book 1

The *Phonics Pupil Books* are designed so that each page is a complete phonics lesson.

The majority of *Phonics Pupil Book 1* is devoted to the letter sound pages, which introduce the children to the main 42 sounds of the English language. With the letter sound pages, the children are not only taught how to recognise each letter sound, but are also introduced to one way of writing each sound. Towards the end of *Phonics Pupil Book 1*, the children are taught how to read and spell the first twelve tricky words and there are a number of activity pages, which help the children to begin to use their letter-sound knowledge for reading and writing.

The letter sound pages

There is one page for each of the letter sounds, but the teaching on each page follows the same pattern and the following four activities are covered daily.

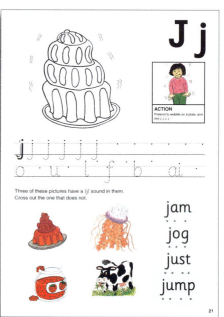

1. Learning the letter sound
- Each letter sound is introduced with a story, which is provided for the teacher in the Daily Lesson Plan.
- Throughout each story, the letter sound of the day is repeatedly emphasised, and a letter-sound action emerges from the story, which helps to make the letter sound more memorable for the children.
- A picture, linked to the story, and an illustration of the action are provided on the pages of *Phonics Pupil Book 1* as a further reminder for the children.

2. Letter formation
- The letter of the day is printed at the top of each page. Both the capital letter and the lower-case letter are shown, but the children need only learn the formation of the lower-case letter at this early stage. The capital letters are taught thoroughly in *Phonics Pupil Book 2*, and should only be referred to incidentally at this point.
- The Daily Lesson Plans give instructions for teaching the children how to form the letters correctly. A corresponding activity on each page in *Phonics Pupil Book 1* shows precisely how each letter is written and provides dotted letters for the children to write over.

3. Blending

- There are words for the children to blend in the coloured panels on each page and a number of extra words for blending practice provided in a daily word bank. All the blending words use only the letter sounds that have been covered at that point.
- For more information about blending, see pages 16 to 22 of the introduction.

4. Identifying the sounds

- A number of pictures are provided on each letter sound page.
- The children say the words corresponding to each picture. When they come across a word that does not contain the sound of the day, they cross out its picture.
- A number of further activities are explained in the Daily Lesson Plan, along with the letters and the words for dictation.

The tricky word pages

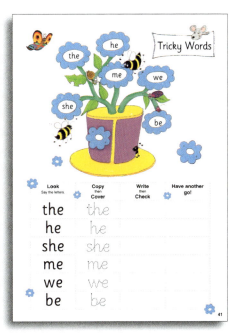

Once the main 42 letter sounds have been introduced, the children are taught to read and spell some of the most common tricky words. For more information, see pages 30 to 33 of this book for the section on tricky words. The tricky words introduced in *Phonics Pupil Book 1* are as follows:

> the, he she, me, we, be,
> I, was, to, do, are, all.

The tricky words are introduced in colour-coded sets in the *Phonics Pupil Books*. This first set of twelve words is referred to as the blue set and the words are displayed in blue flowers in *Phonics Pupil Book 1*.

The reading and writing pages

The reading activities on these pages help the children to consolidate their letter-sound and tricky word knowledge and provide them with the opportunity to practise their blending skills.

Whenever the children are expected to write a word, a line is provided for each sound in that word, with a longer line indicating that a digraph is required. This reminds the children that they have to listen for all the sounds in a word in order to write it. At this point, the children are only expected to write single words.

Letter Sound /s/

Story

· Introduce the sound /s/ using a story, such as the one below, and the action.

It is a sunny morning, and Sam is taking his dog, Sampson, for a walk. They like to walk down to the pond. Sam looks around as they walk along. He sees a toadstool, a red and yellow caterpillar, and a blackbird on her nest. When they get to the pond, Sam and Sampson spend some time watching the fish swim around. After a while, Sampson goes off and snuffles around in the grass. He finds a stick, which he brings back to Sam. Then he barks at Sam, and Sam throws the stick for Sampson to fetch. Sampson runs around, looking for the stick in the grass. Suddenly, Sampson starts barking, 'woof, woof, woof!' Sam skips over to see what Sampson has found. He hears a 'ssssss' sound, 'ssssss!' In front of Sampson is a spotty snake. It is rearing up and hissing loudly. Sam grabs hold of Sampson, and the snake slithers quickly away.

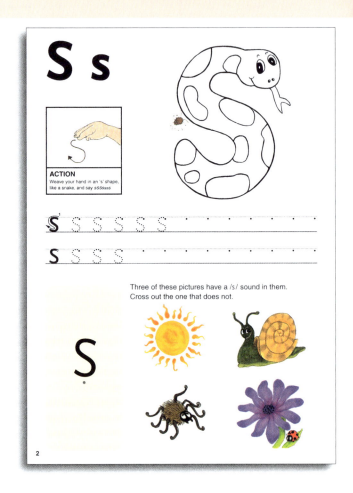

Action

· The children weave their arms like a snake while making a continuous /ssssss/ sound.

Formation

· Explain how the letter ‹s› is written.
· The children write over the dotted letters in their books.

Blending

· Encourage the children to try making the /s/ sound.
· No words can be read at this stage, as the children have only been taught one letter sound. However, even at this early stage, teachers can begin auditory blending can by encouraging the children to listen for the word when they have said the sounds. For example, the teacher says, /s-u-n/ and the children call out *sun*.

Sounding

· Say the words corresponding to the pictures on the children's page: *sun, snail, spider, flower*.
· The children listen for the word without the /s/ sound (*flower*), and cross out its picture.

Further ideas

· Sing the song from the *Jolly Jingles* or the *Jolly Songs*.
· Put up on the wall, or hold up, the /s/ section of the *Wall Frieze*.
· Paint or collage a snake shape.
· Make snake shapes from dough or modelling clay.

Letter Sound /a/

Flash cards
· Revise the sound /s/.

Story
· Introduce the sound /a/ using a story, such as the one below, and the action.

The Smith family is going on a picnic. The children help their mother pack the food. Adam packs the apples and Annie helps to make the jam sandwiches. At last, they are ready and set off for their picnic. When they arrive, they spread out a big picnic blanket and lay all the food on it. Annie rubs her arm. 'Something is tickling me,' she says. 'Something is tickling me, too,' says Adam, eating his apple. Then Annie shouts, 'a, a, a ants!' They all look at Annie and see some ants crawling up her arm. They all jump up. There are ants all over the picnic cloth! 'Oh dear,' says Dad. 'We must have put our cloth over an ants' nest.' They pack up their things and move to a nicer spot.

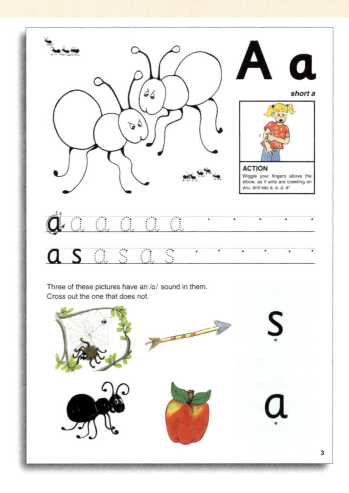

Action
· The children pretend that ants are crawling up their arms and say 'a, a, a'.

Formation
· Explain how the letter ‹a› is written.
· The children write over the dotted letters in their books.

Blending
· Point to the letters and say the sounds /s/ and /a/. No words can be read at this stage, as the children have only been taught two letter sounds. However, teachers can begin auditory blending can by encouraging the children to listen for the word when they have said the sounds.
· For example, the teacher says, /a-n-t/ and the children call out *ant*.

Sounding
· Say the words corresponding to the pictures on the children's page: *cobweb, arrow, ant, apple*.
· The children listen for the word without the /a/ sound (*cobweb*), and cross out its picture.

Dictation
· Call out the sounds /a/ and /s/ for the children to write.

Further ideas
· Sing the /a/ song from the *Jolly Jingles* or the *Jolly Songs*.
· Put up on the wall, or hold up, the /a/ section of the *Wall Frieze*.
· Cut out a large letter ‹a› shape from paper or card for each child. The children collage or paint their letter ‹a›.
· Cut some apples in half and use them to print shapes.

Letter Sound /t/

Flash cards
• Revise the sounds /s/ and /a/.

Story
• Introduce the sound /t/ using a story, such as the one below, and the action.

This morning, Tom and Tamiko watched an important tennis match on television. There was a big crowd waiting for the match to begin. When the players came on to the court, the crowd clapped. Then the match began, and the two tennis players hit the ball to each other, 't, t, t'. The people in the crowd turned their heads from side to side, watching the tennis ball. Now, Tom and Tamiko are outside, pretending to be the tennis players they saw on television. They hit the tennis ball to each other, 't, t, t'. Among the tulips, some animals are watching Tom and Tamiko play. The animals turn their heads from side to side, watching the ball, just like the crowd at the tennis match.

Action
• The children imitate watching tennis, turning their heads from side to side and saying 't, t, t'.

Formation
• Explain how the letter ‹t› is written. It is a tall letter and starts slightly higher up than the letters ‹s› and ‹a›.
• The children write over the dotted letters in their books.

Blending
• Point to the letters and say the sounds /s/ and /a/.
• Blend the words *at* and *sat*.
• Say the sounds with the children, then blend the sounds together and read the words.
• Encourage the children to point to the dot underneath each sound as they say it.

Sounding
• Say the words corresponding to the pictures on the children's page: *teddy bear, tortoise, tennis racket, sun.*
• The children listen for the word without the /t/ sound (*sun*), and cross out its picture.

Dictation
• Call out the sounds /t/, /a/ and /s/ for the children to write.

Further ideas
• Sing the song from the *Jolly Jingles* or the *Jolly Songs*.
• Put up on the wall, or hold up, the /t/ section of the *Wall Frieze*.
• Play tennis.
• Have a teddy bear day.
• Make model tortoises and turtles from modelling clay.

Letter Sound /i/

Flash cards
· Revise the sounds /s/, /a/ and /t/.

Story
· Introduce the sound /i/ using a story, such as the one below, and the action.

Zack has a white pet mouse. She lives in a cage on the desk in his bedroom. One evening, Zack forgets to close the cage door properly. The little mouse climbs out of the cage and starts looking around the desk. Suddenly, she sees the cat watching her. She squeaks, 'i, i, i,' and quickly runs across the top of the desk. Crash! She bumps into a bottle of ink and knocks it over. As the bottle falls, the lid comes off, and the ink spills out everywhere, even over the little mouse. The mouse keeps on running as fast as she can, scampering off the desk and across the room to a mouse hole she had seen from her cage. Safe in the mouse hole, she scrubs and scrubs at her fur, but she cannot get all the ink off. She decides that from now on she will make the mouse hole her new home and call herself 'Inky Mouse'. In the morning, Zack finds the mouse missing and sees a little set of inky footprints across the carpet, leading from the desk to the little mouse hole.

Action
· The children wiggle their fingers on the end of their nose, like whiskers, saying, 'i, i, i'.

Formation
· Explain how the letter ⟨i⟩ is written. The children write over the dotted letters in their books.

Blending
· Point to the letters and say the sounds /a/ and /i/.
· Blend the words *it* and *sit*.
· Say the sounds with the children, then blend the sounds together and read the words.
· Encourage the children to point to the dot underneath each sound as they say it.

Sounding
· Say the words corresponding to the pictures on the children's page: *igloo, arrow, insects, ink*.
· The children listen for the word without the /i/ sound (*arrow*), and cross out its picture.

Dictation
· Call out the sound /i/ and the other sounds already covered for the children to write.

Further ideas
· Sing the song from the *Jolly Jingles* or the *Jolly Songs*.
· Put up on the wall, or hold up, the /i/ section of the *Wall Frieze*.
· Make inky fingerprints.
· Hunt for the letter ⟨i⟩ around the classroom, for example, in books, or on posters on the walls.

Letter Sound /p/

Flash cards
• Revise the sounds /s/, /a/, /t/ and /i/.

Story
• Introduce the sound /p/ using a story such as the one below, and the action.

Paul likes to visit the city zoo near his home. His favourite animal there is the polar bear. 'The polar bear has big paws for paddling in the pool,' says the zookeeper. It is Paul's birthday soon and his mother asks if he would like a teddy bear as his present. Paul thinks about this, and says that he would prefer a polar bear! When his birthday arrives, Paul's friends Peng, Pavlo and Pat come to his party. They all play games and eat the party food: pineapple, pizza and popcorn. Then Paul's mother gives Paul his present. He unwraps the paper to find a perfect toy polar bear. After that, Paul's mother produces a big birthday cake, with purple icing. She has put trick candles on the cake. Every time Paul blows out a candle, it lights up again! He tries to puff out the candles, 'p, p, p, p, p,' but they keep re-lighting. Everyone laughs and claps and tries to puff out the candles, 'p, p, p'.

Action
• The children pretend their finger is a candle and try to puff out the trick candle, saying 'p, p, p'.

Formation
• Explain how the letter ‹p› is written. It has a stick that goes down under the line.
• The children write over the dotted letters in their books.

Blending
• Blend the words *pit, pat, tap, tip*.
• Say the sounds with the children, then blend the sounds together and read the words.
• Encourage the children to point to the dot underneath each sound as they say it.

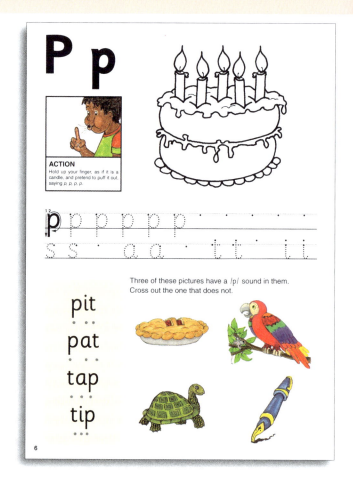

Sounding
• Say the words corresponding to the pictures on the children's page: *pie, parrot, tortoise, pen*.
• The children listen for the word without the /p/ sound (*tortoise*), and cross out its picture.

Word bank
pit, pat, tip, tap, sap, sip, pip.

Dictation
• Call out the sound /p/ and the other sounds already covered for the children to write.
• Call out some words from the word bank.
• The children listen to the words and hold up a finger for each sound.

Further ideas
• Sing the song from the *Jolly Jingles* or the *Jolly Songs* and pin up the /p/ section of the *Wall Frieze*.
• Collage parrot pictures with feathers.
• Paint pictures of things with the /p/ sound in, for example, pink poodles or spiny porcupines.

Letter Sound /n/

Flash cards
• Revise the sounds /s/, /a/, /t/, /i/, /p/.

Story
• Introduce the sound /n/ using a story, such as the one below, and the action.

Nicola has always wanted to go fishing with her Grandfather. Up until now, he has always said, 'No, you will get bored and make too much noise and you will scare the fish away. You can come when you get bigger.' But now Nicola is five and her Grandfather has agreed to take her fishing for an afternoon. Grandfather sets up the fishing rod and puts his net in the pond. Then he places a bucket on the ground and they both settle down to fish. Nicola sits very still and waits very quietly. She watches all the birds and insects flying around over the pond. It is very peaceful. Suddenly, Nicola and her Grandfather hear a very loud and very nasty noise, 'nnnn!' A plane is flying overhead! The plane does a noisy loop-the-loop in the sky above them. Grandfather doesn't like the nasty noise and puts his hands over his ears. Nicola looks at her Grandfather and laughs. 'You were worried I would make too much noise! Even I am never that noisy.' And, with a swoop and a swirl, she runs up and down on the bank, pretending that she is a plane, 'nnnnnnnnnnnn!'

Action
• The children put their arms out and pretend to be a 'nasty noisy aeroplane', making a continuous /nnnnnn/ sound.

Formation
• Explain how the letter ‹n› is written.
• The children write over the dotted letters in their books.

Blending
• Blend the words *nap, ant, pan, tin.*
• Say the sounds with the children, then blend the sounds together and read the words.
• Encourage the children to point to the dot underneath each sound as they say it.

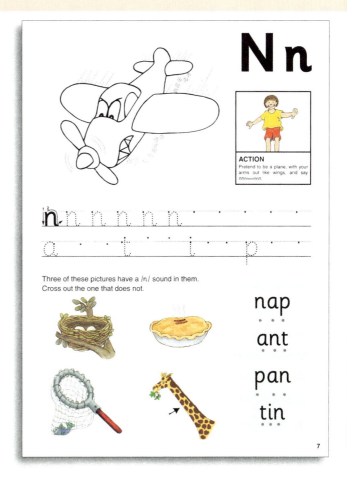

Sounding
• Say the words corresponding to the pictures on the children's page: *nest, pie, net, neck.*
• The children listen for the word without the /n/ sound (*pie*), and cross out its picture.

Word bank
nap, nip, pan, pin, tin, tan, ant, pant, snip, snap, span, spin.

Dictation
• Call out the sound /n/ and the other sounds already covered for the children to write.
• Call out some words from the word bank.
• The children listen to the words and hold up a finger for each sound.

Further ideas
• Sing the song from the *Jolly Jingles* or the *Jolly Songs.*
• Put up on the wall, or hold up, the /n/ section of the *Wall Frieze.*
• Think of some 'nasty, noisy things' and draw pictures of them.

Letter Sound /c k/

Flash cards
- Revise some of the sounds already learnt: /s/, /a/, /t/, /i/, /p/, /n/.

Story
- Introduce the sound /c k/ using a story, such as the one below, and the action.

The Khan family is on holiday in Spain. Mr. Khan has hired a car and the family decides to drive to a nearby village to visit the castle there. On the way, they pass a donkey carrying a big bundle of sticks. After they have seen the castle, the Khan family comes back to the village for a snack. Outside the café is the same donkey they saw before, enjoying a rest and a bucket of water. While the family is eating, a cat and her kittens play outside. As the clock strikes four, some Spanish dancers skip into the courtyard in front of the café. The ladies carry castanets and wear dresses in bright crimson, yellow and black. They clap and dance, swirling their dresses around and clicking their castanets, 'ck, ck, ck!'

Action
- The children click their fingers above their heads saying 'ck, ck, ck'.

Formation
- Explain how the letters ‹c› (caterpillar c) and ‹k› (kicking k) are written. The letter ‹k› is a tall letter and the children need to be careful to come up only a little way before doing the 'loop and kick'.
- The children write over the dotted letters.

Blending
- Blend the words *cat, kip, pick, sack*.
- Say the sounds with the children, then blend the sounds together and read the words.
- Note that there is a single dot underneath the ‹ck› in both *pick* and *sack*. When ‹c› and ‹k› are together in a word, they make a single /ck/ sound. So say /p-i-ck/ and not /p-i-c-k/ when blending these words with the children.
- Encourage the children to point to the dot underneath each sound as they say it.

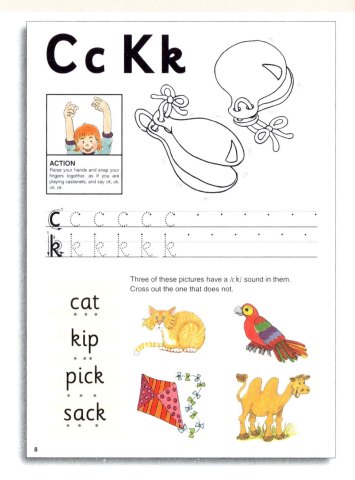

Sounding
- Say the words corresponding to the pictures on the children's page: *cat, parrot, kite, camel*.
- The children listen for the word without the /c k/ sound (*parrot*), and cross out its picture.

Word bank
cat, cap, can, kit, kip, kin, sack, sick, pack, pick, tick, tack, tank, sank, stack, snack, stick.

Dictation
- Call out the sounds /i/, /t/, /p/ and /n/ for the children to write down. Then ask the children to write a 'caterpillar c' and a 'kicking k'.
- Now tell the children that you are going to dictate a word: *it*. The children should say the word to themselves, listening for the sounds in *it*, and then write the word.
- Repeat this exercise with the word *at*.

Further ideas
- Sing the song from the *Jolly Songs* and pin up the /c k/ section of the *Wall Frieze*.
- Collage pictures of cats and kittens.

Letter Sound /e/

Flash cards
- Revise some of the sounds already learnt: /s/, /a/, /t/, /i/, /p/, /n/, /c/, /k/.

Story
- Introduce the sound /e/ using a story, such as the one below, and the action.

It is almost the end of the summer. Eric and his family have gone to stay on Ten Acre Farm for seven days' holiday. Every morning, they get up early to watch the cows being milked. After that, Eric likes to help out with the farm chores. He helps fetch buckets of water from the well. Then he pours the water into troughs for the cows to drink. Then Eric helps to feed the hens and collect the eggs. He takes the eggs into the kitchen for breakfast. Ellie, the farmer's wife, cracks open the eggs by tapping their shells on the side of the pan, 'e, e, e'. Then everyone eats fried eggs for breakfast.

Action
- The children pretend to hold an egg in one hand and tap it against a pan saying 'e, e, e'. Then, they use both hands to open the imaginary eggshell, and say 'e'.

Formation
- Explain how the letter ‹e› is written. It is an unusual letter, as it starts in the middle.
- The children write over the dotted letters in their books.

Blending
- Blend the words *set, pet, tent, neck*.
- Say the sounds with the children, then blend the sounds together and read the words.
- Encourage the children to point to the dot underneath each sound as they say it.

Sounding
- Say the words corresponding to the pictures on the children's page: *egg, ant, nest, hen*.
- The children listen for the word without the /e/ sound (*ant*), and cross out its picture.

Word bank
set, ten, pen, peck, neck, kept, net, pet, sent, tent, step, nest, pest, test, spent.

Dictation
- Call out the sound /e/ and some of the other sounds already covered for the children to write.
- Dictate the words *net* and *pen*.
- Call out some words from the word bank.
- The children listen to the words and hold up a finger for each sound.

Further ideas
- Sing the song from the *Jolly Jingles* or the *Jolly Songs*.
- Put up on the wall, or hold up, the /e/ section of the *Wall Frieze*.
- Paint egg shapes.
- Plant mustard or cress seeds in empty eggshells.

Letter Sound /h/

Flash cards
- Revise some of the sounds already learnt: /s/, /a/, /t/, /i/, /p/, /n/, /c/, /k/, /e/.

Story
- Introduce the sound /h/ using a story, such as the one below, and the action.

It is the school's summer fun day. In the morning, the children do fun things in the classroom, and in the afternoon there are races. Helen, Harry, Hanif and Harriet are in the hopping race. Mr. Heath starts the race. 'One, two, three, GO!' he shouts and waves his hat in the air. Helen, Harry, Hanif and Harriet hop as fast as they can. It is a hot day and hopping is hard work. Harriet is huffing and puffing by the time she finishes, 'h, h, h, h!' Miss Hopkins gives everyone huge drinks.

Action
- The children pretend that they are panting, and say 'h, h, h'.

Formation
- Explain how the letter ‹h› is written. It is a tall letter.
- The children write over the dotted letters in their books.

Blending
- Blend the words *hen, hat, hip, hiss*.
- Say the sounds with the children, then blend the sounds together and read the words.
- Encourage the children to point to the dot underneath each sound as they say it.
- Explain to the children that, when two letters making the same sound are next to each other, the sound is only said once.
- Say /h-i-s/ and not /h-i-s-s/, when blending the word *hiss* with the children.

Sounding
- Say the words corresponding to the pictures on the children's page: *kite, hen, horse, hand*.
- The children listen for the word without the /h/ sound (*kite*), and cross out its picture.

Word bank
hat, hit, hip, hen, hiss, hint, hectic.

Dictation
- Call out the sound /h/ and some of the other sounds already covered for the children to write.
- Dictate the words *hen* and *hat*.
- Call out some words from the word bank.
- The children listen to the words and hold up a finger for each sound.

Further ideas
- Sing the song from the *Jolly Jingles* or the *Jolly Songs*.
- Put up on the wall, or hold up, the /h/ section of the *Wall Frieze*.
- Have a hopping race.
- Make hedgehogs with handprint prickles.

Letter Sound /r/

Flash cards
•Revise some of the sounds already learnt: /s/, /a/, /t/, /i/, /p/, /n/, /c/, /k/, /e/, /h/.

Story
•Introduce the sound /r/ using a story, such as the one below, and the action.

Robert's family has a new puppy. They have to choose a name for him. Robert's parents like 'Rover', but Robert likes 'Ben'. Robert can't decide. He goes up to his bedroom with the puppy to fetch his roller skates. While Robert looks for the roller skates, the puppy explores the bedroom. Suddenly, Robert hears a loud 'ruff, rrrrrrrrrr!' The puppy has found a blanket and is shaking it from side to side. Robert gets hold of the blanket and tries to pull it away, but the puppy hangs on tightly, going, 'rrrrrrrr!' The blanket rips. 'Oh dear,' says Robert, holding up the ripped blanket. 'This looks like a rag now. I know, we'll call you Rags!'

Action
•The children pretend to be a puppy holding the blanket, shaking their heads and making a continuous /rrrrrr/ sound.

Formation
•Explain how the letter ‹r› is written.
•The children write over the dotted letters in their books.

Blending
•Blend the words *rat, rip, ran, rest*.
•Say the sounds with the children, then blend the sounds together and read the words.
•Encourage the children to point to the dot underneath each sound as they say it.

Sounding
•Say the words corresponding to the pictures on the children's page: *rabbit, dress, egg, rocket*.
•The children listen for the word without the /r/ sound (*egg*), and cross out its picture.

Word bank
rat, ran, rack, rip, rest, rap, trap, trip, track, crack, crest, crisp, strap, scrap.

Dictation
•Call out the sound /r/ and some other sounds already covered for the children to write.
•Dictate the words *rat* and *rip*.
•Call out some words from the word bank.
•The children listen to the words and hold up a finger for each sound.

Further ideas
•Sing the song from the *Jolly Jingles* or the *Jolly Songs*.
•Put up on the wall, or hold up, the /r/ section of the *Wall Frieze*.
•Make model rabbits from modelling clay.
•Paint a rocket picture.

Letter Sound /m/

Flash cards
- Revise some of the sounds already learnt: /s/, /a/, /t/, /i/, /p/, /n/, /c/, /k/, /e/, /h/, /r/.

Story
- Introduce the sound /m/ using a story, such as the one below, and the action.

Mrs. Morris and her son Marvin have invited his friends, Milly and Molly for supper. The children are playing outside when they hear the call for supper. They all come inside, wash their hands and sit down at the table. 'I'm hungry!' says Marvin, rubbing his tummy. 'Mmmmm, I hope it's spaghetti and meat balls.' 'I hope it's hot dogs, mmmmm,' says Molly. 'I hope it's hamburgers,' says Milly, rubbing her tummy. Then Mrs. Morris comes in, carrying a steaming dish. 'Lamb and peas,' say the children, 'mmmmm'. 'I like that meal most of all!' says Marvin, 'mmmmmm!'

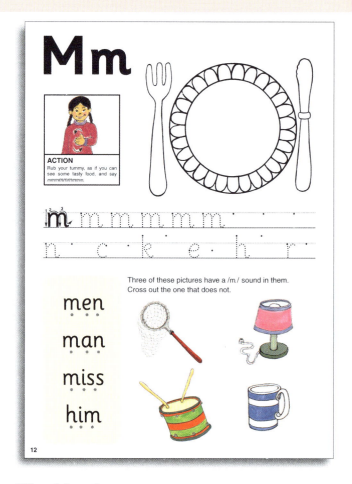

Action
- The children rub their tummies, as though eating their favourite foods, and make a continuous /mmmmmm/ sound.

Formation
- Explain how the letter ‹m› is written.
- The children write over the dotted letters in their books.

Blending
- Blend the words *men, man, miss, him.*
- Say the sounds with the children, then blend the sounds together and read the words.
- Encourage the children to point to the dot underneath each sound as they say it.

Sounding
- Say the words corresponding to the pictures on the children's page: *net, lamp, drum, mug.*
- The children listen for the word without the /m/ sound (*net*), and cross out its picture.

Word bank
mat, met, map, man, men, ram, him, camp, ramp, pram, imp, mill, stem, stamp, smack, mess, miss.

Dictation
- Call out the sound /m/ and some other sounds already covered for the children to write.
- Dictate the words *rim* and *map.*
- Call out some words from the word bank.
- The children listen to the words and hold up a finger for each sound.

Further ideas
- Sing the song from the *Jolly Jingles* or the *Jolly Songs.*
- Put up on the wall, or hold up, the /m/ section of the *Wall Frieze.*
- Make a collage of different foods.

Letter Sound /d/

Flash cards
- Revise some of the sounds already learnt: /s/, /a/, /t/, /i/, /p/, /n/, /c/, /k/, /e/, /h/, /r/, /m/.

Story
- Introduce the sound /d/ using a story, such as the one below and the action.

Dan is tidying his toy cupboard. He pulls out his teddy, his old donkey and a duck. Then, he finds a box of dominoes. He plays with them for a while. Next, he sees his yellow digger and takes it out for a drive. Suddenly, from downstairs, Dad asks, 'Dan, have you finished yet?' 'Not yet,' says Dan, and he goes back to the cupboard. He finds a bag of marbles and some dice. He plays with these for a little while, and then hears his Dad again. 'Dan, have you finished yet?' 'No, not yet,' says Dan, and he goes back to the cupboard. At the very back of the cupboard, he sees his old red and blue drum. He picks it up and marches up and down, banging the drum, 'd, d, d!' Dad comes in to see what all the noise is. 'Do you know you have spent all day tidying your cupboard?' he says. Dan smiles. 'I've found lots of things I had forgotten all about,' he replies.

Action
- The children pretend to be playing a drum, moving their hands up and down, and saying 'd, d, d'.

Formation
- Explain how the letter ‹d› is written. It starts with a 'caterpillar c', and is a tall letter.
- The children write over the dotted letters in their books.

Blending
- Blend the words *dip, dad, pad, hid*.
- Say the sounds with the children, then blend the sounds together and read the words.
- Encourage the children to point to the dot underneath each sound as they say it.

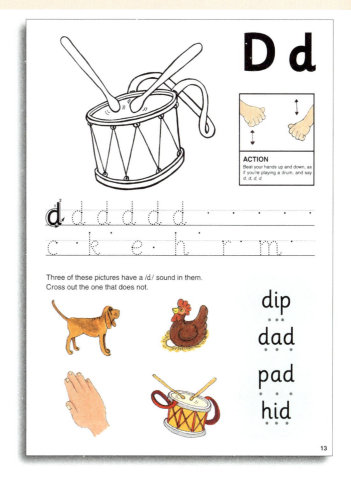

Sounding
- Say the words corresponding to the pictures on the children's page: *dog, hen, hand, drum*.
- The children listen for the word without the /d/ sound (*hen*), and cross out its picture.

Word bank
dad, did, den, din, dip, hid, had, red, deck, pad, sad, mad, end, hand, and, sand, desk, drip, dent, send, skid, spend, add.

Dictation
- Call out the sound /d/ and some other sounds already covered for the children to write.
- Dictate the words *dad* and *hid*.
- Call out some words from the word bank.
- The children listen to the words and hold up a finger for each sound.

Further ideas
- Sing the song from the *Jolly Songs* and pin up the /d/ section of the *Wall Frieze*.
- Look at books about dinosaurs and paint dinosaur pictures. Play the drums.

Letter Sound /g/

Flash cards
- Revise some of the sounds already learnt:
  /s/, /a/, /t/, /i/, /p/, /n/, /c/, /k/, /e/, /h/, /r/, /m/, /d/.

Story
- Introduce the sound /g/ using a story, such as the one below, and the action.

Gail is staying with her grandmother, who has a big garden and keeps some animals. This morning, Gail and Gran went outside to check on the goat and the geese. While they were outside, Gail found a frog next to the water bucket. She watched it hop off under the gate. When they came in, Gran sent Gail to the bathroom to have a wash. Gail put the plug in the sink, filled the basin and washed her hands and face, but when she pulled the plug out, the water didn't go away. Her grandmother came to have a look. 'Oh dear, the sink must be blocked,' she said. Gran phoned the plumber. When he arrived, the plumber unblocked the sink and the water ran gurgling out of the basin, 'g, g, g, g, g'.

Action
- The children pretend their hand is the water spiralling down the drain saying, 'g, g, g'.

Formation
- Explain how the letter ‹g› is written. It starts with a 'caterpillar c' and has a tail that goes down under the line.
- The children write over the dotted letters.

Blending
- Blend the words *get, gap, peg, rag.*
- Say the sounds with the children, then blend the sounds together and read the words.
- Encourage the children to point to the dot underneath each sound as they say it.

Sounding
- Say the words corresponding to the pictures on the children's page: *glass, plug, hen, frog.*
- The children listen for the word without the /g/ sound (*hen*), and cross out its picture.

Word bank
get, gap, peg, dig, tag, gas, rag, gram, grim, grip, grid, grin, snag, stag, grand.

Dictation
- Call out the sound /g/ and some other sounds already covered for the children to write.
- Dictate the words *sag, peg, dig, leg.*
- Call out some words from the word bank.
- The children listen to the words and hold up a finger for each sound.

Further ideas
- Sing the song from the *Jolly Jingles* or the *Jolly Songs.*
- Put up on the wall, or hold up, the /g/ section of the *Wall Frieze.*
- Read the story, *The Three Billy Goats Gruff.*
- Paint some green frogs.

Letter Sound /o/

Flash cards
· Revise some of the sounds already learnt: /s/, /a/, /t/, /i/, /p/, /n/, /c/, /k/, /e/, /h/, /r/, /m/, /d/, /g/.

Story
· Introduce the sound /o/ using a story, such as the one below, and the action.

Oliver and Holly have moved to a new house. They have a new bedroom with bunk beds in it. Near the bed is a light switch, so they can turn the light on and off by themselves when they are in bed. That night, Holly curls up with Oscar, her toy rabbit, and Oliver reads his comic. 'You can turn the light out when you've finished,' says Dad. Oliver leans over to the light switch and turns it off. 'Off it goes,' he says. Then he turns the light back on, saying 'o, on it goes'. He turns the light on and off, saying, 'o, on it goes. Off it goes. O, on it goes'. Then he hears Dad's voice. 'Stop turning the light on and off, Oliver! You will break it. Turn it off, and go to sleep.' Oliver turns the light off and goes to sleep.

Action
· The children point their finger, as if pushing a switch on and off saying 'o, o, o, o'.

Formation
· Explain how the letter ‹o› is written. It starts with a 'caterpillar c'.
· The children write over the dotted letters in their books.

Blending
· Blend the words *hot, mop, pots, dog*.
· Say the sounds with the children, then blend the sounds together and read the words.
· Encourage the children to point to the dot underneath each sound as they say it.

Sounding
· Say the words corresponding to the pictures on the children's page: *bat, octopus, sock, pond*.
· The children listen for the word without the /o/ sound (*bat*), and cross out its picture.

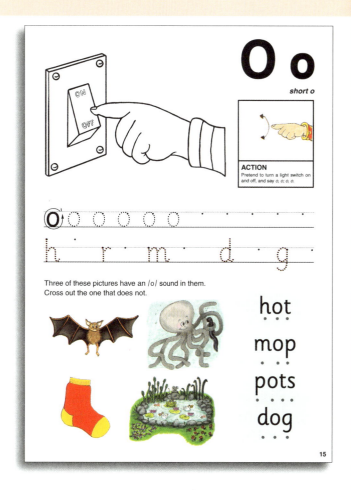

Word bank
top, pot, dot, pod, dog, sock, tock, rock, mock, dock, hop, mop, hog, pond, spot, cod, cog, cot, got, hot, nod, not, pop, rod, drop, trod, stop, cost, odd, moss, cross.

Dictation
· Call out the sound /o/ and some other sounds already covered for the children to write.
· Dictate the words *hog, hop, dot* and *mop*.
· Call out some words from the word bank.
· The children listen to the words and hold up a finger for each sound.

Further ideas
· Sing the song from the *Jolly Jingles* or the *Jolly Songs*.
· Put up on the wall, or hold up, the /o/ section of the *Wall Frieze*.
· Print ‹o› shapes using the end of cardboard tubes.
· Make an octopus.

Letter Sound /u/

Flash cards
- Revise some of the sounds already learnt: /s/, /a/, /t/, /i/, /p/, /n/, /c/, /k/, /e/, /h/, /r/, /m/, /d/, /g/, /o/.

Story
- Introduce the sound /u/ using a story, such as the one below, and the action.

Uncle Bud often comes to visit his niece and nephew, Anna and Ulric. Today, he has brought them each a big umbrella. Anna's umbrella is spotty, and Ulric's umbrella has red and white stripes. In the afternoon, the whole family goes out for a walk. Although it is a sunny day, Anna and Ulric insist on bringing their umbrellas with them. Everyone laughs, except Uncle Bud. 'I'll take my umbrella, too,' he says. The family sets off for their walk in brilliant sunshine. After a while, they notice some big black clouds on the horizon. A little while later, they feel the first raindrops starting to fall. Soon it is pouring with rain! Uncle Bud, Anna and Ulric put up their umbrellas, shouting, 'u, u, up umbrellas!' They are the ones laughing now! They have a lovely time, splashing in the puddles and dancing under their umbrellas.

Action
- The children pretend to be putting up an umbrella, with one hand holding the umbrella and the other moving up, saying 'u, u, u'.

Formation
- Explain how the letter ⟨u⟩ is written.
- The children write over the dotted letters in their books.

Blending
- Blend the words sun, mud, cup, dug.
- Say the sounds with the children, then blend the sounds together and read the words.
- Encourage the children to point to the dot underneath each sound as they say it.

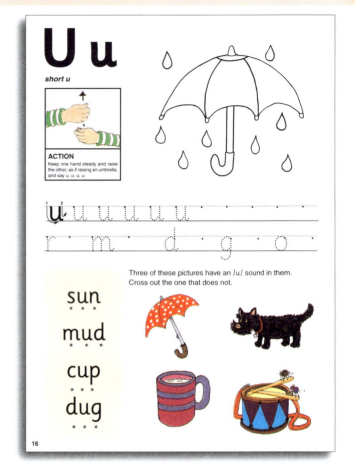

Sounding
- Say the words corresponding to the pictures on the children's page: umbrella, dog, mug, drum.
- The children listen for the word without the /u/ sound (dog), and cross out its picture.

Word bank
up, us, sun, run, mug, tug, dug, rug, hug, cup, cut, hum, hut, mud, nut, pup, sum, snug, suck, duck, muck, gulp, hunt, dump, hump, pump, dusk, tusk, dust, must, crust, trust, skunk, stump, truck, stuck.

Dictation
- Call out the sound /u/ and some other sounds already covered for the children to write.
- Dictate the words run, sum, cut and mug.
- Call out some words from the word bank.
- The children listen to the words and hold up a finger for each sound.

Further ideas
Sing the song from the *Jolly Songs* and pin up the /u/ section of the *Wall Frieze*.

Letter Sound /l/

Flash cards
- Revise some of the sounds already learnt: /s/, /a/, /t/, /i/, /p/, /n/, /c/, /k/, /e/, /h/, /r/, /m/, /d/, /g/, /o/, /u/.

Story
- Introduce the sound /l/ using a story, such as the one below, and the action.

It is Luca's birthday and he is having a party. Luca's friends have brought lots of presents for him. Luca and his friends play some party games while the food is set out. There are lettuce sandwiches, little cakes, liquorice laces and lemonade to drink. Most importantly, there is a big birthday cake in the shape of a lion. Luca and his friends play 'blind man's buff' and 'pin the tail on the donkey'. Lucy wins 'pin the tail on the donkey' and gets a lime lollipop as a prize. She licks her lollipop, going 'lllllllll'.

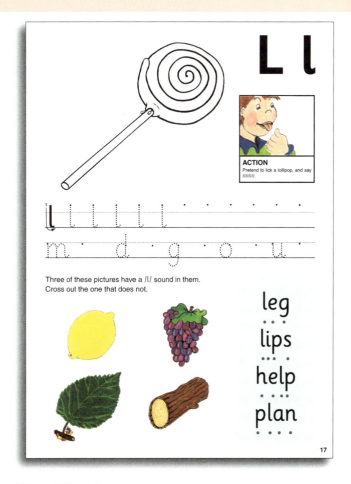

Action
- The children stick out their tongues, pretending to be licking a lollipop, and say /llllll/.

Formation
- Explain how the letter ⏻ is written. It is a tall letter.
- The children write over the dotted letters in their books.

Blending
- Blend the words *leg, lips, help, plan*.
- Say the sounds with the children, then blend the sounds together and read the words.
- Encourage the children to point to the dot underneath each sound as they say it.

Sounding
- Say the words corresponding to the pictures on the children's page: *lemon, grapes, leaf, log*.
- The children listen for the word without the /l/ sound (*grapes*), and cross out its picture.

Word bank
lap, lad, leg, lip, led, let, lid, lit, lot, clap, clip, clog, glad, glum, plan, plot, plug, plum, plus, slam, slip, slug, held, milk, help, lent, lump, list, slept, ill, hill, mill, pill, till, doll, loss, spell, smell, lick, lock, luck, click, trick, stick, clock.

Dictation
- Call out the sound /l/ and some other sounds already covered for the children to write.
- Dictate the words *lap, log, lad* and *lit*.
- Call out some words from the word bank.
- The children listen to the words and hold up a finger for each sound.

Further ideas
- Sing the song from the *Jolly Jingles* or the *Jolly Songs*.
- Put up on the wall, or hold up, the /l/ section of the *Wall Frieze*.
- Make lemon ice lollies.
- Play 'pin the tail on the donkey'.

Letter Sound /f/

Flash cards
- Revise some of the sounds already learnt: /s/, /a/, /t/, /i/, /p/, /n/, /c/, /k/, /e/, /h/, /r/, /m/, /d/, /g/, /o/, /u/, /l/.

Story
- Introduce the sound /f/ using a story, such as the one below, and the action.

Freda, Fred and their friend Felix are at the beach. Freda has a new sun hat and a bucket and spade. Fred has a large, floating, inflatable fish. At first, all the children play in the water with the inflatable fish. Then, Freda and Felix decide to build sand castles and Fred leaves his inflatable fish on the sand to dry. Freda's castle has four towers and she puts a flag on each one. Felix finds some shells and seaweed for his castle. Fred puts on his flippers and goes off for a swim. Suddenly, Fred calls out. When the others look around, they see his inflatable fish getting smaller and smaller. The plug has come out and the all air is escaping, 'ffffffff!'

Action
- The children bring their hands together, as if the fish is deflating, and make a continuous /ffffff/ sound.

Formation
- Explain how the letter f is written. It is a tall letter and has a tail that goes under the line.
- The children write over the dotted letters.

Blending
- Blend the words *fit, fat, puff, soft*.
- Say the sounds with the children, then blend the sounds together and read the words.
- Encourage the children to point to the dot underneath each sound as they say it.

Sounding
- Say the words corresponding to the pictures on the children's page: *flag, umbrella, frog, fox*.
- The children listen for the word without the /f/ sound (*umbrella*), and cross out its picture.

Word bank
fit, fat, fun, fan, fed, fig, fin, fog, flag, flap, flat, flop, frog, from, elf, self, golf, film, felt, left, gift, lift, loft, soft, tuft, fund, fist, frost, fill, fuss, flock.

Dictation
- Call out the sound /f/ and some other sounds already covered for the children to write.
- Dictate the words *fan, fin, fog* and *fun*.
- Call out some words from the word bank.
- The children listen to the words and hold up a finger for each sound.

Further ideas
- Sing the song from the *Jolly Jingles* or the *Jolly Songs*.
- Put up on the wall, or hold up, the /f/ section of the *Wall Frieze*.
- Paint a fish picture.
- Find out about different sorts of fish.

Letter Sound /b/

Flash cards
• Revise some of the sounds already learnt.

Story
• Introduce the sound /b/ using a story, such as the one below and the action.

Gran is looking after Bill and his baby brother, Ben. Gran takes Bill and baby Ben to the park. Gran stops to watch the boats on the lake, and to listen to the band playing. She finds a bench and sits down. Soon she and baby Ben are dozing in the sun. Bill sees his friend, Rob, who has a bat and ball set. They find some more of their friends and have a game of baseball. Bill throws the ball for Rob. As the bat hits the ball, it goes 'b'. Then, it is Betty's turn. She bashes the ball as hard as she can. It just misses Gran, but bounces and hits the bench. Gran and baby Ben wake up. 'I think I had better keep a safe distance from the baseball,' says Gran and she pushes baby Ben along the path at the side of the boating lake.

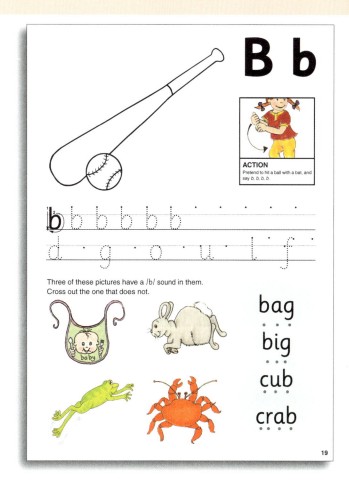

Action
• The children pretend to hold a bat and hit a ball saying 'b b b'.

Formation
• Explain how the letter ‹b› is written. It is a tall letter. Tell the children to go down for the bat and bounce up and around for the ball.
• The children write over the dotted letters in their books.

Blending
• Blend the words *bag, big, cub* and *crab*.
• Say the sounds with the children, then blend the sounds together and read the words.
• Encourage the children to point to the dot underneath each sound as they say it.

Sounding
• Say the words corresponding to the pictures on the children's page: *bib, rabbit, frog, crab*.
• The children listen for the word without the /b/ sound (*frog*), and cross out its picture.

Word bank
bat, bad, bag, ban, cab, bed, beg, bet, bib, big, bin, bit, rob, bud, bug, bus, but, cub, rub, club, crab, crib, grab, scab, bulb, belt, bent, bend, bump, best, bill, bell, boss, back, beck, buck, black, block, brick, blend.

Dictation
• Call out the sound /b/ and some other sounds already covered for the children to write.
• Dictate the words *bed, but, bat* and *bib*.
• Call out some words from the word bank.
• The children listen to the words and hold up a finger for each sound.

Further ideas
• Sing the song from the *Jolly Jingles* or the *Jolly Songs*.
• Put up on the wall, or hold up, the /b/ section of the *Wall Frieze*.
• Play bat and ball.
• Make up a band.

Letter Sound /ai/

Flash cards
- Revise some of the sounds already learnt: /s/, /a/, /t/, /i/, /p/, /n/, /c/, /k/, /e/, /h/, /r/, /m/, /d/, /g/, /o/, /u/, /l/, /f/, /b/.
- The sound /ai/ is written using two letters.
- When these two letters come together they make a different sound.
- When two letters make one sound it is called a digraph.

Story
- Introduce the sound /ai/ using a story, such as the one below, and the action.

Ainsley has been having trouble with his hearing. Whenever his mother speaks to him, he puts his hand to his ear and says, 'ai?' His mother tells him that he should say 'pardon', not 'ai'. After a while, his mother takes him to the doctor to have his hearing checked. In the waiting room there is a box of toys. Ainsley plays with a whale and a sailing boat and a train. As he is pushing the train around the room, Dr. Ail comes out and calls his name. Dr. Ail looks in Ainsley's ears. 'You have a lot of wax in your ears, Ainsley. That's why you're having trouble with your hearing.' Dr. Ail gives him some eardrops. 'Not another "ai" now, Ainsley,' says his mother.

Action
- The children cup one hand over an ear and say 'ai, ai, ai'.

Formation
- Explain how the digraph ‹ai› is written.
- This is a good opportunity to introduce joined-up handwriting.
- The children write over the dotted letters.

Blending
- Blend the words *rain, tail, paid, snail.*
- Say the sounds with the children, then blend the sounds together and read the words.
- Encourage the children to point to the dot underneath each sound as they say it.

Sounding
- Say the words corresponding to the pictures on the children's page: *ink, rain, train, snail.*
- The children listen for the word without the /ai/ sound (*ink*), and cross out its picture.

Word bank
aid, aim, bait, fail, hail, laid, maid, mail, main, nail, paid, pail, pain, raid, rail, rain, sail, tail, claim, plain, brain, drain, trail, train, snail, strain, faint, paint, saint.

Dictation
- Call out the sound /ai/ and some other sounds already covered for the children to write.
- Dictate the words *aid, rail, pain* and *bait.*
- Call out some words from the word bank.
- The children listen to the words and hold up a finger for each sound.

Further ideas
- Sing the song from the *Jolly Songs* and pin up the /ai/ section of the *Wall Frieze.*
- Paint a rainy day picture on a raindrop shape.

Letter Sound /j/

Flash cards
• Revise some of the sounds already learnt: /s/, /a/, /t/, /i/, /p/, /n/, /c/, /k/, /e/, /h/, /r/, /m/, /d/, /g/, /o/, /u/, /l/, /f/, /b/, /ai/.

Story
• Introduce the sound /j/ using a story, such as the one below, and the action.

Jane loves jelly. Jane's mother has promised to make her some jelly this afternoon. When Jane gets home from school, she eats a slice of bread and jam and has a glass of orange juice. She tells her mother that she and her friend Javinda made a giant jigsaw of a juggler at school. Jane's mother shows Jane the jelly she has made. 'Wow,' says Jane. The jelly is tall and red and has four layers. As Jane carries it to the table, it wobbles and wobbles. Jane pretends to wobble just like the jelly, saying, 'jelly on a plate, jelly on a plate, j, j, j, j, jelly on a plate.'

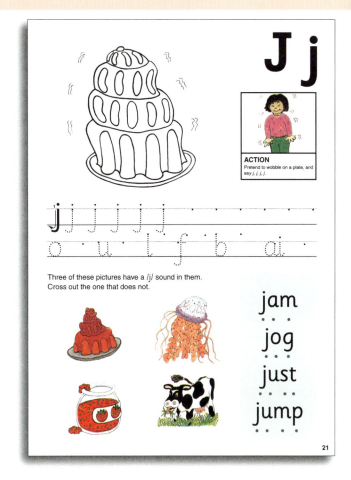

Action
• The children pretend to be the jelly and wobble, saying 'j, j, j'.

Formation
• Explain how the letter ⟨j⟩ is written. It has a tail that goes down and under the line.
• The children write over the dotted letters in their books.

Blending
• Blend the words *jam, jog, just, jump*.
• Say the sounds with the children, then blend the sounds together and read the words.
• Encourage the children to point to the dot underneath each sound as they say it.

Sounding
• Say the words corresponding to the pictures on the children's page: *jelly, jellyfish, jam, cow*.
• The children listen for the word without the /j/ sound (*cow*), and cross out its picture.

Word bank
jet, job, jab, jug, jog, jig, jot, jut, just, jacket, jail, jam, jump, junk.

Dictation
• Call out the sound /j/ and some other sounds already covered for the children to write.
• Dictate the words *jet, job, jab* and *jug*.
• Call out some words from the word bank.
• The children listen to the words and hold up a finger for each sound.

Further ideas
• Sing the song from the *Jolly Jingles* or the *Jolly Songs*.
• Put up on the wall, or hold up, the /j/ section of the *Wall Frieze*.
• Make a multi-coloured jelly.
• Make a jellyfish with a paper cup body and crêpe paper tentacles.

Letter Sound /oa/

Flash cards
- Revise some of the sounds already learnt: /s/, /a/, /t/, /i/, /p/, /n/, /c/, /k/, /e/, /h/, /r/, /m/, /d/, /g/, /o/, /u/, /l/, /f/, /b/, /ai/, /j/.

Story
- Introduce the sound /oa/ using a story, such as the one below, and the action.

A bad-tempered goat lives in a field at the side of a road. The goat gets very cross if any other animal comes into his field. Mona and her brother, Jonah, often walk past the field and talk to the goat. One windy day, Mona and Jonah are going to the park to have a picnic and to sail Jonah's model boat. As they pass by, they can see the goat is very cross. He is stamping his hooves and snorting beside an oak tree, which is blowing in the wind. Up in the tree are two cheeky robins and a squirrel. The robins have been flying down and stealing oats from the goat. The goat charges at the tree and butts the trunk as hard as he can. CRASH! The tree falls on top of the goat. 'Oh!' say Mona and Jonah. They run to get the farmer, who rescues the goat.

Action
- The children bring one hand up to their mouth, as if they see something go wrong, and say 'oh!'

Formation
- Explain how the digraph ‹oa› is written.
- Digraphs can be a good way to introduce joined handwriting.
- Write the ‹o› as usual and then go across to where the letter ‹a› should start and stop. Then come back around in a 'caterpillar c' shape, before finishing the letter ‹a›.
- The children write over the dotted letters.

Blending
- Blend the words goat, soak, road, foam.
- Say the sounds with the children, then blend the sounds together and read the words.
- Encourage the children to point to the dot underneath each sound as they say it.

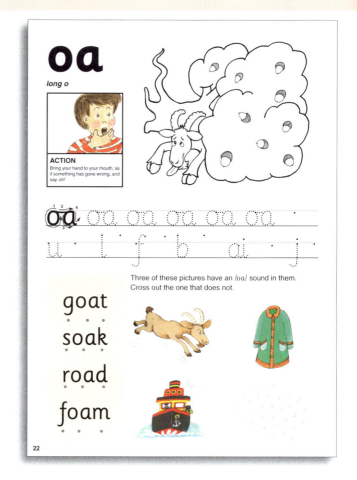

Sounding
- Say the words corresponding to the pictures on the children's page: goat, coat, boat, rain.
- The children listen for the word without the /oa/ sound (rain), and cross out its picture.

Word bank
oak, oats, boat, coal, coat, foal, foam, goal, goat, load, loaf, moan, moat, road, soak, soap, toad, cloak, float, croak, groan, boast, coast, roast, toast.

Dictation
- Call out the sound /oa/ and some other sounds already covered for the children to write.
- Dictate the words oak, moan, soap and coat.
- Call out some words from the word bank.
- The children listen to the words and hold up a finger for each sound.

Further ideas
- Sing the song from the Jolly Songs and pin up the /oa/ section of the Wall Frieze.
- Make paper boats and see if they float.

Letter Sound /ie/

Flash cards
• Revise some of the sounds already learnt: /s/, /a/, /t/, /i/, /p/, /n/, /c/, /k/, /e/, /h/, /r/, /m/, /d/, /g/, /o/, /u/, /l/, /f/, /b/, /ai/, /j/, /oa/.

Story
• Introduce the sound /ie/ using a story, such as the one below, and the action.

Clive has been invited to a party. Clive's dad is a sailor in the navy and he has given Clive a hat from his ship. Clive wants to dress up as a sailor like his dad and wear the hat to the party. His mother makes him a sailor's outfit. Just before the party, Clive's dad comes home on leave. Clive insists on wearing his new outfit to meet him off the ship. He waves and waves when he sees his dad and runs up and gives him a big hug. Dad admires his outfit and says, 'If you are a sailor, you will have to learn how to salute and say, ie, ie!' When they get home, he shows Clive how to salute. Clive has a go in front of the mirror, saluting and saying, 'ie, ie!'

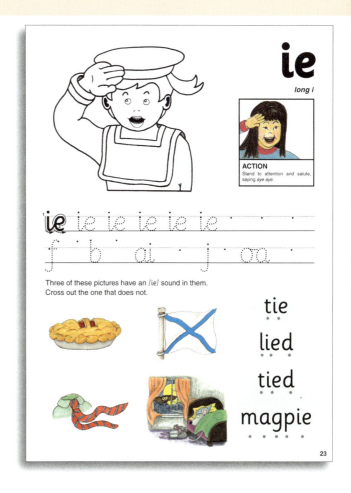

Action
• The children pretend to be the sailor and salute, saying 'ie, ie'.

Formation
• Explain how the digraph ‹ie› is written.
• Digraphs can be a good way to introduce joined handwriting.
• The children write over the dotted letters.

Blending
• Blend the words *tie, lied, tied,* and *magpie.*
• Say the sounds with the children, then blend the sounds together and read the words.
• Encourage the children to point to the dot underneath each sound as they say it.

Sounding
• Say the words corresponding to the pictures on the children's page: *pie, flag, tie, night.*
• The children listen for the word without the /ie/ sound (*flag*), and cross out its picture.

Word bank
pie, tie, lie, die, died, lied, magpie, tried, spied, fried, cried, dried.

Dictation
• Call out the sound /ie/ and some other sounds already covered for the children to write.
• Dictate the words *pie, tie, lie* and *die.*
• Call out some words from the word bank.
• The children listen to the words and hold up a finger for each sound.

Further ideas
• Sing the song from the *Jolly Jingles* or the *Jolly Songs.*
• Put up on the wall, or hold up, the /ie/ section of the *Wall Frieze.*
• Cut out paper tie shapes for the children to decorate.

Letter Sounds /ee/ and /or/

Flash cards
- Revise some of the sounds already learnt.

Story
- Introduce the sounds /ee/ and /or/ using a story, such as the one below, and the action.

An old donkey and some sheep live next to a small cornfield. Nora and Jakeem like to go and talk to the donkey. The donkey is always very pleased to see them. When he sees them coming, he brays, 'ee or!' and waggles his ears up and down in greeting. One August morning, the children go for a walk to see the donkey. He brays happily, 'ee or!' Jakeem gives the donkey a carrot. 'The carrot comes from my garden,' says Nora. 'I have carrots and sweetcorn growing there.' As the children talk to the donkey, big raindrops begin to fall. Behind the children is an enormous rain cloud. 'I think we had better get home quickly,' says Jakeem. 'There is a storm coming. We will have to run home as fast as we can.' The children run off, waving to the donkey.

Action
- The children pretend their hands are the donkey's ears. Their hands point straight up for the /ee/ sound and point down for /or/.

Formation
- Explain how the digraphs ‹ee› and ‹or› are written.
- The children write over the dotted letters.

Blending
- Blend the following words with the children: *tree, seen, bee*; *corn, fork, sort*.
- Encourage the children to point to the dot underneath each sound as they say it.

Sounding
- Say the words corresponding to the pictures on the children's page: *bee, crab, sheep; goat, fork, horse*. The children listen for the words without the /ee/ or /or/ sounds (*crab; goat*), and cross out these pictures.

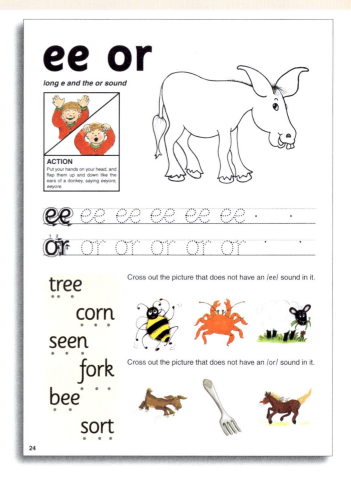

Word bank
- /ee/ words

  eel, bee, beef, been, deep, feed, feel, feet, heel, jeep, keen, keep, leek, meet, need, peel, peep, reef, see, seed, seek, seem, seen, bleed, sleep, creep, free, greed, green, tree, speed.
- /or/ words

  lord, cork, fork, form, born, corn, horn, morn, fort, port, sort, sport, stork, storm.

Dictation
- Call out the sounds /ee/ and /or/ and some other sounds already covered for the children to write.
- Dictate the words *feet, seed, born, form*.
- Call out some words from the word banks.
- The children listen to the words and hold up a finger for each sound.

Further ideas
- Sing the song from the *Jolly Songs* and pin up the /ee/-/or/ section of the *Wall Frieze*.
- Collage a storm picture with scrap-paper trees.

Letter Sound /z/

Flash cards
- Revise some of the sounds already learnt: /s/, /a/, /t/, /i/, /p/, /n/, /c/, /k/, /e/, /h/, /r/, /m/, /d/, /g/, /o/, /u/, /l/, /f/, /b/, /ai/, /j/, /oa/, /ie/, /ee/, /or/.

Story
- Introduce the sound /z/ using a story, such as the one below, and the action.

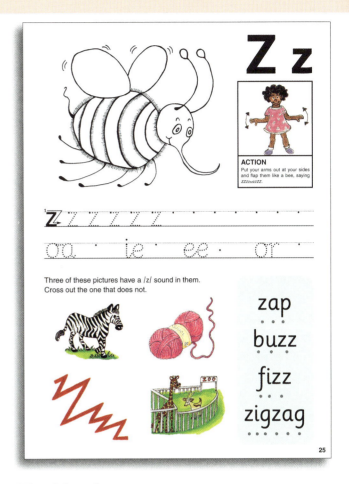

Zara is sitting outside on the grass one sunny morning. She is playing with Zebadee, her toy zebra. Suddenly, Zara hears a loud buzzing sound, 'zzzZZZzzz'. She looks around and sees a big honeybee, buzzing around the flowers. The bee is collecting pollen to be made into honey, back at the hive. Zara watches the bee as it buzzes from flower to flower, landing on each one and collecting the pollen. Then Zara stands up and runs around, flapping her arms like the wings of the bee and saying, 'zzzZZZzzz!' She stops by a gazania and bends down to pretend to collect the pollen from the flower. Then, 'zzzZZZzzz', she buzzes and off she goes to collect more pollen from the daisies.

Action
- The children pretend to be a bee, flapping their arms up and down like wings, and saying /zzzzzz/.

Formation
- Explain how the letter ‹z› is written.
- The children write over the dotted letters.

Blending
- Blend the words *zap, buzz, fizz, zigzag*.
- Say the sounds with the children, then blend the sounds together and read the words.
- Encourage the children to point to the dot underneath each sound as they say it.

Sounding
- Say the words corresponding to the pictures on the children's page: *zebra, wool, zigzag, zoo*.
- The children listen for the word without the /z/ sound (*wool*), and cross out its picture.

Word bank
zip, zit, zed, jazz, zigzag, zest.

Dictation
- Call out the sound /z/ and some other sounds already covered for the children to write.
- Dictate the words *zip, zest, zit* and *zed*.
- Call out some words from the word bank.
- The children listen to the words and hold up a finger for each sound.

Further ideas
- Sing the song from the *Jolly Jingles* or the *Jolly Songs*.
- Put up on the wall, or hold up, the /z/ section of the *Wall Frieze*.
- Make a zoo with toy animals.
- Make bees by painting paper plates with black and yellow stripes and adding paper wings.

Letter Sound /w/

Flash cards
- Revise some of the sounds already learnt: /s/, /a/, /t/, /i/, /p/, /n/, /c/, /k/, /e/, /h/, /r/, /m/, /d/, /g/, /o/, /u/, /l/, /f/, /b/, /ai/, /j/, /oa/, /ie/, /ee/, /or/, /z/.

Story
- Introduce the sound /w/ using a story, such as the one below, and the action.

Aesop told a fable about the wind and the sun. The west wind and the sun are having an argument about which of them is the strongest. The west wind says to the sun, 'You see that man down there? I bet I can blow so hard that his coat comes off.' The west wind blows and blows, 'wwwwwww,' but the man hangs on to his warm coat. The harder the wind blows, the more tightly the man holds on to his coat. 'My turn! Let me try,' says the sun. The sun shines and shines and the man gets warmer and warmer, then hotter and hotter. Then the man gets too hot and takes off his coat. 'I win,' smiles the sun, and the west wind storms off, 'wwwwww!'

Action
- The children cup their hands and blow on them, saying 'w, w, w'.

Formation
- Explain how the letter ‹w› is written.
- The children write over the dotted letters in their books.

Blending
- Blend the words *web, wig, swam, wind*.
- Say the sounds with the children, then blend the sounds together and read the words.
- Encourage the children to point to the dot underneath each sound as they say it.

Sounding
- Say the words corresponding to the pictures on the children's page: *window, swan, apple, well*.
- The children listen for the word without the /w/ sound (*apple*), and cross out its picture.

Word bank
web, wig, swim, swam, wind, went, well, wait, will, twist, sweet, sweep, waist, twig, weep, weekend.

Dictation
- Call out the sound /w/ and some other sounds already covered for the children to write.
- Dictate the words *wag, win, wet* and *swim*.
- Call out some words from the word bank.
- The children listen to the words and hold up a finger for each sound.

Further ideas
- Sing the song from the *Jolly Jingles* or the *Jolly Songs*.
- Put up on the wall, or hold up, the /w/ section of the *Wall Frieze*.
- Paint the view from the classroom window.
- Make a spider's web with wool.

Letter Sound /ng/

Flash cards
· Revise some of the sounds already learnt.

Story
· Introduce the sound /ng/ using a story, such as the one below, and the action.

It is Saturday afternoon, and Bing has come to play at Mark's house. They start by having a game of ping-pong. Then they play with a racing car. 'Let's see what's on television,' says Mark, 'There might be some motor racing.' They put on the television. 'Look at that man!' says Bing. 'He's a weightlifter,' says Mark. Bing and Mark watch the man as he lifts some huge weights. The man grunts as he lifts, 'ngngngng!' 'He must be strong,' says Bing. 'Let's be weightlifters,' says Mark. They use a broom and a mop as weights. As they pretend to lift the heavy weights, they go 'ngngngngng,' just like the weightlifter.

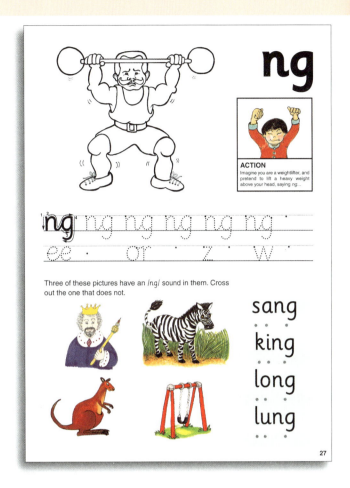

Action
· The children pretend to lift a heavy weight and say, 'ng, ng, ng'.

Formation
· Explain how the digraph ‹ng› is written.
· Write the letter ‹n›, then take the joining tail up to where the letter ‹g› begins and stop, then come back in a 'caterpillar c' shape, before finishing the letter ‹g›.
· The children write over the dotted letters.

Blending
· Blend the words *sang, king, long, lung*.
· Say the sounds with the children, then blend the sounds together and read the words.
· Encourage the children to point to the dot underneath each sound as they say it.

Sounding
· Say the words corresponding to the pictures on the children's page: *king, zebra, kangaroo, swing*.
· The children listen for the word without the /ng/ sound (*zebra*), and cross out its picture.

Word bank
sang, king, long, lung, ping-pong, song, sing, bang, gang, hang, rang, ring, wing, zing, hung, rung, cling, sling, bring, sting, swing, string, strong, clung, stung, swung.

Dictation
· Call out the sound /ng/ and some other sounds already covered for the children to write.
· Dictate the words *song, bang, lung* and *wing*.
· Call out some words from the word bank. The children listen to the words and hold up a finger for each sound.

Further ideas
· Sing the song from the *Jolly Jingles* or the *Jolly Songs*.
· Put up on the wall, or hold up, the /ng/ section of the *Wall Frieze*.
· Play ping-pong.

Letter Sounds /v/

Flash cards
- Revise some of the sounds already learnt: /s/, /a/, /t/, /i/, /p/, /n/, /c/, /k/, /e/, /h/, /r/, /m/, /d/, /g/, /o/, /u/, /l/, /f/, /b/, /ai/, /j/, /oa/, /ie/, /ee/, /or/, /z/, /w/, /ng/.

Story
- Introduce the sound /v/ using a story, such as the one below, and the action.

One day during the summer, Uncle Vic arrives at Zack and Jess's house. 'Would you like to come and help me, today?' he asks. 'Yes, please,' they reply. 'Come on, then, we have a lot to do,' says Uncle Vic. They all drive off to the station in his van, 'vvvvv!' 'I need to collect an order from Val's Fruit and Veg,' says Uncle Vic. 'Vvvvvv!' They stop outside the door and Uncle Vic collects the order. Then, 'vroom,' they are off again. Next, Uncle Vic delivers the vegetables to old Mrs. Vernon. They are busy all day, driving around, 'vvvvv!' Eventually, it is time for Zack and Jess to go home. 'Good-bye,' call Zack and Jess, as they wave to Uncle Vic.

Action
- The children pretend to be driving, holding the steering wheel and saying /vvvvvv/.

Formation
- Explain how the letter ‹v› is written.
- The children write over the dotted letters.

Blending
- Blends the words *van, vim, vat, vest*.
- Say the sounds with the children, then blend the sounds together and read the words.
- Encourage the children to point to the dot underneath each sound as they say it.

Sounding
- Say the words corresponding to the pictures on the children's page: *violin, van, fish, volcano*.
- The children listen for the word without the /v/ sound (*fish*), and cross out its picture.

Word bank
van, vat, vet, vent, vain, velvet, vest, vivid, visit.

Dictation
- Call out the sound /v/ and some other sounds already covered for the children to write.
- Dictate the words *vat, van, vent* and *vet*.
- Call out some words from the word bank.
- The children listen to the words and hold up a finger for each sound.

Further ideas
- Sing the song from the *Jolly Jingles* or the *Jolly Songs*.
- Put up on the wall, or hold up, the /v/ section of the *Wall Frieze*.
- Wrap up some parcels for Uncle Vic to deliver.
- Set up a vet's surgery for toy animals.

Letter Sounds /oo/ and /oo/

Flash cards
- Revise some of the sounds already learnt.
- The digraph ‹oo› has two sounds, the /oo/ in *book* and the /oo/ in *moon*.
- Initially the two sounds are represented by two sizes of letter.

Story
- Introduce the /oo/ sounds using a story, such as the one below, and the action.

Oona is going to visit Great Aunt Ivy. Oona likes visiting Great Aunt Ivy because she has lots of interesting things and a large friendly cat called Noodle. The thing Oona likes best is Great Aunt Ivy's cuckoo clock. On the hour, a little wooden cuckoo pops out from the little wooden door at the top, calling, '00 **oo**, 00 **oo**'. Noodle and Oona like to wait underneath the clock, knowing that the cuckoo will come out soon. As the cuckoo goes in and out, Oona pretends to be the cuckoo, and says, '00 **oo**, 00 **oo**!'

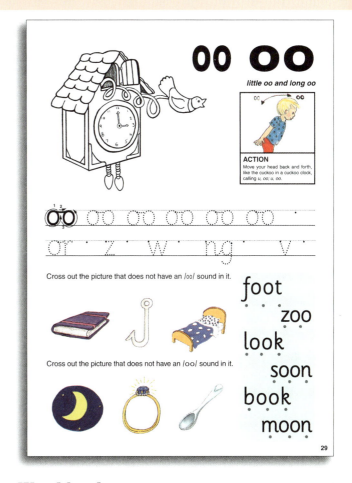

Action
- The children pretend to be the cuckoo in the clock, moving their heads forward for the short /oo/ sound and back for the long /oo/ sound.

Formation
- Explain how the digraph ‹oo› is written. One size of writing is used for the two /oo/ sounds.
- The children write over the dotted letters.

Blending
- Blend the words *foot, look, book; zoo, soon* and *moon* with the children.
- Say the sounds with the children, then blend the sounds together and read the words.
- Encourage the children to point to the dot underneath each sound as they say it.

Sounding
- Say the words corresponding to the pictures on the children's page: *book, hook, bed; moon, ring, spoon*. The children listen for the words without the /oo/ or /oo/ sounds (*bed; ring*), and cross out the pictures.

Word bank
- /oo/ words
  look, foot, woof, wool, hook, book, cook, good, rook, took, wood, stood.
- /oo/ words
  zoo, hoop, zoom, moon, boot, boo, moo, too, boom, cool, food, hoot, mood, noon, pool, roof, root, soon, tool, bloom, scoop, spook, spoon, stool.

Dictation
- Call out the /oo/ sounds and some other sounds already covered for the children to write.
- Dictate the words *wood, good, boot* and *zoom*.
- Call out some words from the word banks.
- The children listen to the words and hold up a finger for each sound.

Further ideas
- Sing the song from the *Jolly Songs* and pin up the /oo/ section of the *Wall Frieze*.
- Make a model cuckoo clock.
- Paint designs on some boot shapes.

Letter Sound /y/

Flash cards
• Revise some of the sounds already learnt: /s/, /a/, /t/, /i/, /p/, /n/, /c/, /k/, /e/, /h/, /r/, /m/, /d/, /g/, /o/, /u/, /l/, /f/, /b/, /ai/, /j/, /oa/, /ie/, /ee/, /or/, /z/, /w/, /ng/, /v/, /oo/, /oo/.

Story
• Introduce the sound /y/ using a story, such as the one below, and the action.

It is lunchtime and Yasmin, Ron and Yamal are having something to eat. Yamal eats his sandwiches quickly, so that he can play with his yo-yo. Yasmin's mum has given her some yogurt. 'That looks nice,' says Ron. 'Yes, it is,' says Yasmin. 'I chose it when we went shopping yesterday. It's a yellow banana yogurt. I love yellow.' 'Please may I try some?' asks Ron. 'Yes,' says Yasmin. 'It's nice,' says Ron, 'a yummy, yellow yogurt!'

Action
• The children pretend to be eating yogurt from a spoon and say, 'y, y, y'.

Formation
• Explain how the letter ‹y› is written. It has a tail that goes under the line.
• The children write over the dotted letters.

Blending
• Blend the words yes, yak, yell, yelp.
• Say the sounds with the children, then blend the sounds together and read the words.
• Encourage the children to point to the dot underneath each sound as they say it.

Sounding
• Say the words corresponding to the pictures on the children's page: cat, yolk, yo-yo, yogurt.
• The children listen for the word without the /y/ sound (cat), and cross out its picture.

Word bank
yes, yak, yell, yelp, yet, yuck, yam, yap.

Dictation
• Call out the sound /y/ and some other sounds already covered for the children to write.
• Dictate the words yam, yet, yap and yen.
• Call out some words from the word bank.
• The children listen to the words and hold up a finger for each sound.

Further ideas
• Sing the song from the Jolly Jingles or the Jolly Songs.
• Put up on the wall, or hold up, the /y/ section of the Wall Frieze.
• Paint a yellow picture.
• Collage a yak using wool.

Letter Sound /x/

Flash cards
- Revise some of the sounds already learnt: /s/, /a/, /t/, /i/, /p/, /n/, /c/, /k/, /e/, /h/, /r/, /m/, /d/, /g/, /o/, /u/, /l/, /f/, /b/, /ai/, /j/, /oa/, /ie/, /ee/, /or/, /z/, /w/, /ng/, /v/, /oo/, /oo/, /y/.
- The sound /x/ is really two sounds: a /k/ and a /s/. However, when the children see the letter ‹x›, they need to be able to say /ks/ together in order to hear the word.

Story
- Introduce the sound /x/ using a story such as the one below, and the action.

Max and Ti are playing. They are pretending to be spacemen. Max, the alien, chases Ti, the astronaut, up a tree. Ti falls out of the tree and hurts his arm. Dad takes Ti and Max to hospital, where Ti has to have an x-ray. Ti has to keep his arm very still while the nurse takes the x-ray, 'ks, ks, ks, ks, ks, ks'. 'Ti's arm is broken,' explains the doctor. The nurse puts a plaster cast on Ti's arm, so that he cannot move it and the bones will mend properly.

Action
- The children pretend to take an x-ray picture of someone and say 'x, x, x'.

Formation
- Explain how the letter ‹x› is written.
- The children write over the dotted letters in their books.

Blending
- Blend the words *box, six, exit, next*.
- Say the sounds with the children, then blend the sounds together and read the words.
- Encourage the children to point to the dot underneath each sound as they say it.

Sounding
- Say the words corresponding to the pictures on the children's page: *box, sheep, six, fox*.
- The children listen for the word without the /x/ sound (*sheep*), and cross out its picture.

Word bank
fox, fax, box, six, mix, tax, wax, sax, exit, fix, sixteen, next, boxing, toolbox, expect, exam, flex, fixing.

Dictation
- Call out the sound /x/ and some other sounds already covered for the children to write.
- Dictate the words *fox, sax, mix* and *fax*.
- Call out some words from the word bank.
- The children listen to the words and hold up a finger for each sound.

Further ideas
- Sing the song from the *Jolly Jingles* or the *Jolly Songs*.
- Put up on the wall, or hold up, the /x/ section of the *Wall Frieze*.
- Look at pictures of skeletons and x-rays.
- Make x-ray pictures with white straws and black paper.

Letter Sound /ch/

Flash cards
• Revise some of the sounds already learnt: /s/, /a/, /t/, /i/, /p/, /n/, /c/, /k/, /e/, /h/, /r/, /m/, /d/, /g/, /o/, /u/, /l/, /f/, /b/, /ai/, /j/, /oa/, /ie/, /ee/, /or/, /z/, /w/, /ng/, /v/, /oo/, /oo/, /y/, /x/.

Story
• Introduce the sound /ch/ using a story, such as the one below, and the action.

The children in Charlie's class are studying transport. Their teacher has arranged an outing to a transport museum. In the afternoon, the children get to ride on a steam train. They are very excited. They all climb into the carriage. The train starts chugging, 'ch, ch, ch, ch.' The train goes faster, 'ch, ch, ch, ch!' Then, steam comes out of the funnel, and the whistle blows. 'Choo! Choo!' The next day at school, all the children pretend to be trains, going, 'ch, ch, ch, ch!' They chuff around, pretending to stop at lots of different places so the passengers can get on and off.

Action
• The children move their arms at their sides, as though they are a steam train and say, 'ch, ch, ch'.

Formation
• Explain how the digraph ‹ch› is written.
• The children write over the dotted letters in their books.

Blending
• Blend the words *chops, chips, bunch, chain.*
• Say the sounds with the children, then blend the sounds together and read the words.
• Encourage the children to point to the dot underneath each sound as they say it.

Sounding
• Say the words corresponding to the pictures on the children's page: *cheese, chimney, butterfly, chick.*
• The children listen for the word without the /ch/ sound (*butterfly*), and cross out its picture.

Word bank
chat, chest, chess, check, chin, chip, chill, chick, chimp, chop, rich, much, such, bench, drench, pinch, bunch, lunch, munch, chain, cheek, speech, coach, torch.

Dictation
• Call out the sound /ch/ and some other sounds already covered for the children to write.
• Dictate the words *much, such, chat* and *chin.*
• Call out some words from the word bank.
• The children listen to the words and hold up a finger for each sound.

Further ideas
• Sing the song from the *Jolly Jingles* or the *Jolly Songs.*
• Put up on the wall, or hold up, the /ch/ section of the *Wall Frieze.*
• Pretend to be a train and chuff around saying 'ch, ch, ch!'

Letter Sound /sh/

Flash cards
- Revise some of the sounds already learnt: /s/, /a/, /t/, /i/, /p/, /n/, /c/, /k/, /e/, /h/, /r/, /m/, /d/, /g/, /o/, /u/, /l/, /f/, /b/, /ai/, /j/, /oa/, /ie/, /ee/, /or/, /z/, /w/, /ng/, /v/, /oo/, **/oo/**, /y/, /x/, /ch/.

Story
- Introduce the sound /sh/ using a story such as the one below, and the action.

Mrs. Shaw has just had a baby. The baby is called Shannon. Sam is the baby's elder brother. Sam thinks Shannon is all right, but she cries a lot. While his mother tries to get Shannon to sleep, Sam goes and plays with his toys. He plays in his shop, with his cash register. It makes a very loud 'ting' when the cash drawer opens. 'Shshshshsh,' whispers Mrs Shaw, putting her finger to her lips. 'Shannon is nearly asleep. Let's go downstairs for a while.' 'OK,' says Sam, adding, 'shshshsh,' as they tiptoe quietly from the room.

Action
- The children place their finger over their lips, saying, 'sh, sh, shhhh!'

Formation
- Explain how the digraph ‹sh› is written.
- The children write over the dotted letters in their books.

Blending
- Blend the words *shop, fish, sheep, brush*.
- Say the sounds with the children, then blend the sounds together and read the words.
- Encourage the children to point to the dot underneath each sound as they say it.

Sounding
- Say the words corresponding to the pictures on the children's page: *sheep, fish, shell, teddy bear*.
- The children listen for the word without the /sh/ sound (*teddy bear*), and cross out its picture.

Word bank
shed, shelf, shell, shin, ship, shift, shop, shot, shock, shut, shrimp, ash, bash, cash, mash, rash, dish, fish, wish, hush, rush, crash, splash, fresh, brush, sheep, sheet, shoot, shook, short, shampoo, mushroom, shopping, paintbrush.

Dictation
- Call out the sound /sh/ and some other sounds already covered for the children to write.
- Dictate the words *ash, wish, sheet* and *shed*.
- Call out some words from the word bank.
- The children listen to the words and hold up a finger for each sound.

Further ideas
- Sing the song from the *Jolly Jingles* or the *Jolly Songs*.
- Put up on the wall, or hold up, the /sh/ section of the *Wall Frieze*.
- Make sheep with cotton wool fleeces.
- Have a class shop.

Letter Sounds /th/ and /th/

Flash cards
- Revise some of the sounds already learnt.
- The digraph ‹th› has two sounds, the voiced sound /th/, in *this, that, then*, and the unvoiced /**th**/, in *thin, thick, three*.

Story
- Introduce the /th/ sounds using a story, such as the one below, and the action.

Matthew and Nathan have gone to the circus. The ringmaster opens the circus and introduces the acts. First, there is a juggler, throwing three rings high into the air. Then, two naughty clowns throw water at the ringmaster, who tells them off. One clown, a thin fellow, is rather rude. He sticks his tongue out at the ringmaster, but only a little way; 'th,' he goes. The other clown, who is much bigger, is very rude. He sticks his tongue right out; 'ththth!' he goes. Then the clowns chase one another and tickle each other with feathers. Everyone laughs at them.

Action
- The children pretend to be naughty clowns and stick out their tongues, a little way for the /th/ sound and further for the /**th**/ sound.

Formation
- Explain how the digraph ‹th› is written.
- The children write over the dotted letters in their books. One size of writing is used for the two /th/ sounds.

Blending
- Blend the words *this, that, them; moth, three, thin.*
- Say the sounds with the children, then blend the sounds together and read the words.

Sounding
- Say the words corresponding to the pictures on the children's page: *three, feather, frog, moth.*
- The children listen for the words without a /th/ sound or a /**th**/ sound (*frog*), and cross out its picture.

Word bank
- /th/ words
  than, them, this, that, then, with, smooth.
- /**th**/ words
  thank, theft, thin, thing, think, thick, throb, thump, sixth, moth, cloth, froth, teeth, three, throat, tooth, north, thud, thorn, toothbrush.

Dictation
- Call out the /th/ sounds and some other sounds already covered for the children to write.
- Dictate the words *than, with, tooth* and *thud.*
- Call out some words from the word banks.
- The children listen to the words and hold up a finger for each sound.

Further ideas
- Sing the song from the *Jolly Songs* and pin up the /th/ section of the *Wall Frieze.*
- Make a picture using feathers.
- Find out about moths.

Letter Sound /qu/

Flash cards
- Revise some of the sounds already learnt.
- The sound /qu/ is really two sounds: a /k/ and a /w/. However, when the children see the letters ‹qu› they need to be able to say /kw/ together in order to hear the word.

Story
- Introduce the sound /qu/ using a story, such as the one below, and the action.

Quentin quite enjoys going to the park with his family. They always take some stale bread so that they can feed the ducks and Quentin likes to give some to the squirrels too. When they see Quentin with a bag of bread, the squirrels scamper over quickly. Two squirrels grab the same slice. They begin to quarrel, squeaking at each other and tugging at the bread. The ducks also see the bread and rush to the side of the pond, quacking loudly, 'qu, qu, qu!' Quentin throws pieces of bread into the pond for the ducks. Then Quentin pretends that he is a duck. He goes, 'qu, qu, qu,' and opens and shuts his hands like a beak.

Action
- The children make their hands into a duck's bill and say, 'qu, qu, qu'.

Formation
- Explain how the digraph ‹qu› is written.
- The children write over the dotted letters.

Blending
- Blend the words *quick, quilt, liquid, squid*.
- Say the sounds with the children, then blend the sounds together and read the words.
- Encourage the children to point to the dot underneath each sound as they say it.

Sounding
- Say the words corresponding to the pictures on the children's page: *queen, squirrel, map, question mark*.
- The children listen for the word without the /qu/ sound (*map*), and cross out its picture.

Word bank
quit, quiz, quick, quilt, quins, squid, liquid, queen, quill, quack, quest, quench, quail.

Dictation
- Call out the sound /qu/ and some other sounds already covered for the children to write.
- Dictate the words *quit, quiz, queen* and *quail*.
- Call out some words from the word bank.
- The children listen to the words and hold up a finger for each sound.

Further ideas
- Sing the song from the *Jolly Jingles* or the *Jolly Songs*.
- Put up on the wall, or hold up, the /qu/ section of the *Wall Frieze*.
- Draw a picture of ducks on a pond.
- Collage a squirrel with a wool tail.

Letter Sound /ou/

Flash cards
· Revise some of the sounds already learnt: /s/, /a/, /t/, /i/, /p/, /n/, /c/, /k/, /e/, /h/, /r/, /m/, /d/, /g/, /o/, /u/, /l/, /f/, /b/, /ai/, /j/, /oa/, /ie/, /ee/, /or/, /z/, /w/, /ng/, /v/, /oo/, /**oo**/, /y/, /x/, /ch/, /sh/, /th/, /**th**/ and /qu/.

Story
· Introduce the sound /ou/ using a story, such as the one below, and the action.

Emily has gone to stay at her grandmother's house. Emily's grandmother does a lot of sewing. Emily asks if she can do some sewing, too. Gran gets out a piece of cloth from her sewing basket. Emily has found a reel of brown cotton and Gran helps her to thread the needle. Emily sits down on the couch and does a few stitches. Then, as she pushes the needle through the cloth, she pricks her thumb. She frowns and shouts, 'ou, ou! That hurt!' 'You must be careful, Emily,' says Gran. By the end of her visit, Emily has done a lot of sewing. She is much better at it now, and she has made a little mat as a present for her parents. She has embroidered a brown owl on it.

Action
· The children pretend that their finger is a needle and use it to prick their thumb, saying 'ou, ou, ou'.

Formation
· Explain how the digraph ‹ou› is written.
· The children write over the dotted letters in their books.

Blending
· Blend the words *cloud, proud, mouth, shout.*
· Say the sounds with the children, then blend the sounds together and read the words.
· Encourage the children to point to the dot underneath each sound as they say it.

Sounding
· Say the words corresponding to the pictures on the children's page: *cloud, cheese, house, mouth.*

· The children listen for the word without the /ou/ sound (*cheese*), and cross out its picture.

Word bank
out, loud, noun, cloud, trout, scout, snout, spout, sprout, joust, found, round, sound, ground, count, shout, couch, mouth, south, crouch, about, around, aloud.

Dictation
· Call out the sound /ou/ and some other sounds already covered for the children to write.
· Dictate the words *out, loud* and *noun.*
· Call out some words from the word bank.
· The children listen to the words and hold up a finger for each sound.

Further ideas
· Sing the song from the *Jolly Songs* and pin up the /ou/ section of the *Wall Frieze.*
· Do some sewing or lacing.
· Draw houses and describe them.

Letter Sound /oi/

Flash cards

- Revise some of the sounds already learnt: /s/, /a/, /t/, /i/, /p/, /n/, /c/, /k/, /e/, /h/, /r/, /m/, /d/, /g/, /o/, /u/, /l/, /f/, /b/, /ai/, /j/, /oa/, /ie/, /ee/, /or/, /z/, /w/, /ng/, /v/, /oo/, /**oo**/, /y/, /x/, /ch/, /sh/, /th/, /**th**/, /qu/, /ou/.

Story

- Introduce the sound /oi/ using a story, such as the one below, and the action.

Roy's dad has a little boat, called Sailor Boy. Sometimes, in the summer, Roy is allowed to join his dad on the boat. One morning, Roy, Dad and Uncle Martin are taking the boat out. They pack all their things, climb aboard and set off. They are really enjoying themselves, when, BANG! There is a loud noise as they hit something in the water. It is an oil drum. 'Oh dear,' says Dad. 'It's made a hole.' Just then, they see a ship, steaming along. 'Quick,' says Dad, pointing at the ship. 'We'll shout for help. Oi, oi, ship ahoy!' The sailors from the ship hear their voices and yell back, 'oi, ship ahoy, are you in trouble?' 'Yes, we're sinking. Help!' they cry. The sailors help Roy and his dad get the boat back to port.

Action

- The children cup their hands around their mouth and shout, 'oi, oi, ship ahoy!'

Formation

- Explain how the digraph ‹oi› is written.
- The children write over the dotted letters in their books.

Blending

- Blend the words *soil, joint, point* and *void*.
- Say the sounds with the children, then blend the sounds together and read the words.
- Encourage the children to point to the dot underneath each sound as they say it.

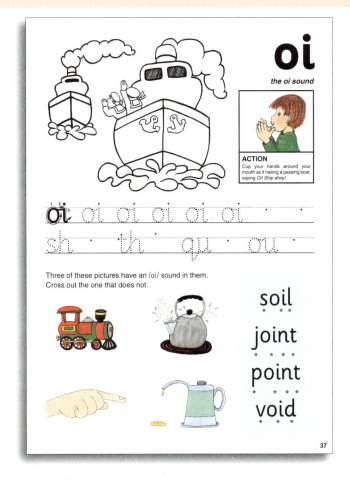

Sounding

- Say the words corresponding to the pictures on the children's page: *train, boil, point, oil*.
- The children listen for the word without the /oi/ sound (*train*), and cross out its picture.

Word bank

oil, boil, coil, coin, foil, join, soil, toil, spoil, joint, point, moist, boiling, toilet, tinfoil, oilcan, avoid.

Dictation

- Call out the sound /oi/ and some other sounds already covered for the children to write.
- Dictate the words *oil, boil, join* and *coin*.
- Call out some words from the word bank.
- The children listen to the words and hold up a finger for each sound.

Further ideas

- Sing the song from the *Jolly Songs* and pin up the /oi/ section of the *Wall Frieze*.
- Make boats.

Letter Sound /ue/

Flash cards

- Revise some of the sounds already learnt: /s/, /a/, /t/, /i/, /p/, /n/, /c/, /k/, /e/, /h/, /r/, /m/, /d/, /g/, /o/, /u/, /l/, /f/, /b/, /ai/, /j/, /oa/, /ie/, /ee/, /or/, /z/, /w/, /ng/, /v/, /oo/, /oo/, /y/, /x/, /ch/, /sh/, /th/, /**th**/, /qu/, /ou/, /oi/.
- The digraph ‹ue› is sometimes pronounced as a long /oo/ sound, for example in the words: *glue, blue, clue.*

Story

- Introduce the sound /ue/ using a story, such as the one below, and the action.

It is Samuel's birthday and he is having a party. First, Samuel and his friends play musical chairs. After that, a magician performs a magic show. He is very amusing. He uses a magic wand and he has a big magic box with a unicorn on the side. The magician does a few card tricks, and then he asks for someone to come and help him. 'You,' he says, pointing at Samuel, 'You are the birthday boy', he continues, 'will you come and help me?' 'Me?' asks Samuel. 'You!' shout the children. Samuel helps the magician do a special trick. He has to wave the magic wand and say, 'ue, ue, ue.' Right on cue, a rabbit pops out from under the magician's table! After the magic show, they all go outside and have a barbecue.

Action

- The children point to people around them and say, 'ue, ue, ue'.

Formation

- Explain how the digraph ‹ue› is written.
- The children write over the dotted letters in their books.

Blending

- Blend the words *fuel, statue, value, rescue.*
- Say the sounds with the children, then blend the sounds together and read the words.
- Encourage the children to point to the dot underneath each sound as they say it.

Sounding

- Say the words corresponding to the pictures on the children's page: *drum, cube, statue, barbecue.*
- The children listen for the word without the /ue/ sound (*drum*), and cross out its picture.

Word bank

cue, duel, fuel, value, rescue, statue, tissue.

Dictation

- Call out the sound /ue/ and some other sounds already covered for the children to write.
- Dictate the words *value, cue* and *duel.*
- Call out some words from the word bank.
- The children listen to the words and hold up a finger for each sound.

Further ideas

- Sing the song from the *Jolly Songs* pin up the /ue/ section of the *Wall Frieze.*
- Paint a unicorn.
- Build a model with cubes and tubes.

Letter Sound /er/

Flash cards
• Revise some of the sounds already learnt.

Story
• Introduce the sound /er/ using a story, such as the one below, and the action.

Bert's teacher, Mr. Bird, has been reading *The Gingerbread Man* to his class. When Bert gets home, he asks if he can make some gingerbread for supper. First, he and his sister, Jennifer, help to weigh the butter, sugar, flour, eggs and the ground ginger. Then they put all the ingredients in a bowl and stir. 'Erererer,' goes the mixer. Bert and Jennifer roll their hands over and over, pretending to be the mixer; 'er, er, er, er, er,' they go. Next, Bert and Jennifer roll out their mixture, cut out the gingerbread shapes, and bake them in the oven. When the gingerbread has cooked and cooled, Bert decorates the biscuits with frosting and currants. He makes a special biscuit to take into school for his teacher.

Action
• The children roll their hands over each other, like a mixer, and say 'er, er, er'.

Formation
• Explain how the digraph ‹er› is written.
• The children write over the dotted letters in their books.

Blending
• Blend the words *verb, letter, winter, runner*.
• Say the sounds with the children, then blend the sounds together and read the words.
• Encourage the children to point to the dot underneath each sound as they say it.

Sounding
• Say the words corresponding to the pictures on the children's page: *spider, tiger, letter, kite*.
• The children listen for the word without the /er/ sound (*kite*), and cross out its picture.

Word bank
her, herb, silver, deeper, summer, dinner, ladder, longer, stronger, sister, chatter, helper, sender, jester, blender, litter, printer, singer, trucker, jumper, zipper, duster, waiter, thunderstorm, cooker, helicopter, corner, understand.

Dictation
• Call out the sound /er/ and some other sounds already covered for the children to write.
• Dictate the words *her, silver, winter* and *fern*.
• Call out some words from the word bank.
• The children listen to the words and hold up a finger for each sound.

Further ideas
• Sing the song from the *Jolly Songs* and pin up the /er/ section of the *Wall Frieze*.
• Make gingerbread people and decorate them.
• Make summer and winter pictures.

Letter Sound /ar/

Flash cards
• Revise some of the sounds already learnt: /s/, /a/, /t/, /i/, /p/, /n/, /c/, /k/, /e/, /h/, /r/, /m/, /d/, /g/, /o/, /u/, /l/, /f/, /b/, /ai/, /j/, /oa/, /ie/, /ee/, /or/, /z/, /w/, /ng/, /v/, /oo/, /**oo**/, /y/, /x/, /ch/, /sh/, /th/, /**th**/, /qu/, /ou/, /oi/, /ue/, /er/.

Story
• Introduce the sound /ar/ using a story, such as the one below, and the action.

Barbara has not been feeling very well. She has a sore throat and it is hard for her to talk. Barbara's mum takes her to see the doctor. It is not very far in the car. Mum makes sure Barbara wears a warm scarf. The doctor starts by asking Barbara to open her mouth and say 'ah.' 'Ah,' says Barbara. The doctor looks into her mouth. 'Ah, you have a throat infection,' he says. He gives her some tablets, and soon the sore throat has gone. Now Barbara is able to go and play in the park with all her friends.

Action
• The children open their mouths wide and say, 'aahhhh'.

Formation
• Explain how the digraph ‹ar› is written.
• The children write over the dotted letters in their books.

Blending
• Blend the words *jar, dark, shark, scarf.*
• Say the sounds with the children, then blend the sounds together and read the words.
• Encourage the children to point to the dot underneath each sound as they say it.

Sounding
• Say the words corresponding to the pictures on the children's page: *star, arm, goat, car.*
• The children listen for the word without the /ar/ sound (*goat*), and cross out its picture.

Word bank
art, ark, bar, car, arm, jar, bark, barn, card, cart, dark, dart, farm, hard, harm, harp, park, part, tart, yard, star, scar, spark, start, scarf, smart, shark, sharp, charm, chart, marsh, arch, march, farmer, farmyard, cartoon.

Dictation
• Call out the sound /ar/ and some other sounds already covered for the children to write.
• Dictate the words *art, card, star* and *march.*
• Call out some words from the word banks.
• The children listen to the words and hold up a finger for each sound.

Further ideas
• Sing the song from the *Jolly Jingles* or the *Jolly Songs.*
• Put up on the wall, or hold up, the /ar/ section of the *Wall Frieze.*
• Make stars from shiny paper.
• Design a park using a construction set.

Tricky Words

Flash cards
- Revise some of the basic 42 sounds:
/s/, /a/, /t/, /i/, /p/, /n/, /c/, /k/, /e/, /h/, /r/, /m/, /d/, /g/, /o/, /u/, /l/, /f/, /b/, /ai/, /j/, /oa/, /ie/, /ee/, /or/, /z/, /w/, /ng/, /v/, /oo/, /**oo**/, /y/, /x/, /ch/, /sh/, /th/, /**th**/, /qu/, /ou/, /oi/, /ue/, /er/ and /ar/.

Tricky words
- Explain that some words are not written exactly as they sound, and that we call these words 'tricky words'.
- We also use this term to describe words that have alternative spellings that have not yet been taught.
- To remember how to spell these words, the children have to look for, and remember, the 'tricky bits'.
- Introduce the tricky words: *the, he, she, me, we*, and *be*. The children look at these words in the flowers on the page.
- Point out that the /ee/ sound at the end of each word is written with only one ‹e›, even though it sounds like there should be two.
- The children might find it helpful to underline the ‹e› at the end of each of these words in purple, to remind them that this is the 'tricky bit'.
- Whilst the sound /th/ is written ‹th›, the tricky word *the*, has an ‹e› on the end.
- Point out to the children that they must remember to add the ‹e› when writing the tricky word *the*.

Look, copy, cover, write, check
- Look at the first word, *the*, with the children.
- Say the letter names (not the letter sounds) in that word.
- The children write over the dotted word *the*.
- Then the children cover up all instances of the word *the* on their page and try writing the word in the next column.
- Once the children have had one try at writing *the*, they check their spelling.
- Then they cover up all instances of the word *the* again, and have another go at writing *the* in the final column.
- Repeat these steps with the other words.

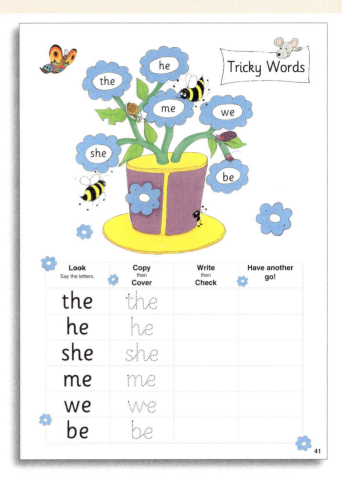

Further blending practice
- Write the following list of words on the board and blend them with the children:
    joint,
    winner,
    cartoon,
    thorn,
    sound.

Reading sentences
- Write the following sentences on the board, pointing out the tricky words and blending any unknown words with the children.
1. The dog jumps on the cat.
2. She is sleeping in the barn.
3. We must not drop litter.
4. The king had a red cloak.

Reading and Writing Activities

Flash cards
- Revise some of the basic 42 sounds:
/s/, /a/, /t/, /i/, /p/, /n/, /c/, /k/, /e/, /h/, /r/, /m/,
/d/, /g/, /o/, /u/, /l/, /f/, /b/, /ai/, /j/, /oa/, /ie/, /ee/,
/or/, /z/, /w/, /ng/, /v/, /oo/, /**oo**/, /y/, /x/, /ch/, /sh/,
/th/, /**th**/, /qu/, /ou/, /oi/, /ue/, /er/ and /ar/.
- Use the flash cards, or the *Tricky Word Wall Flowers*, to revise the tricky words *the, he, she, me, we,* and *be*.

Reading words with short vowels
- The children read the words under the picture frames and draw a picture in the frames to illustrate each word.
- The words are: *ant, van, cup.*

Writing short words
- The children look at each picture, say the word and listen for the sounds. They might need some help hearing each individual sound.
- For the first row of pictures, the children write over the dotted letters and fill in the missing sounds.
- For the next two rows of pictures, the children are expected to listen for the sounds and write the whole word on the lines provided.
- A line is provided for each sound in the words.
- A longer line indicates a digraph is needed.
- The pictures are:
    mixer, queen, chin
    hen, sun, ant
    wood, six, ring

Further blending practice
- Write the following list of words on the board and blend them with the children:
    quit,
    throat,
    rubbish,
    ostrich,
    mix.

Reading sentences
- Write the following sentences on the board, pointing out the tricky words and blending any unknown words with the children.
  1. He can finish the job next week.
  2. This will be the best toolbox.
  3. The rocket zooms up and up.
  4. Can we feed the ducks?

Tricky Words

Flash cards
- Revise some of the basic 42 sounds already learnt.
- Use the flash cards, or the *Tricky Word Wall Flowers*, to revise the tricky words *the, he, she, me, we,* and *be.*

Tricky words
- Introduce the new tricky words: *I, was, to, do, are,* and *all.* The children look at these words in the flowers in their books.
- Explain that the letter ‹i› is shy, so when it appears on its own as the tricky word *I*, it puffs itself up and uses its capital letter.
- When introducing the tricky word *was*, say it first by blending its sounds and tell the children that *was* (pronouncing it to rhyme with *mass*), says /woz/.
- Point out that *to* and *do* both have an /oo/ sound at the end, but they are written with only one ‹o›.
- The children might find it helpful to underline the ‹o› at the end of these two words in purple, to remind them that this is the 'tricky bit'.
- Point out that the sound /ar/ is written ‹ar›, but the tricky word *are* has an ‹e› at the end.
- When the children can read *all*, they can also read words with ‹all› at the end, such as *ball* and *call*.

Look, copy, cover, write, check
- Look at the first word, *I*, with the children.
- Say the letter names (not the letter sounds) in that word. The children write over the dotted word *I*.
- Point out the capital letter in this word.
- Then the children cover up all instances of the word *I* on their page and try writing the word in the next column.
- Once the children have had one try at writing *I*, they check their spelling. Then they cover up all instances of the word *I* again, and have another go at writing *I* in the final column.
- Repeat these steps with the other words.

Further blending practice
- Write the following list of words on the board and blend them with the children:
  > took,
  > toadstool,
  > dinner,
  > coin,
  > sharper.

Reading sentences
- Write the following sentences on the board, pointing out the tricky words and blending any unknown words with the children.
  1. I can do the dishes in the morning.
  2. All the fish are in the pond.
  3. She went to the park.
  4. He sat on the picnic rug.

Reading and Writing Activities

Flash cards
- Revise some of the basic 42 sounds:
/s/, /a/, /t/, /i/, /p/, /n/, /c/, /k/, /e/, /h/, /r/, /m/,
/d/, /g/, /o/, /u/, /l/, /f/, /b/, /ai/, /j/, /oa/, /ie/, /ee/,
/or/, /z/, /w/, /ng/, /v/, /oo/, /**oo**/, /y/, /x/, /ch/, /sh/,
/th/, /**th**/, /qu/, /ou/, /oi/, /ue/, /er/ and /ar/.
- Use the flash cards, or the *Tricky Word Wall
Flowers*, to revise the tricky words *the, he,
she, me, we, be, I, was, to, do, are* and *all*.

Words with digraphs and consonant blends
- Look at the pictures with the children, and
say the word for each one.
- The children listen for the sounds in each
word, and write the words underneath the
pictures.
- A line is provided for each sound in the words.
- A longer line indicates a digraph is needed.
- The pictures are:
    moth, tree, star
    fish, boat, moon
    snail, flag, nest

Look at the pictures and write the words underneath.

Read the sentences and draw a picture in each frame.

This is me.   I can run.

44

Reading and illustrating sentences
- Many tricky words are very common words
and it is difficult to read or write a sentence
that does not have a tricky word in it.
- Although, so far, you have concentrated on
teaching the lower case letters, point out to
the children that sentences start with a
capital letter.
- Point to the capitals *T* and *I* on this page, and
refer the children to the capital letters on the
/t/ and /i/ pages in their pupil books.
- Point out that each sentence ends with a full
stop.
- The children read each sentence, and
illustrate the sentences in the picture
frames.
- The sentences are:
    This is me.
    I can run.

Further blending practice
- Write the following list of words on the board
and blend them with the children:
    thanks,
    quick,
    footsteps,
    yes,
    toffee.

Reading sentences
- Write the following sentences on the board,
pointing out the tricky words and blending
any unknown words with the children.
1. We can all sing the songs.
2. I do not need the stool.
3. He was good at tennis.
4. We are clever.

Tricky Words

Flash cards
- Revise some of the basic 42 sounds:
/s/, /a/, /t/, /i/, /p/, /n/, /c/, /k/, /e/, /h/, /r/, /m/,
/d/, /g/, /o/, /u/, /l/, /f/, /b/, /ai/, /j/, /oa/, /ie/, /ee/,
/or/, /z/, /w/, /ng/, /v/, /oo/, /oo/, /y/, /x/, /ch/, /sh/,
/th/, /**th**/, /qu/, /ou/, /oi/, /ue/, /er/ and /ar/.
- Use the flash cards, or the *Tricky Word Wall Flowers*, to revise the tricky words *the, he, she, me, we, be, I, was, to, do, are* and *all*.

Reading CVC words
- Look at the words and pictures at the top of the page with the children.
- Read the first word, *cat*, to the children. Point out that it is joined to the picture of the cat.
- The children read the remaining words and join each word to the corresponding picture.
- All the words are CVC words (consonant-vowel-consonant words), and have short vowel sounds.
- Once the children have joined each word to the right picture, they can colour the pictures.

Tricky words word search
- Look at the tricky word flowers surrounding the word search and read the tricky words with the children.
- The children have to find each tricky word in the word search, and lightly shade the squares blue.
- As they find each tricky word, the children cross out the corresponding flower.

Reading sentences
- Write the following sentences on the board, pointing out the tricky words and blending any unknown words with the children.
1. The snail left a long trail.
2. Do not groan or moan.
3. We all had fun.
4. The dog was wagging his tail.

Further blending practice
- Write the following list of words on the board and blend them with the children:
    sheet,
    think,
    bumper,
    blend,
    sack.

Reading and Writing Activities

Flash cards
- Revise some of the basic 42 sounds:
/s/, /a/, /t/, /i/, /p/, /n/, /c/, /k/, /e/, /h/, /r/, /m/,
/d/, /g/, /o/, /u/, /l/, /f/, /b/, /ai/, /j/, /oa/, /ie/, /ee/,
/or/, /z/, /w/, /ng/, /v/, /oo/, /oo/, /y/, /x/, /ch/, /sh/,
/th/, /th/, /qu/, /ou/, /oi/, /ue/, /er/ and /ar/.
- Use the flash cards, or the *Tricky Word Wall Flowers*, to revise the tricky words *the, he, she, me, we, be, I, was, to, do, are* and *all*.

Sentence reading
- The children read each sentence, and then draw a picture in the frame to illustrate the sentence.
- The sentences are:
    He can sing.
    She is sad.
    I can jump.
    We can hop.
    The sun is hot.
    Drums are loud.

Further blending practice
- Write the following list of words on the board and blend them with the children:
    windmill,
    foghorn,
    weep,
    zigzag,
    wedding.

Reading sentences
- Write the following sentences on the board, pointing out the tricky words and blending any unknown words with the children.
1. Bring all the books to me.
2. We are to sit and wait on the bench.
3. I ran to the helicopter.
4. We are all about to jump in the pool.

Reading and Writing Activities

Flash cards

- Revise some of the basic 42 sounds:
/s/, /a/, /t/, /i/, /p/, /n/, /c/, /k/, /e/, /h/, /r/, /m/,
/d/, /g/, /o/, /u/, /l/, /f/, /b/, /ai/, /j/, /oa/, /ie/, /ee/,
/or/, /z/, /w/, /ng/, /v/, /oo/, /**oo**/, /y/, /x/, /ch/, /sh/,
/th/, /**th**/, /qu/, /ou/, /oi/, /ue/, /er/ and /ar/.
- Use the flash cards, or the *Tricky Word Wall Flowers*, to revise the tricky words *the, he, she, me, we, be, I, was, to, do, are* and *all*.

Missing words

- The children read each sentence and write the missing word in the gap. The adjacent picture provides the clue.
- The sentences (with missing words in brackets) are:
  The (pie) is hot.
  The (frog) is green.
  The (tent) is big.
  The (bee) flies.
- On the second half of the page the children not only have to fill in the missing words, but also have to colour the picture so that it corresponds to the sentence.
- The sentences (with missing words in brackets) are:
  The (car) is red.
  I see the green (tree).
  The (fish) is pink.
  The (pen) is blue.

Further blending practice

- Write the following list of words on the board and blend them with the children:
  cooker,
  sharp,
  plain,
  float,
  steer.

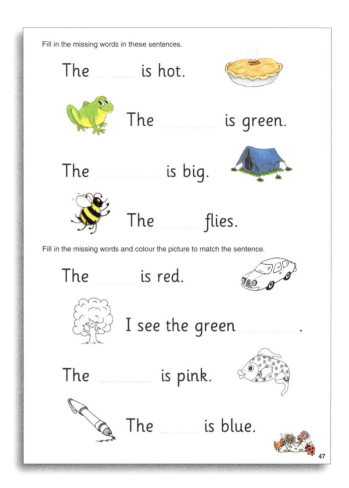

Reading sentences

- Write the following sentences on the board, pointing out the tricky words and blending any unknown words with the children.
  1. He must be a twin.
  2. We all need to bring our food.
  3. His footprints are big.
  4. I must not crash the car.

Revision page

- Page 48 is a revision page for the children.
- The children read the tricky words in the flowers.
- Then they trace inside the outline letters and digraphs.

Teaching with Phonics Pupil Book 2

In *Phonics Pupil Book 1*, the basic 42 sounds were introduced and the children were taught one way of writing each of these sounds. Towards the end of *Phonics Pupil Book 1*, the children were taught how to read and spell the first twelve tricky words.

The basic letter-sound skills taught in *Phonics Pupil Book 1* enable the children to tackle their first reading books. Once *Phonics Pupil Book 1* has been completed, any children who are able to decode regular words independently and know the first twelve tricky words can start reading decodable books. If the *Jolly Phonics Readers* are available, these more able children can be given books from the Red Level.

If the *Jolly Phonics Readers*, or similar decodable books, are not available, the children can practise their blending skills by reading the Further Blending Practice words and the Reading Sentences provided in the Daily Lesson Plans.

The exercises in *Phonics Pupil Book 2* provide the children with numerous opportunities to practise reading and writing the letter sounds they have learnt. *Phonics Pupil Book 2* also introduces some of the common alternative spellings for these sounds, as well as teaching the capital letters and introducing more tricky words. The blending activities in *Phonics Pupil Book 2* encourage the children towards greater fluency in their reading and the various writing activities help them to become independent and confident writers

Like *Phonics Pupil Book 1*, *Phonics Pupil Book 2* is designed so that each page is a complete lesson. The teaching covered in each lesson follows a pattern and the following types of activities are covered on a regular basis.

Alternatives

In *Phonics Pupil Book 1*, one way of writing each sound was introduced. However, in the English language there are often a number of ways to write an individual sound and these alternative spellings also need to be taught. To begin with, the children should only be expected to recognise these alternative letter-sound spellings when reading; they should not be expected to use the correct alternative letter-sound spellings consistently in their writing. The children need to revise the alternative letter-sound spellings frequently. The Further Blending Practice words give the children the opportunity to practise blending words containing these alternatives.

The following alternative letter-sound spellings are introduced in *Phonics Pupil Book 2*.

⟨y⟩ making an /**ee**/ sound at the end of a word, as in *holly*
⟨ck⟩ making a /**ck**/ sound in words with a short vowel sound, as in *back*
double letters in words with short vowels, as in *rabbit*
'**hop-over e**' digraphs, as in the words *cake, eve, kite, rope, mule*
⟨ay⟩ spelling for the /**ai**/ sound, as in *day*
⟨oy⟩ spelling for the /**oi**/ sound, as in *boy*
⟨ea⟩ making the /**ee**/ sound, as in *leaf*
⟨y⟩ making the /**ie**/ sound, as in *my*
⟨ow⟩ making the /**oa**/ sound in *snow* and the /**ou**/ sound in *owl*
⟨ir⟩ and ⟨ur⟩ making the /**er**/ sound, as in *bird* and *curl*

Handwriting and dictation

In *Phonics Pupil Book 2*, dictation and handwriting activities are covered on the same page.

Dictation
The teacher calls out the dictation words provided in the Daily Lesson Plans. The children listen for each sound in the words and then write the words on the lines in their books. For more information about dictation, see page 25 of the introduction.

Handwriting
The handwriting exercises in *Phonics Pupil Book 2* concentrate first on the formation capital letters and later on the revision of certain types of letter, for example tall letters, tail letters and letters that start with a 'caterpillar c'.

- The children trace inside the outline letters and write over the line of dotted letters.
- On the pages where there are starting dots above the line, the children have to write the letters by themselves. The children need to remember to start each letter at the dots and ensure that all their letters sit on the line.
- When the capital letters are being introduced, teachers should explain how each letter is formed before the children start writing.

Letter formation is very important and it is worth taking the time to ensure it is correct. For more information, see pages 13 to 15 of the introduction for the section on letter formation. When children are learning the capital letters, they need to be taught the letter names as well as the sound each letter makes.

Tricky words

These pages introduce the children to more of the tricky words and help them to revise the tricky words that have already been taught. For more information, see pages 30 to 33 of this book for the section on tricky words.

The following tricky words are introduced in *Phonics Pupil Book 2*.

> you, your, come, some, said, here, there, they, go, no, so my
> > (yellow words)
> one, by, only, old, like, have, live, give, little, down, what, when
> > (red words)
> why, where, who, which
> > (green words)

Comprehension

There are a number of reading activities in *Phonics Pupil Book 2*, which aim to improve the children's blending and comprehension skills.

Teachers can also improve children's levels of comprehension by discussing the Further Blending Practice words and sentences and explaining any words the children do not understand.

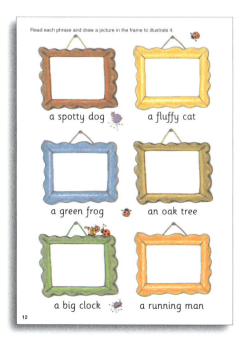

Words and sentences

These pages help the children to start writing independently. To begin with, children need plenty of help and guidance when writing.

- The guided writing pages provide the children with a writing topic and a model sentence to get them started.
- The teacher uses the picture to help initiate a class discussion. He or she then selects some key words from the discussion to write on the board, pointing out any alternative spelling patterns in these words.
- The teacher uses the model sentence provided in the Daily Lesson Plan as an opportunity to explain basic sentence structure. The following things can be pointed out as the teacher writes the model sentence on the board.
    - All sentences start with a capital letter and end with a full stop.
    - Leave a space between words.
    - Read what you have written and make sure that it makes sense.
- All the children copy the model sentence from the board and try to write some more sentences by themselves. Some children will be able to write independently at an early stage, but others may take more time.

The more able children can move on to the Yellow Level of *Jolly Phonics Readers* when the have learnt the tricky words up to and including *they* and once they know that ‹y› can make the /ee/ sound when it comes at the end of a word. This knowledge is covered on pages 1 to 17 of *Phonics Pupil Book 2*.

Alternatives: ‹y› Making an /ee/ Sound

Flash cards
- Revise some of the basic 42 sounds.

Alternatives: ‹y› as /ee/
- Explain that the letter ‹y› only says the sound /y/ when it comes at the beginning of a word (as in the words *yummy, yellow, yoghurt*), or sometimes in the middle (as in the word *beyond*). When a ‹y› comes at the end of the word it makes an /ee/ sound.
- Remind the children that, when two letters making the same sound are next to each other, the sound is only said once.
- Read the words at the top of the page.
     jolly, daisy, muddy, teddy,
     sunny, funny, daddy, spotty.
- Point out the letter that is making the /ee/ sound at the end of the words (the letter ‹y›).
- The sound made by the ‹y› may vary slightly according to accent.

Note 1: double letters
- The blending words with short vowel sounds have double consonant letters after the vowel. When two letters that make the same sound are next to each other, the sound is only said once.
- Consonant letters are often doubled after a short vowel sound so that the 'magic' from any subsequent vowels cannot 'hop back' over the consonants and change the short vowel into a long vowel.
- For example, when one consonant is removed from the word *holly* (which has a short vowel sound, /o/, followed by two consonants), it leaves *holy* (which has a long vowel sound /oa/ and one consonant).
- As the ‹y› is replacing a vowel sound in the reading words, it has borrowed the 'magic' of a vowel. So, if the consonants after the short vowel were not doubled, the ‹y› at the end of the word would change the short vowel sound into a long vowel.
- There are, however, some exceptions to this rule; in the words *body, lily* and *copy*, the consonant is not doubled.

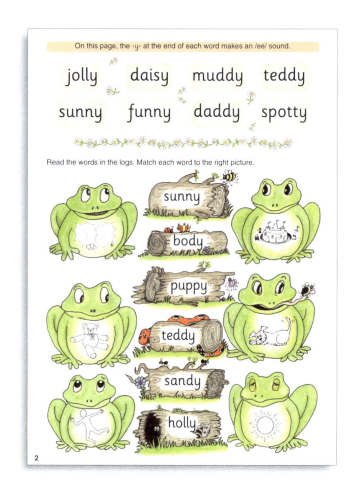

Word and picture matching
- The children read the words in the logs. They join each word to the frog containing the corresponding picture. The children can then colour the pictures.
- The pictures (top to bottom) are as follows:
     (left)   (right)
     holly,   sandy,
     teddy,   puppy,
     body,   sunny.

Reading sentences
- Write the following sentences on the board, pointing out the tricky words and blending any unknown words with the children.
  1. Do sheep sleep in beds?
  2. The farmyard is a mess.
  3. The shark swam in the reef.
  4. Did she do her job well?

Handwriting and Dictation

Flash cards
· Revise some of the basic 42 sounds that were introduced in *Phonics Pupil Book 1*.

Dictation words
· Dictate the following words:

cat,
dog,
hen,
step,
drum,
chin,
than,
sheep,
rain,
cobweb.

· The children write these words on the lines in their *Phonics Pupil Books*.

The alphabet
· Look at a copy of the alphabet with the children.
· Say the alphabet, pointing to each letter as you say it and pausing between each group: A–E, F–M, N–S, T–Z.

Handwriting
· Revise the sounds and formation for the letters ‹s›, ‹a›, ‹t›, ‹i›, ‹p› and ‹n›.
· Teach the children how to write the capital letters: ‹S›, ‹A›, ‹T›, ‹I›, ‹P› and ‹N›.
· All capital letters start at the top.
· The children trace inside the outline letters and then write over the dotted letters, saying the letter names as they do so.

Capitals and lower-case letters
· The children join each upper-case letter to its corresponding lower-case letter.
· Then they trace inside the outline letters using a different colour for each pair of letters.

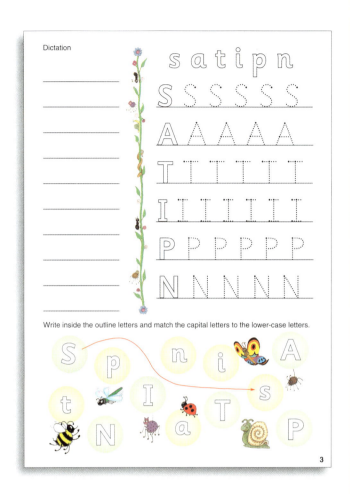

Further blending practice
· Write the following list of words on the board and blend them with the children:

sandwich,
barn,
weekend,
skunk,
limping.

Reading sentences
· Write the following sentences on the board, pointing out the tricky words and blending any unknown words with the children.
1. We do not jump on the bed.
2. The big dog has black spots.
3. Her coat was pink and blue.
4. He brushes his teeth in the morning.

Tricky Words

Flash cards
- Use the flash cards, or *Tricky Word Wall Flowers*, to revise the tricky words that were introduced in *Phonics Pupil Book 1*.

Tricky words
- Introduce the two new tricky words: *you* and *your*.
- The children look at the two words in yellow flowers at the top of the page: *you* and *your*.
- Point out that *your* is the same as *you*, but it has a letter ‹r› at the end.
- The children write inside the outline letters using a yellow pen or pencil.

Look, copy, cover, write, check
- Look at the first word, *you*, with the children.
- Say the letter names (not the letter sounds) in that word. The children write over the dotted word *you*.
- Then the children cover up all instances of the word *you* on their page and try writing the word in the next column.
- Once the children have had one try at writing *you*, they check their spelling. Then they cover up all instances of the word *you* again, and have another go at writing the word in the final column.
- Repeat these steps with the word *your*, reminding the children that *your* is the same as *you*, but with an ‹r› at the end.

Short vowels
- Explain that the five vowel letters are ‹a›, ‹e›, ‹i›, ‹o› and ‹u›. These letters have a short vowel sound, which the children know.
- The children look at the outline letters at the side of their page.
- Say the short vowel sounds with the children.
- The children write inside the outline letters using a blue pencil.
- Then the children look at the letters in the grid.
- They find all the vowel letters and colour these squares blue.

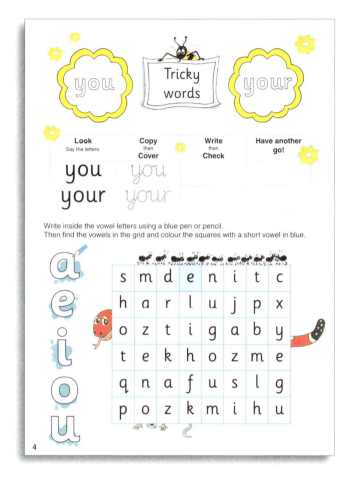

Further blending practice
- Write the following list of words on the board and blend them with the children:
  > black,
  > paid,
  > soak,
  > street,
  > fork.

Reading sentences
- Write the following sentences on the board, pointing out the tricky words and blending any unknown words with the children.
  1. Is your jumper red or green?
  2. You must stop at the kerb to cross the road.
  3. This is the bin for your rubbish.
  4. You will get your wish.

Words and Sentences

Flash cards
- Revise some of the basic 42 sounds, plus ‹y› as /ee/.

Words and sentences
- Look at the picture and discuss it with the children.
- Ask a child to say one sentence about the picture. For example, 'I can see a hen.' 'The chick is on the hen's back.' 'The hen is on the nest.'
- Choose some words to blend and write them on the board; examples could be: *hen*, *nest*, *her*, *eggs*, *chicks*.
- Some words will be straightforward to spell by listening for the sounds, but others will need some guidance.
- *Eggs*: explain that the ‹s› on the end of a plural often makes a /z/ sound.
- *Chicks*: explain that in short words with a short vowel followed by a /c/ sound, the /c/ is often spelt ‹ck›; as in the words *sack*, *neck* and *chick*.
- Write the following sentence on the board.
    A hen just sits on her nest.
- Discuss it as you write, saying:
- Sentences start with a capital letter.
- Capital letters are always tall.
- Listen for the sounds in the words.
- Leave a space between each word.
- Don't forget the full stop.
- All the children copy the sentence. Those children who can write independently can try to write some more sentences on their own.
- At this stage, the children only know one way of writing each sound, so their spelling will not always be accurate, but their work will be readable. Spelling gradually improves through reading many books and learning the alternative letter-sound spellings.

Short vowels
- Revise the five vowel letters and their sounds: ‹a›, ‹e›, ‹i›, ‹o› and ‹u›.
- The children look at the grid at the bottom of the page.

- Each word is missing a short vowel.
- The children look at the first word: *f_n*.
- Encourage them to try saying this word using all the different short vowel sounds, *fan, fen, fin, fon, fun*.
- Point out that the words *fun, fin* and *fan* all make sense. The children write over the dotted ‹u› to make the word *fun*.
- The children complete all the other words in the same way. When they come across a sound that makes sense in the word, like the ‹u› in *fun*, they write the vowel in the gap.
- There may be several different correct answers for each word:
f_n: *fan, fin, fun*; **h_p:** *hip, hop*;
r_d: *red, rid, rod*; **b_g:** *bag, beg, big, bug*;
m_n: *man, men*; **p_t:** *pat, pet, pit, pot*;
c_p: *cap, cop, cup*; **m_p:** *map, mop*;
s_ck: *sack, sick, sock, suck*; **sh_p:** *ship, shop*;
cl_p: *clap, clip, clop*; **qu_ck:** *quack, quick*.

Short Vowels

Flash cards
- Revise some of the basic 42 sounds, plus ‹y› as /ee/.

Reading short vowel words
- Remind the children that the short vowel sounds are: /a/, /e/, /i/, /o/ and /u/.
- Together with the children, read the short vowel words at the top of the page.
- The words are: *bag, net, bin, box* and *mug*.
- Point out the position of Inky Mouse in the pictures above the short vowel words.
- Inky is: **a**gainst the b**a**g,
        resting on the **e**dge of the n**e**t,
        in the b**i**n,
        on t**o**p of the b**o**x,
        under the m**u**g.
- Emphasise the short vowels as you say where Inky is in each picture.
- The children trace inside the outline vowel letters.

Writing short vowel words
- The children look at the picture of the box.
- Say the word *box* and ask the children to listen out for the short vowel sound, /o/.
- Point out that, in the line of short vowels above the picture of the box, the ‹o› has been circled.
- The children write over the dotted word, *box*, underneath the picture.
- Then the children look at the rest of the pictures.
- They say each word to themselves, listening first for the short vowel sound, which they ring, and then for all the sounds in the word, which they write on the lines underneath the picture.
- The pictures are as follows:
        box, bus, frog,
        duck, nest, ring,
        hat, shell, crab.
- When the children have finished writing, they can colour the pictures.

Further blending practice
- Write the following list of words on the board and blend them with the children:
        noisy,
        starting,
        groan,
        pail,
        street.

Reading sentences
- Write the following sentences on the board, pointing out the tricky words and blending any unknown words with the children.
  1. Your jumper is not too big for you.
  2. He had a train set in his room.
  3. You must be good at the shops.
  4. I went to the dentist.

Handwriting and Dictation

Flash cards
· Revise some of the basic 42 sounds, plus ‹y› as /ee/.

Dictation words
· Dictate the following words:

cap,
dot,
men,
stop,
drip,
boat,
chip,
thin,
shoot,
nutmeg.

· The children write these words on the lines in their *Phonics Pupil Books*.

The alphabet
· Look at a copy of the alphabet with the children.
· Say the alphabet, pointing to each letter as you say it and pausing between each group: A–E, F–M, N–S, T–Z.

Handwriting
· Revise the sounds and formation for the letters ‹c›, ‹k›, ‹e›, ‹h›, ‹r›, ‹m› and ‹d›.
· Teach the children how to write the capital letters: ‹C›, ‹K›, ‹E›, ‹H›, ‹R›, ‹M› and ‹D›.
· All capital letters start at the top.
· The children trace inside the outline letters and then write over the dotted letters, saying the letter names as they do so.

Capitals and lower-case letters
· The children join each upper-case letter to its corresponding lower-case letter.
· Then they trace inside the outline letters, using a different colour for each pair of letters.

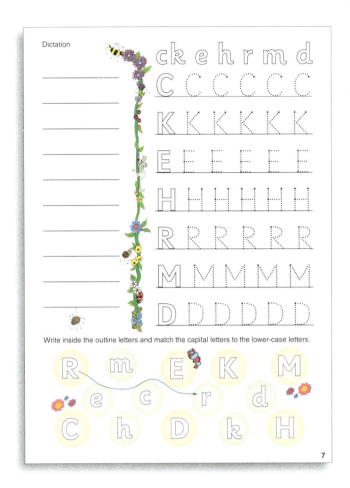

Further blending practice
· Write the following list of words on the board and blend them with the children:

barbecue,
foggy,
louder,
happy,
handstand.

Reading sentences
· Write the following sentences on the board, pointing out the tricky words and blending any unknown words with the children.
1. You must be hungry.
2. The car went north along the road.
3. Your hat is floppy.
4. Can you help me?

Tricky Words

Flash cards
- Use the flash cards, or *Tricky Word Wall Flowers*, to revise the tricky words already taught, including *you* and *your*.

Tricky words
- Introduce the two new tricky words: *come* and *some*.
- The children look at the two words in yellow flowers at the top of the page: *come* and *some*.
- Point out that *some* is the same as *come*, but it has a letter ‹s› at the beginning.
- The children might find it helpful to underline the ‹o_e› at the end of these two words in purple, to remind them that this is the 'tricky bit'.
- The children write inside the outline letters using a yellow pen or pencil.

Tricky word flowers
- The children read all the tricky words inside the flowers and join the matching pairs.
- Then the children find the flowers containing the words *some* and *come* and colour these flowers yellow.

Look, copy, cover, write, check
- Look at the first word, *come*, with the children.
- Say the letter names (not the letter sounds) in that word. The children write over the dotted word *come*.
- Then the children cover up all instances of the word *come* on their page and try writing the word in the next column.
- Once the children have had one try at writing *come*, they check their spelling. Then they cover up all instances of the word *come* again, and have another go at writing the word in the final column.
- Repeat these steps with the word *some*.

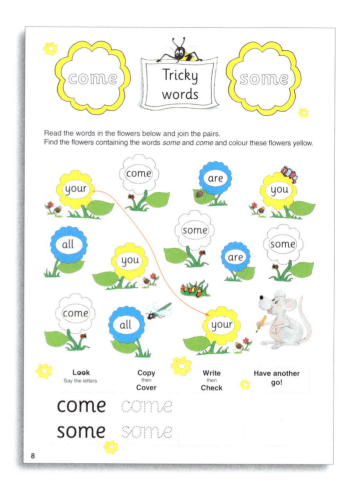

Further blending practice
- Write the following list of words on the board and blend them with the children:
  - *sandy,*
  - *lorry,*
  - *family,*
  - *soapy,*
  - *berry.*

Reading sentences
- Write the following sentences on the board, pointing out the tricky words and blending any unknown words with the children.
  1. Your dog has muddy feet.
  2. Some cats are greedy.
  3. Can we come to your party?
  4. His fingers are all sticky.

Words and Sentences

Flash cards
- Revise some of the basic 42 sounds, plus ‹y› as /ee/.

Words and sentences
- Look at the picture and discuss it with the children.
- Ask a child to say one sentence about the picture. For example, 'I can see a dog.' 'The boy is throwing the ball.'
- Choose some words to blend and write them on the board; examples could be: *boy, dog, ball, park.*
- Some words will be straightforward to spell by listening for the sounds, but others will need some guidance.
- *Boy*: point that the /oi/ sound in this word is written ‹oy›.
- Explain that ‹y› often replaces ‹i› at the end of a word. Tell the children that the letter ‹i› is shy and does not like to be at the end of a word in English, so its cousin 'toughy y' takes its place.
- *Park*: point out that the /ck/ sound at the end of *park* is spelt with a 'kicking k'.
- Explain that when a short word ending in a /ck/ sound does not have short vowel sound, the /ck/ sound is usually spelt ‹k›, as in the words *week, rook, oak* and *park*.
- Write the following sentence on the board.
  I can see a big dog.
- Discuss it as you write, saying:
- Sentences start with a capital letter.
- Capital letters are always tall.
- Listen for the sounds in the words.
- Leave a space between each word.
- Don't forget the full stop.
- All the children copy the sentence. Those children who can write independently can try to write some more sentences on their own.
- At this stage, the children only know one way of writing each sound, so their spelling will not always be accurate, but their work will be readable. Spelling gradually improves through reading many books and learning the alternative letter-sound spellings.

Reading words
- The children read each park-related word at the bottom of the page and join it to the matching picture.

Further blending practice
- Write the following list of words on the board and blend them with the children:
  magpie, fern, roasting, foil, thunderstorm.

Reading sentences
- Write the following sentences on the board, pointing out the tricky words and blending any unknown words with the children.
  1. Did you see the cartoons in that comic book?
  2. Some children are painting in the corner.
  3. Will you come to the shops with us?
  4. The man was rescued in a helicopter.

Alternatives: ‹ck›

Flash cards
- Revise some of the basic 42 sounds, plus ‹y› as /ee/.

Alternatives: ‹ck›
- Remind the children that when two letters that make the same sound are next to each other, the sound is only said once.
- Explain that when a short vowel is followed by a /ck/ sound in short words, the /ck/ sound is spelt ‹ck›; both a caterpillar ‹c› and a kicking ‹k› are needed.
- Revise the short vowel sounds, /a/, /e/, /i/, /o/ and /u/.
- The children look at the blending words at the top of the page.
- Read out the first word: *duck*.
- The children listen for and identify the short vowel sound: /u/.
- Read the other words with the children:
  duck, bricks, sack, peck, black,
  sock, jacket, tick, kick, clock.

Note 1: ‹ck› and ‹k›
- In short words with a short vowel sound followed by a /ck/, the /ck/ sound is spelt with both a ‹c› and a ‹k›, as in the words, *duck* and *lack*.
- However, in short words where a /ck/ sound follows any other vowel sound (for example, /ai/, /ee/, /ie/, /oa/, /ar/, /er/, or /oo/) then the /ck/ sound is spelt with a ‹k› only, as in the words *rake*, *peek*, *look* and *mark*.

Rockets
- The children look at the dotted words written in the rockets.
- They write over the first dotted word, *stick*, and draw a picture in the rocket to illustrate this word.
- They do the same with the remaining words.
- The words (clockwise from *stick*) are as follows:
  stick, black, socks, rocket,
  duck, brick, neck.

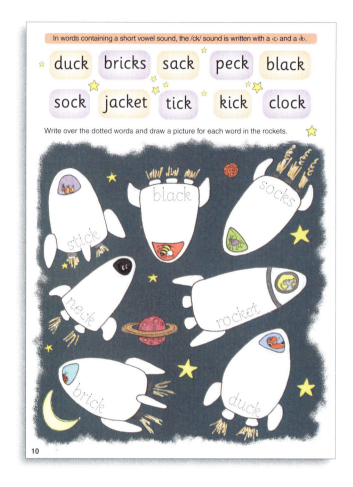

Further blending practice
- Write the following list of words on the board and blend them with the children:
  bedroom,
  beetroot,
  cricket,
  haddock,
  packing.

Reading sentences
- Write the following sentences on the board, pointing out the tricky words and blending any unknown words with the children.
  1. I swam ten lengths in the pool.
  2. You are very clever indeed.
  3. Did you get a book for me?
  4. We laid out some nuts for the squirrels.

Handwriting and Dictation

Flash cards
· Revise some of the basic 42 sounds, plus ‹y› as /ee/.

Dictation words
· Dictate the following words:

> set,
> hit,
> box,
> plum,
> snap,
> port,
> sharp,
> chop,
> quiz,
> redwood.

· The children write these words on the lines in their *Phonics Pupil Books*.

The alphabet
· Look at a copy of the alphabet with the children.
· Say the alphabet, pointing to each letter as you say it and pausing between each group: A–E, F–M, N–S, T–Z.

Handwriting
· Revise the sounds and formation for the letters ‹g›, ‹o›, ‹w›, ‹b›, ‹f› and ‹b›.
· Teach the children how to write the capital letters: ‹G›, ‹O›, ‹U›, ‹L›, ‹F› and ‹B›.
· All capital letters start at the top.
· The children trace inside the outline letters and then write over the dotted letters. Saying the letter names as they do so.

Capitals and lower-case letters
· The children join each upper-case letter to its corresponding lower-case letter.
· Then they trace inside the outline letters, using a different colour for each pair of letters.

Further blending practice
· Write the following list of words on the board and blend them with the children:

> south,
> yummy,
> pest,
> twig,
> hurry.

Reading sentences
· Write the following sentences on the board, pointing out the tricky words and blending any unknown words with the children.
1. Pack all your things in the bag.
2. Dad poaches eggs for our lunch.
3. Come and feed ducks with me.
4. She has three pet rabbits.

Comprehension

Flash cards
• Revise some of the basic 42 sounds, plus ‹y› as /ee/.

Comprehension: read and draw
• Read the first phrase, *a spotty dog*, with the children.
• Point out that in the word *spotty*, the ‹y› makes an /ee/ sound.
• The children draw a picture in the picture frame to illustrate this phrase.
• The children read all the other phrases and draw a picture to illustrate each one.
• The phrases are as follows:

> *a spotty dog*
> *a fluffy cat*
> *a green frog*
> *an oak tree*
> *a big clock*
> *a running man.*

Read each phrase and draw a picture in the frame to illustrate it.

a spotty dog   a fluffy cat

a green frog   an oak tree

a big clock   a running man

12

Further blending practice
• Write the following list of words on the board and blend them with the children:

> *sleeping,*
> *waist,*
> *velvet,*
> *spooky,*
> *thump*
> *socks,*
> *amber,*
> *shopping,*
> *best,*
> *understand*

Reading sentences
• Write the following sentences on the board, pointing out the tricky words and blending any unknown words with the children.
1. Did he look at the paintings?
2. The clock was on the shelf.
3. We went to the park for a picnic.
4. He had a smart green scarf.
5. Her dog just fell off the bed!
6. She has a blue party dress.
7. Do cats go swimming?
8. The rabbit has black spots.
9. I got some stickers with that comic.
10. Can you come to the shops with us?

Tricky Words

Flash cards
· Use the flash cards, or *Tricky Word Wall Flowers*, to revise the tricky words already taught, including *you*, *your*, *some* and *come*.

Tricky words
· Introduce the three new tricky words: *said*, *here* and *there*. The children look at the words in flowers at the top of the page.
· Point out that *there* is spelt like *here*, but with a letter ‹t› at the beginning.
· The children could underline the ‹ere› at the end of these two words in purple, to remind them that this is the 'tricky bit'.
· The children write inside the outline letters using a yellow pen or pencil.

Look, copy, cover, write, check
· Look at the first word, *said*, with the children.
· Say the letter names (not the letter sounds) in that word. The children write over the dotted word *said*.
· Then the children cover up all instances of the word *said* on their page and try writing the word in the next column.
· Once the children have had one try at writing *said*, they check their spelling. Then they cover up all instances of the word *said* again, and have another go at writing the word in the final column.
· Repeat these steps for *here* and *there*.

Writing activities
· Look at the first picture with the children and say the word, *bed*.
· The children listen for the sounds in the word bed: /b/, /e/, /d/ and write over the dotted word *bed* underneath the picture.
· The children look at the rest of the pictures.
· They say each word to themselves and identify all the sounds in each word.
· The children write the words on the lines underneath the picture.
· There is a line for each sound in the words.
· The pictures are as follows:
    bed, jam, six, web, fox, dog.

Further blending practice
· Write the following list of words on the board and blend them with the children:
    clever,
    sorry,
    march,
    toddler,
    seven.

Reading sentences
· Write the following sentences on the board, pointing out the tricky words and blending any unknown words with the children.
1. There are some happy children here.
2. Dad said that some dogs are silly.
3. There is a teddy on her bed.
4. Here is her blue hat.

Words and Sentences

Flash cards
- Revise some of the basic 42 sounds, plus ‹y› as /ee/.

Words and sentences
- Look at the picture and discuss it with the children.
- Ask a child to say one sentence about the picture. For example, 'The pond is big.' 'The duckling quacks at a frog.' 'I can see a boat.'
- Choose some words to blend and write them on the board; examples could be: *pond, frog, fish, duck*.
- Some words will be straightforward to spell by listening for the sounds, but others will need some guidance.
- Write the following sentence on the board.
  A boat sails on the pond.
- Discuss it as you write, saying:
- Sentences start with a capital letter.
- Capital letters are always tall.
- Listen for the sounds in the words.
- Leave a space between each word.
- Don't forget the full stop.
- All the children copy the sentence.
- Those children who can write independently can try to write some more sentences on their own.
- At this stage, the children only know one way of writing each sound, so their spelling will not always be accurate, but their work will be readable.
- Spelling gradually improves through reading many books and learning the alternative letter-sound spellings.

Reading words
- The children read each pond-related word at the bottom of the page and join it to the corresponding picture.

Further blending practice
- Write the following list of words on the board and blend them with the children:
  sticky,
  tricky,
  rocky,
  dizzy,
  start.

Reading sentences
- Write the following sentences on the board, pointing out the tricky words and blending any unknown words with the children.
1. She found some duck eggs.
2. There is a crack in this egg.
3. He painted his truck with black paint.
4. Here is an empty box.

Alternatives: Double Letters

Flash cards
· Revise some of the basic 42 sounds, plus ‹y› as /ee/.

Alternatives: double letters
· Remind the children that, when two letters that make the same sound are next to each other, the sound is only said once.
· Consonants are often doubled after a short vowel sound so that the 'magic' from any subsequent vowels cannot 'hop back' over the consonants and change the short vowel into a long vowel.
· The children look at the blending words at the top of the page.
· Read out the first word: *parrot.*
· The children listen for and identify the first short vowel sound: /a/.
· The second vowel letter ‹o› makes a schwa sound in this word.
· Point out the double ‹r› in this word.
· Read the other words with the children:
> *parrot, egg, bell, jazz, button,*
> *kitten, huff, bill, doll, miss.*

Double letters rabbit
· Read the word in the first of the rabbit's patches: *rabbit.*
· Point out the short vowel and the double ‹b› in this word.
· The children colour the picture of the rabbit.
· Then they read the words in the rest of the rabbit's patches and draw a picture in the patches to illustrate each word.
· The words (clockwise from *rabbit*) are as follows:
> *rabbit, dress, shell, carrot, puppet, duck.*

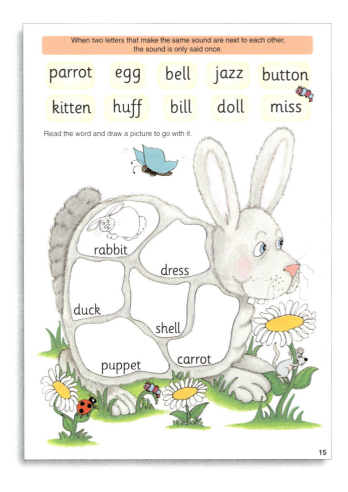

Further blending practice
· Write the following list of words on the board and blend them with the children:
> *cannot,*
> *puppet,*
> *hiccup,*
> *sniff,*
> *tick.*

Reading sentences
· Write the following sentences on the board, pointing out the tricky words and blending any unknown words with the children.
1. Your hands are very grubby.
2. She has a scarf around her neck.
3. There are green bugs on this log.
4. Here is a red toadstool.

Handwriting and Dictation

Flash cards
· Revise some of the basic 42 sounds, plus ‹y› as /ee/.

Dictation words
· Dictate the following words:
> *bat,*
> *let,*
> *cup,*
> *swim,*
> *flat,*
> *much,*
> *coin,*
> *loud,*
> *teeth,*
> *herself.*

· The children write these words on the lines in their *Phonics Pupil Books.*

The alphabet
· Look at a copy of the alphabet with the children.
· Say the alphabet, pointing to each letter as you say it and pausing between each group: A–E, F–M, N–S, T–Z.

Handwriting
· Revise the sounds and formation of the letter ‹j› and the digraphs ‹ai›, ‹oa›, ‹ie›, ‹ee›, ‹or›.
· Teach the children how to write the capital letter ‹J›.
· The children trace inside the outline letters and then write over the dotted letters.
· Revise writing the digraphs ‹ai›, ‹oa›, ‹ie›, ‹ee›, and ‹or›. Explain to the children how the letters in the digraphs are joined.
· The children trace inside the outline letters.

Capitals and lower-case letters
· Revise writing the capital letters:
S, A, T, I, P, N, C, K, E, H, R, M, D, G, O, U, L, F, B and J.

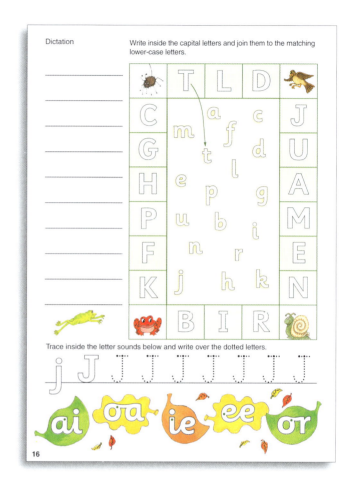

· The children trace inside the outline letters and then join the capital letters around the edge to the lower-case letters in the middle.

Further blending practice
· Write the following list of words on the board and blend them with the children:
> *hissing,*
> *explain,*
> *froth,*
> *snap,*
> *finish.*

Reading sentences
· Write the following sentences on the board, pointing out the tricky words and blending any unknown words with the children.
1. There are some big animals at the zoo.
2. She said that she missed her train.
3. Your cat has such a long tail.
4. The bees buzz happily.

Tricky Words

Flash cards
· Use the flash cards, or *Tricky Word Wall Flowers*, to revise the tricky words already taught, including *you, your, some, come, said, here* and *there*.

Tricky words
· Introduce the new tricky word: *they*.
· The children look at the word in the yellow flower at the top of the page: *they*.
· The children write inside the outline letters using a yellow pen or pencil.

Look, copy, cover, write, check
· Look at the word *they* with the children.
· Say the letter names (not the letter sounds) in that word. The children write over the dotted word *they*.
· Then the children cover up all instances of the word *they* on their page and try writing the word in the next column.
· Once the children have had one try at writing *they*, they check their spelling. Then they cover up all instances of the word *they* again, and have another go at writing the word in the final column.

Choose the correct word
· Look at the first picture with the children.
· Read the words underneath the picture: *met, mat, man*. Ask the children if the picture illustrates *met, mat,* or *man*.
· The children choose the correct word and write over the dotted word *mat* underneath the picture.
· The children look at the remaining pictures.
· They read the three words under each picture and decide which word matches that picture.
· They write this word on the lines underneath.
· The pictures are:
  mat, dog, cup, egg, net, ant, tree, book, jar.

Further blending practice
· Write the following list of words on the board and blend them with the children:
  flatter,
  traffic,
  letter,
  plum,
  umbrella.

Reading sentences
· Write the following sentences on the board, pointing out the tricky words and blending any unknown words with the children.
1. They do not drop litter.
2. They all had pies for supper.
3. The farmer was digging in the soil.
4. I found all the pens in the box.

Words and Sentences

Flash cards
- Revise some of the basic 42 sounds, plus ‹y› as /ee/.

Words and sentences
- Look at the picture and discuss it with the children.
- Ask a child to say one sentence about the picture. For example, 'The bat is flying.' 'The moon and stars are shining.' 'I can see a fox.'
- Choose some words to blend and write them on the board; examples could be: *fox, moon, tree.*
- Some words will be straightforward to spell by listening for the sounds, but others will need some guidance.
- Write the following sentence on the board.
    The fox looks up at the moon.
- Discuss it as you write, saying:
- Sentences start with a capital letter.
- Capital letters are always tall.
- Listen for the sounds in the words.
- Leave a space between each word.
- Don't forget the full stop.
- All the children copy the sentence.
- Those children who can write independently can try to write some more sentences on their own.
- At this stage, the children only know one way of writing each sound, so their spelling will not always be accurate, but their work will be readable.
- Spelling gradually improves through reading many books and learning the alternative letter-sound spellings.

Reading words
- The children read each word at the bottom of the page and join it to the corresponding picture.

Further blending practice
- Write the following list of words on the board and blend them with the children:
    jester,
    windy,
    empty,
    filling,
    sweeps.

Reading sentences
- Write the following sentences on the board, pointing out the tricky words and blending any unknown words with the children.
1. We need butter and flour for our cooking.
2. The moth flaps its wings.
3. The trip to the zoo was fun.
4. Three men went out in a boat.

Alternatives: Hop-Over ‹e› Digraphs

Flash cards
- Revise some of the basic 42 sounds, plus ‹y› as /ee/.

Alternatives: hop-over ‹e› digraphs
- Explain to the children that, when a word has more than one vowel, the 'magic' from the second vowel can sometimes hop back over one letter and change the first short vowel into a long vowel.
- Point out that the 'magic' can only hop back over one consonant.
- Encourage the children to say, 'When two vowels go walking, the first does the talking.'
- This saying explains both the vowel digraphs that the children already know, like ‹ai›, ‹ee›, ‹ie› ‹oa› and ‹ue›, and the split digraphs like the ‹i_e› in *bike*.
- The children look at the blending words at the top of the page.
- Read the first word to the children: *smoke*.
- The children listen for, and identify, the long vowel sound: /oa/.
- Point out the letters that make the /oa/ sound in the word *smoke*, ‹o_e›.
- Read the other words with the children:
    smoke, use, game, eve, mule,
    hive, these, joke, shave, side.
- Point out to the children that they know one way of writing the long vowels: ‹ai›, ‹ee›, ‹ie›, ‹oa› and ‹ue›.
- Explain to the children that there are other ways to write these long vowel sounds.
- Write ‹a_e›, ‹e_e›, ‹i_e›, ‹o_e› and ‹u_e› on the board and get the children to say each letter sound as you point to it.

Vowel forest trees
- The children look at the words written in the leaves.
- Read out the first word: *Pete*.
- The children listen for, and identify, the long vowel sound: /ee/.
- Ask the children which letters are making the /ee/ sound in this word.
- They should say the ‹e_e› digraph.

- The children circle the letters making the /ee/ sound.
- Point out that the word *Pete* is joined to the tree containing the picture of *Pete*. The children colour in this picture.
- The children read the remaining words. They circle the letters making the long vowel sound in each word and then join the word to the matching picture.
- When they have joined all the words to the correct pictures, the children can colour the pictures.

Reading sentences
- Write the following sentences on the board, pointing out the tricky words and blending any unknown words with the children.
  1. Do not argue with the queen.
  2. We made a cake with blackberry jam.
  3. She lent me her skates.
  4. There are a hundred bees in the hive.

103

Handwriting and Dictation

Flash cards
• Revise the basic 42 sounds, plus ⟨y⟩ as /ee/.

Dictation words
• Dictate the following words:
>   *hid,*
>   *hum,*
>   *ant,*
>   *from,*
>   *slip,*
>   *shed,*
>   *them,*
>   *chain,*
>   *harp,*
>   *mushroom.*

• The children write these words on the lines in their *Phonics Pupil Books*.

The alphabet
• Look at a copy of the alphabet with the children.
• Say the alphabet, pointing to each letter as you say it and pausing between each group.

Handwriting
• Revise writing the capital letters:
S, A, T, I, P, N, C, K, E, H, R, M, D.
• The children trace inside the outline letters in the boxes.
• If the outline letter is a lower-case letter, the children write the corresponding capital letter in the second half of the box, as with the example, ⟨S⟩.
• If the outline letter is a capital letter, the children write the corresponding lower-case letter in the second half of the box.
• At the bottom of the page, the children revise writing the lower-case letters ⟨z⟩, ⟨w⟩ and ⟨v⟩.
• Teach the children how to write the capital letters ⟨Z⟩, ⟨W⟩ and ⟨V⟩. The children trace inside the outline letters and write over the dotted letters.

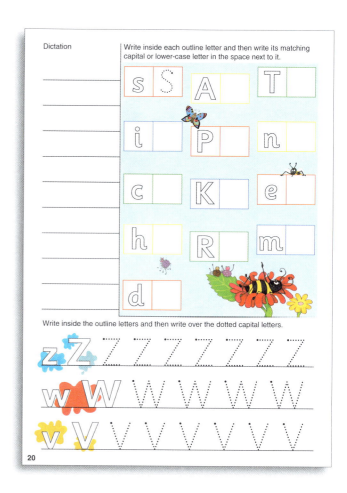

Further blending practice
• Write the following list of words on the board and blend them with the children:
>   *spoon,*
>   *sour,*
>   *tenth,*
>   *eggshell,*
>   *throat.*

Reading sentences
• Write the following sentences on the board, pointing out the tricky words and blending any unknown words with the children.
1. I can fix the bench in the shed.
2. She hangs up her coat on the peg.
3. This is a long road.
4. She points to the clouds.

Tricky Words

Flash cards
- Use the flash cards, or *Tricky Word Wall Flowers*, to revise the tricky words already taught, including *you, your, some, come, said, here, there* and *they*.

Tricky words
- Introduce the three new tricky words: *go, no* and *so*. The children look at these words in the yellow flowers at the top of the page.
- Point out that, judging from their spelling, these words should have the short vowel sound, /o/ at the end, but they actually have the long vowel sound /oa/.
- Encourage the children to say:
  'If one way doesn't work, try the other.'
- The children should first say the words as they are spelt and, if this pronunciation does not make sense, they should try saying the word with the long vowel sound instead.
- The children could underline the ‹o› at the end of each of these words in purple, to remind them that this is the 'tricky bit'.
- The children write inside the outline letters using a yellow pen or pencil.

Word search
- The children read the tricky words written in the yellow flowers surrounding the grid.
- They search for each word in the grid and circle the word when they find it.

Look, copy, cover, write, check
- Look at the first word, *go*, with the children.
- Say the letter names (not the letter sounds) in that word. The children write over the dotted word *go*.
- Then the children cover up all instances of the word *go* on their page and try writing the word in the next column.
- Once the children have had one try at writing *go*, they check their spelling. Then they cover up all instances of the word *go* again, and have another go at writing the word in the final column.
- Repeat these steps with the words *no* and *so*.

Further blending practice
- Write the following list of words on the board and blend them with the children:

  sprain,   *shame,*
  feel,   *theme,*
  like,   *truck,*
  flick,   *smell,*
  cherry,   *poppy.*

Reading sentences
- Write the following sentences on the board, pointing out the tricky words and blending any unknown words with the children.
  1. It is so hilly here.
  2. They will go and ring the bells soon.
  3. No, you cannot go out alone.
  4. They can go to the farm in March.

Words and Sentences

Flash cards
· Revise some of the basic 42 sounds, plus ‹y›
as /ee/, ‹a_e›, ‹e_e›, ‹i_e›, ‹o_e›, ‹u_e›.

Words and sentences
· Look at the picture and discuss it with the
children.
· Ask a child to say one sentence about the
picture. For example, 'I can see a crab.' 'The
fish is swimming.' 'There is a shell in the
weeds.'
· Choose some words to blend and write them
on the board; examples could be: *fish, crab,
weeds*.
· Some words will be straightforward to spell
by listening for the sounds, but others will
need some guidance.
· Write the following sentence on the board.
　　That fish has a long tail.
· Discuss it as you write, saying:
· Sentences start with a capital letter.
· Capital letters are always tall.
· Listen for the sounds in the words.
· Leave a space between each word.
· Don't forget the full stop.
· All the children copy the sentence.
· Those children who can write independently
can try to write some more sentences on their
own.
· At this stage, the children only know one way
of writing each sound, so their spelling will
not always be accurate, but their work will
be readable.
· Spelling gradually improves through reading
many books and learning the alternative
letter-sound spellings.

Reading words
· The children read each word at the bottom of
the page and join it to the corresponding fish
picture.
· If the children have trouble with this activity,
encourage them to join up the words they
know and then see what they are left with.

Match each word to the right sea creature.

catfish　starfish　flatfish　eel

22

Further blending practice
· Write the following list of words on the board
and blend them with the children:
　　stale,
　　stile,
　　milkshake,
　　cloth,
　　mole.

Reading sentences
· Write the following sentences on the board,
pointing out the tricky words and blending
any unknown words with the children.
1. The boat is so strong.
2. We must go and sort out the books.
3. The roof shook in the storm.
4. There are no fish in this pond.

Handwriting and Dictation

Flash card
- Revise some of the basic 42 sounds, plus ‹y› as /ee/, ‹a_e›, ‹e_e›, ‹i_e›, ‹o_e›, ‹u_e›.

Dictation words
- Dictate the following words:
    - *van,*
    - *jug,*
    - *yes,*
    - *west,*
    - *jump,*
    - *shin,*
    - *thud,*
    - *cheep,*
    - *quilt,*
    - *starfish.*
- The children write these words on the lines in their *Phonics Pupil Books.*

The alphabet
- Look at a copy of the alphabet with the children.
- Say the alphabet, pointing to each letter as you say it and pausing between each group.

Outline letters
- At the bottom of the page, revise writing the lower-case letters ‹y›, ‹x› and ‹q›.
- Teach the children how to write the capital letters ‹Y›, ‹X› and ‹Q›.
- The children trace inside the outline letters and write over the dotted letters, making sure that they start each letter at the dot.

Handwriting
- Revise writing the capital letters: G, O, U, L, F, B, J, Z, W, V, Y, X, Q. The children trace inside the outline letters in the boxes.
- If the outline letter is a capital letter, the children write the corresponding lower-case letter in the second half of the box, as with the example, ‹g›.

- If the outline letter is a lower-case letter, the children write the corresponding capital letter in the second half of the box.

Further blending practice
- Write the following list of words on the board and blend them with the children: *raincoat, shouting, fire, shade, charming.*

Reading sentences
- Write the following sentences on the board, pointing out the tricky words and blending any unknown words with the children.
    1. This foal was born in the spring.
    2. She spoke so quickly.
    3. The thorn on this twig is very sharp.
    4. This popcorn is too sweet.

Tricky Words

Flash cards

- Use the flash cards, or *Tricky Word Wall Flowers*, to revise the tricky words already taught, including *you, your, some, come, said, here, there, they, go, no* and *so*.

Tricky words

- Introduce the three new tricky words: *my, one* and *by*.
- The children look at the words in flowers at the top of the page: *my, one* and *by*.
- Point out that the word *by* is the same as *my*, but with a ‹b› at the beginning.
- The children could underline the ‹y› at the end of each of these words in purple, to remind them that this is the 'tricky bit'.
- The children write inside the word *my* using a yellow pencil and the words *one* and *by* using a red pencil.

Look, copy, cover, write, check

- Look at the first word, *my*, with the children.
- Say the letter names (not the letter sounds) in that word. The children write over the dotted word *my*.
- Then the children cover up all instances of the word *my* on their page and try writing the word in the next column.
- Once the children have had one try at writing *my*, they check their spelling. Then they cover up all instances of the word *my* again, and have another go at writing the word in the final column.
- Repeat these steps with the words *one* and *by*.

Writing activities

- Look at the first picture with the children and say the word, *cue*.
- The children listen for the sounds in the word *cue*: /c/, /ue/.
- They write over the dotted word *cue* underneath the picture.
- The children look at the rest of the pictures. They say each word to themselves and identify all the sounds in each word.

- The children write the words on the lines underneath the picture.
- There is a line for each sound in the words.
- A longer line indicates that a digraph is needed.
- The pictures are:
    cue, sheep, coat,
    road, barn, pie,
    three, snail, goat.

Further blending practice

- Write the following list of words on the board and blend them with the children:
  smoke, hive, kite, date, perfume.
- Write the following sentences on the board, pointing out the tricky words and blending any unknown words with the children.
  1. My garden is bigger than this one.
  2. They go by train to the theme park.
  3. You can take one cake with you.
  4. Did you invite my sister as well?

Words and Sentences

Flash cards
• Revise some of the basic 42 sounds, plus ‹y› as /ee/, ‹a_e›, ‹e_e›, ‹i_e›, ‹o_e›, ‹u_e›.

Words and sentences
• Look at the picture and discuss it with the children.
• Ask a child to say one sentence about the picture. For example, 'A bat is flying' 'A moon shines in the dark.' 'I can see an owl.'
• Choose some words to blend and write them on the board; examples could be: *owl, moth, tree*.
• Some words will be straightforward to spell by listening for the sounds, but others will need some guidance.
• *Owl*: point out that the /ou/ sound at the beginning of this word is written ‹ow›.
• Write the following sentence on the board.
    The moth is on the tree.
• Discuss it as you write, saying:
• Sentences start with a capital letter.
• Capital letters are always tall.
• Listen for the sounds in the words.
• Leave a space between each word.
• Don't forget the full stop.
• All the children copy the sentence.
• Those children who can write independently can try to write some more sentences on their own.
• At this stage, the children only know one way of writing each sound, so their spelling will not always be accurate, but their work will be readable.
• Spelling gradually improves through reading many books and learning the alternative letter-sound spellings.

Reading words
• The children read each night time word at the bottom of the page and join it to the corresponding picture.

Join each word to the right picture.

star   moth   sleeping   moon

25

Further blending practice
• Write the following list of words on the board and blend them with the children:
    file,
    inflate,
    athlete,
    flagpole,
    liquid.

Reading sentences
• Write the following sentences on the board, pointing out the tricky words and blending any unknown words with the children.
1. We can sweep up with this broom.
2. They run by the river.
3. My dog has a blue collar.
4. In this tank there are twenty fish, one squid and three lobsters.

Alternatives: ‹ay› and ‹oy›

Flash cards
- Revise some of the basic 42 sounds, plus ‹y› as /ee/, ‹a_e›, ‹e_e›, ‹i_e›, ‹o_e›, ‹u_e›.

Alternatives: ‹ay› as /ai /
- When an /ai/ sound comes at the end of a word, it is usually written ‹ay›.
- Say the word *stay*.
- Ask the children what sound they hear at the end of this word. The children should say an /ai/ sound.
- Ask them how an /ai/ sound is usually written. The children should say with an ‹a› and an ‹i›.
- Explain that the letter ‹i› is shy and does not like to come at the end of words in English, so its cousin, 'toughy y' takes its place.
- Explain that when the /ai/ sound is at the end of a word it is usually written ‹ay›, as in the words *day* and *pay*.
- The children write inside the outline digraphs ‹ai› and ‹ay› on their page.

Alternatives: ‹oy› as /oi/
- When an /oi/ sound comes at the end of a word, it is usually written ‹oy›.
- Say the word *joy*.
- Ask the children what sound they hear at the end of this word. The children should say an /oi/ sound.
- Ask them how an /oi/ sound is usually written. The children should say with an ‹o› and an ‹i›.
- Remind the children that the letter ‹i› is shy and does not like to come at the end of words in English, so its cousin, 'toughy y' takes its place.
- Explain that when the /oi/ sound is at the end of a word it is usually written ‹oy›, as in the words *annoy* and *boy*.
- The children write inside the outline digraphs ‹oi› and ‹oy› on their page.

Choose the spelling
- Look at the pictures with the children.
- Say the word *tray*, so that the children can listen for where the /ai/ sound comes in the word.
- The children decide how tray is spelt and write either ‹ai› or ‹ay› in the space.
- The children continue with the rest of the words, listening for the position of the /ai/ and /oi/ sounds and completing the each word by writing the correct spellings of the /ai/ and /oi/ sounds on the lines.
- The words are:
   tray, snail, rain,
   hay, spray, paint;

   oil, point, boy,
   boil, coin, toy box.

Handwriting and Dictation

Flash cards
· Revise some of the basic 42 sounds, plus ‹y›
as /ee/, ‹a_e›, ‹e_e›, ‹i_e›, ‹o_e›, ‹u_e›.

Dictation words
· Dictate the following words:
> log,
> jam,
> bat,
> loft,
> hunt,
> shut,
> chest,
> tooth,
> tree,
> oilcan.

· The children write these words on the lines
in their *Phonics Pupil Books*.

The alphabet
· Look at the alphabet
with the children.
· Say the alphabet,
pointing to each letter
as you say it and
pausing between each
group.

Handwriting
· The children revise writing the capital
letters.
· On this page, the capital letters are in
alphabetical order. The children write inside
the outline letters, using a red pencil for the
letters A-E, a yellow pencil for the letters F-
M, a green pencil for the letters N-S and a
blue pencil for the letters T-Z.

Capitals and lower-case letters
· The children write the lower-case letter next
to each capital letter.

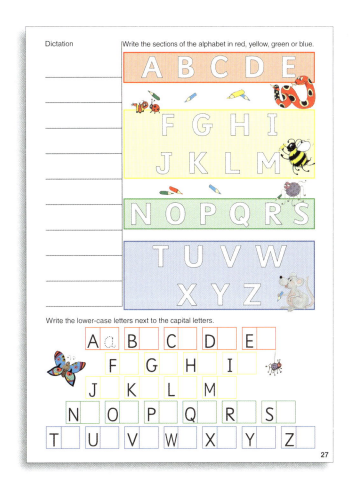

Further blending practice
· Write the following list of words on the board
and blend them with the children:
> sometimes,
> dragonflies,
> choke,
> crane,
> tunes.

Reading sentences
· Write the following sentences on the board,
pointing out the tricky words and blending
any unknown words with the children.
1. He felt unwell and had to go home.
2. She made a bee costume for the party.
3. My cat had one kitten.
4. The ducklings jumped into the pond one
by one.

Tricky Words

Flash cards
- Use the flash cards, or *Tricky Word Wall Flowers*, to revise the tricky words already taught, including *you, your, some, come, said, here, there, they, go, no, so, my, one* and *by*.

Tricky words
- Introduce the two new tricky words: *only* and *old*. The children look at the words in red flowers at the top of the page: *only* and *old*.
- The children write inside the outline letters using a red pencil.

Look, copy, cover, write, check
- Look at the first word, *only*, with the children.
- Say the letter names (not the letter sounds) in that word. The children write over the dotted word *only*.
- Then the children cover up all instances of the word *only* on their page and try writing the word in the next column.
- Once the children have had one try at writing *only*, they check their spelling. Then they cover up all instances of the word *only* again, and have another go at writing the word in the final column.
- Repeat these steps with the word *old*.

Animal anagrams
- Look at the first picture with the children and say the word, *ant*.
- The children listen carefully and try to work the sounds in this word and the order in which the sounds come.
- The children look at the letters at the side of the picture and decide which order the letters should be placed in the word.
- The children write the word on the lines underneath the picture of the ant.
- The children solve the remaining anagrams in the same way.
- There is a line for each sound in the word. The slightly longer lines indicate a digraph is needed.
- The pictures are: *ant, snail, goat, sheep, shark, crab, yak, chick, fox.*

Further blending practice
- Write the following list of words on the board and blend them with the children:
  - *wife,*
  - *lake,*
  - *choke,*
  - *plane,*
  - *safely.*

Reading sentences
- Write the following sentences on the board, pointing out the tricky words and blending any unknown words with the children.
  1. My old teddy is lonely.
  2. I only need some wire.
  3. She only gave me five grapes.
  4. Inside the shell is an old crab.

Words and Sentences

Flash cards
- Revise some of the basic 42 sounds, plus ⟨y⟩ as /ee/, ⟨a_e⟩, ⟨e_e⟩, ⟨i_e⟩, ⟨o_e⟩, ⟨u_e⟩, ⟨ay⟩, ⟨oy⟩.

Words and sentences
- Look at the picture and discuss it with the children.
- Ask a child to say one sentence about the picture. For example, 'The ducks are quacking.' 'The man has caught a fish.' 'I can see some ducks.'
- Choose some words to blend and write them on the board; examples could be: *ducks, quack, fisherman.*
- Some words will be straightforward to spell by listening for the sounds, but others will need some guidance.
- Write the following sentence on the board.
  The ducks on the pond are quacking.
- Discuss it as you write, saying:
- Sentences start with a capital letter.
- Capital letters are always tall.
- Listen for the sounds in the words.
- Leave a space between each word.
- Don't forget the full stop.
- All the children copy the sentence.
- Those children who can write independently can try to write some more sentences on their own.
- At this stage, the children only know one way of writing each sound, so their spelling will not always be accurate, but their work will be readable.
- Spelling gradually improves through reading many books and learning the alternative letter-sound spellings.

Animal anagrams
- Look at the first picture with the children and say the word, *duck.*
- The children listen carefully and try to work the sounds in the word and the order in which the sounds come.
- The children look at the letters at the side of the picture and decide which order the letters should be placed in the word.

- The children write the word on the lines underneath the picture of the duck.
- The children solve the remaining anagrams in the same way.
- There is a line for each sound in the word. The slightly longer lines indicate that digraph is needed.
- The pictures are: *duck, frog, fish.*

Further blending practice
- Write the following list of words on the board and blend them with the children:
  daytime, toys, employ, playing, pays.
- Write the following sentences on the board, pointing out the tricky words and blending any unknown words with the children.
  1. He was such a good boy on Tuesday.
  2. We made pots from clay.
  3. The plane is still on the runway.
  4. The snail left a silver trail.

113

Alternatives: ‹ee› and ‹ea›

Flash cards

- Revise some of the basic 42 sounds, plus ‹y› as /ee/, ‹a_e›, ‹e_e›, ‹i_e›, ‹o_e›, ‹u_e›, ‹ay›, ‹oy›.

Alternatives: ‹ea› as /ee/

- Say the word *free* and ask the children what sound they can hear at the end of this word. The children should say an /ee/ sound.
- Ask the children how an /ee/ sound is usually written; they should say ‹ee›.
- Write *free* on the board and point out the ‹ee› at the end.
- Now say the word *eve* and ask the children what sound they can hear at the beginning of this word. The children should say an /ee/ sound.
- Write *eve* on the board and point out the ‹e_e› digraph that makes the /ee/ sound in this word.
- Remind the children that the /ee/ sound can be written in more than one way.
- Point to the words *free* and *eve* on the board and tell the children that they already know two ways to write the /ee/ sound, ‹ee› and ‹e_e›.
- Now say the word *leap* and ask the children what sound they can hear in the middle of this word. Again, the children should say an /ee/ sound.
- Tell the children that, in the word *leap*, the /ee/ sound is not written ‹ee› or ‹e_e›, but ‹ea›.
- Write *leap* on the board and point out the ‹ea› in the middle.
- Blend all three words with the children, pointing to the letters as you say each sound.
- The children look at the blending words at the top of their page.
- Read the blending words with the children and point out the letters making the ‹ee› soundin each word.
- The words are:
    three, teeth, tree,
    leaf, feet, sheep,
    seal, bee, sea.

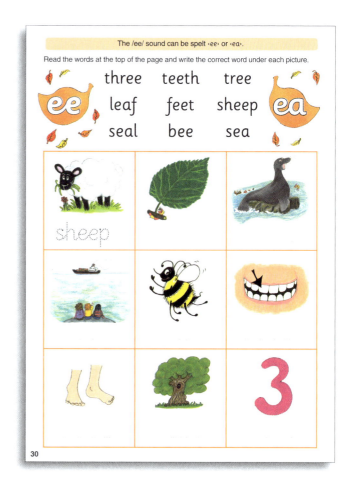

Word and picture matching

- The children look at the pictures in the grid at the bottom of the page.
- They read each blending word again and write it in the grid, on the lines underneath the corresponding picture.
- There is a line for each of the sounds in the word. A longer line indicates that a digraph is needed.

Reading sentences

- Write the following sentences on the board, pointing out the tricky words and blending any unknown words with the children.
    1. There are some old bikes in this shed.
    2. We can only cross the sea in the boats.
    3. This hill is far too steep.
    4. I made some tea for my sister.

Handwriting and Dictation

Flash cards
· Revise some of the basic 42 sounds, plus ‹y›
as /ee/, ‹a_e›, ‹e_e›, ‹i_e›, ‹o_e›, ‹u_e›, ‹ay›, ‹oy›.

Dictation words
· Dictate the following words:
>   *big,*
>   *bag,*
>   *men,*
>   *sand,*
>   *belt,*
>   *wish,*
>   *north,*
>   *lunch,*
>   *sort,*
>   *without.*
· The children write these words on the lines
in their *Phonics Pupil Books*.

The alphabet
· Look at the alphabet
with the children.
· Say the alphabet,
pointing to each letter
as you say it and
pausing between each
group.

Handwriting
· The children revise writing the capital letters
for the first half of the alphabet.
· Take down, or cover, any visible copies of the
alphabet so that the children have to
remember how the capital letters are written.
· The children write inside each lower-case
outline letter and then write the
corresponding capital letter next to it.
· They use a red pencil for the letters A-E and
a yellow pencil for the letters F-M.

Writing ‹b› and ‹d›
· These two letters are often confused.
· One way to help prevent confusion is to
remind the children how these letters are
formed.

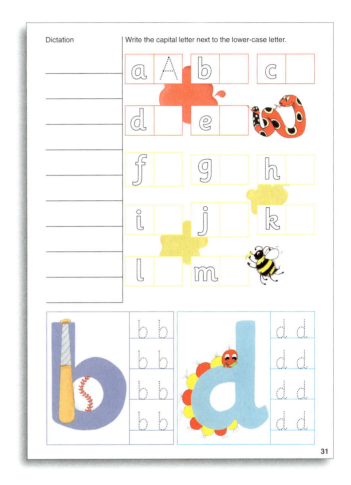

· Tell the children to remember that the letter
‹b› starts at the top with a down stroke (the
bat) and then bounces up and round for the
ball.
· Then say that the letter ‹d› is a 'caterpillar c'
letter, so it starts in the middle with a ‹c›
shape.
· The children write over the letters ‹b› and ‹d›
making sure that they start at the blue dots.

Further blending practice
· Write the following list of words on the board
and blend them with the children:
railway, Sunday, joy, annoy, yesterday.
· Write the following sentences on the board,
pointing out the tricky words and blending
any unknown words with the children.
1. She had some toys in her bag.
2. The boy only needs one pen.
3. They spent the day at the park.
4. The old man is very rich indeed.

Tricky Words

Flash cards
- Use the flash cards, or *Tricky Word Wall Flowers*, to revise the tricky words already taught, including *one, by, only* and *old*.

Tricky words
- Introduce the two new tricky words: *like* and *have*.
- The children look at the words in red flowers at the top of the page: *like* and *have*.
- Point out that *like* is not really tricky because the children now know that ‹i_e› says /ie/.
- Explain that English words ending in a /v/ sound do not end with a letter ‹v›, but have a silent ‹e› added to the end.
- Point out the ‹e› at the end of the word *have*.
- The children write inside the outline letters using a red pencil.

Look, copy, cover, write, check
- Look at the first word, *like*, with the children.
- Say the letter names (not the letter sounds) in that word. The children write over the dotted word *like*.
- Then the children cover up all instances of the word *like* on their page and try writing the word in the next column.
- Once the children have had one try at writing *like*, they check their spelling. Then they cover up all instances of the word *like* again, and have another go at writing the word in the final column.
- Repeat these steps with the word *have*.

Revising ‹b› and ‹d›
- Revise the formation of the letters ‹b› and ‹d›.
- The children look at the pictures.
- Say the first word, *bed*, to the children.
- The children listen out for the sounds /b/ and /d/.
- They trace over the dotted ‹b› and ‹d› in the word *bed*, making sure that they start at the starting dots.
- The children say the remaining ‹b› and ‹d› words to themselves and add the correct letters to each word.

Further blending practice
- Write the following list of words on the board and blend them with the children:
  crayons,
  joystick,
  underneath,
  neaten,
  shampoo.

Reading sentences
- Write the following sentences on the board, pointing out the tricky words and blending any unknown words with the children.
  1. We like to have a holiday in May.
  2. The boys like to play with toy cars.
  3. They have a long playtime.
  4. Do you like tea or coffee?

Words and Sentences

Flash cards
·Revise some of the basic 42 sounds, plus ‹y› as /ee/, ‹a_e›, ‹e_e›, ‹i_e›, ‹o_e›, ‹u_e›, ‹ay›, ‹oy›, ‹ea›.

Words and sentences
·Look at the picture and discuss it with the children.
·Ask a child to say one sentence about the picture. For example, 'I can see a queen.' 'She has a long cloak.' 'The queen waves.'
·Choose some words to blend and write them on the board; examples could be: *queen, cloak, wave.*
·Some words will be straightforward to spell by listening for the sounds, but others will need some guidance.
·*Wave*: point out that the /ai/ sound in the word *wave* is spelt ‹a_e›.
·Write the following sentence on the board.
   The queen has a red cloak.
·Discuss it as you write, saying:
·Sentences start with a capital letter.
·Capital letters are always tall.
·Listen for the sounds in the words.
·Leave a space between each word.
·Don't forget the full stop.
·All the children copy the sentence. Those children who can write independently can try to write some more sentences on their own.
·At this stage, the children only know one way of writing each sound, so their spelling will not always be accurate, but their work will be readable. Spelling gradually improves through reading many books and learning the alternative letter-sound spellings.

Revising ‹b› and ‹d›
·Remind the children that the letter ‹b› starts at the top with a down stroke (the bat) and then bounces up and round for the ball, whilst the letter ‹d› is a 'caterpillar c' letter, so it starts in the middle with a ‹c› shape.
·The children write inside the outline letters ‹b› and ‹d› and trace over the dotted letters, making sure that they start at the starting dots.

the queen

Practise writing ‹b› and ‹d›.

b b b b b b b

d d d d d d d

33

Further blending practice
·Write the following list of words on the board and blend them with the children:
   peanuts,
   sunshine,
   salute,
   speaking,
   seagull.

Reading sentences
·Write the following sentences on the board, pointing out the tricky words and blending any unknown words with the children.
1. Our teacher likes us to be good.
2. Do you like peaches?
3. Have you got a torch?
4. We have toads and frogs in the stream in our garden.

Alternatives: ‹ie›, ‹y› and ‹i_e›

Flash cards

- Revise some of the basic 42 sounds, plus ‹y› as /ee/, ‹a_e›, ‹e_e›, ‹i_e›, ‹o_e›, ‹u_e›, ‹ay›, ‹oy›, ‹ea›.

Alternatives: ‹ie›, ‹y› and ‹i_e› as /ie/

- Say the word *pie* and ask the children what sound they can hear at the end of this word. The children should say an /ie/ sound.
- Ask the children how an /ie/ sound is usually written; they should say ‹ie›.
- Write the word *pie* on the board.
- Explain that the /ie/ sound can be written in a number of different ways.
- Write the different spellings for the /ie/ sound on the board: ‹ie› as in *pie,* ‹y› as in *my* and ‹i_e› as in *like.*
- Remind the children that they already know the ‹ie› spelling for the /ie/ sound and they know that a 'hop-over e' turns a short vowel into a long vowel, so they can also read words containing ‹i_e›.
- Remind the children of the tricky words *my* and *by.* Point out that, in these words, the ‹y› makes an /ie/ sound.
- The children look at the words at the top of their page.
- Read the words with the children and point out the letters making the /ie/ sound in each word.
- The words are:
      pie, lie, tried, cries, tie, die;
      line, time, sunshine, drive, slide;
      my, flying, shy, sky, drying, try.

Reading activities

- The children read the words in the stars and draw a picture to illustrate them in the adjoining moons.
- The words in the stars are:
      tie, pie, fly, sky,
      bike, kite, slide, crying.

Further blending practice

- Write the following list of words on the board and blend them with the children:
      nylon,
      satisfy,
      spy,
      pylon,
      sly.

Reading sentences

- Write the following sentences on the board, pointing out the tricky words and blending any unknown words with the children.
1. We must eat the crusts too.
2. The roses have thorns on the stem.
3. I like the green socks best.
4. The boy is unhappy about the hole in his jumper.

Handwriting and Dictation

Flash cards
· Revise some of the basic 42 sounds, plus ‹y› as /ee/, ‹a_e›, ‹e_e›, ‹i_e›, ‹o_e›, ‹u_e›, ‹ay›, ‹oy›, ‹ea›.

Dictation words
· Dictate the following words:
> *dug,*
> *mix,*
> *leg,*
> *help,*
> *soft,*
> *rang,*
> *this,*
> *shout,*
> *coach,*
> *raindrop.*

· The children write these words on the lines in their *Phonics Pupil Books.*

The alphabet
· Look at the alphabet with the children.
· Say the alphabet, pointing to each letter as you say it and pausing between each group.

Handwriting
· The children revise writing the capital letters for the second half of the alphabet.
· Take down, or cover, any visible copies of the alphabet so that the children have to remember how the capital letters are written.
· The children write inside each lower-case outline letter and then write the corresponding capital letter next to it.
· They use a green pencil for the letters N-S and a blue pencil for the letters T-Z.

Read and draw
· The children read each sentence and illustrate it in the frame above.
· The sentences are:
The sun is hot.   She is running.

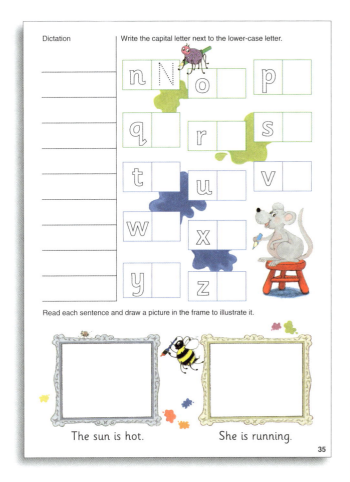

Further blending practice
· Write the following list of words on the board and blend them with the children:
> *bedtime,*
> *meaning,*
> *flashing,*
> *flicking,*
> *amused.*

Reading sentences
· Write the following sentences on the board, pointing out the tricky words and blending any unknown words with the children.
1. We have a set of silver teaspoons at home.
2. The king and queen have a throne each.
3. Dad cooks shrimps on the grill.
4. I like my blue dress best.

Tricky Words

Flash cards
- Use the flash cards, or *Tricky Word Wall Flowers*, to revise the tricky words already taught, including *one, by, only, old, like* and *have*.

Tricky words
- Introduce the two new tricky words: *live* and *give*.
- The children look at the words in red flowers at the top of the page: *live* and *give*.
- Remind the children that English words ending in a /v/ sound do not end with a letter ‹v›, but have a silent ‹e› added to the end.
- Point out the ‹e› at the end of the words *live* and *give*.
- The children write inside the outline letters using a red pencil.

Tricky flowers
- The children write over the dotted words *like, have, live,* and *give* and colour the flowers red.

Look, copy, cover, write, check
- Look at the first word, *live*, with the children.
- Say the letter names (not the letter sounds) in that word. The children write over the dotted word *live*.
- Then the children cover up all instances of the word *live* on their page and try writing the word in the next column.
- Once the children have had one try at writing *live*, they check their spelling. Then they cover up all instances of the word *live* again, and have another go at writing the word in the final column.
- Repeat these steps with the word *give*.

Word and picture matching
- Look at the first picture with the children and read the two words written underneath, *cub* and *cube*.
- Ask the children if the picture shows a *cub* or a *cube*.
- They should say a *cube*.

- The children write this word on the line underneath the picture.
- The children repeat these steps with the remaining words and pictures, writing the correct word on the line each time.
- Point out that the ‹g› in the word *huge* makes a /j/ sound
- The words are:
  > *cub*, **cube**; **fin**, *fine*; **hug**, *huge*;
  > *tub*, **tube**; **hat**, *hate*; *rid*, **ride**.
- The words in bold type are the correct answers.

Reading sentences
- Write the following sentences on the board, pointing out the tricky words and blending any unknown words with the children.
  1. They live near the beach.
  2. Can you give me some teabags?
  3. Your teacher will give you a book to read.
  4. Three slugs live underneath this rock.

Words and Sentences

Flash cards

- Revise some of the basic 42 sounds, plus ‹y› as /ee/ and /ie/, ‹a_e›, ‹e_e›, ‹i_e›, ‹o_e›, ‹u_e›, ‹ay›, ‹oy›, ‹ea›.

Words and sentences

- Look at the picture and discuss it with the children.
- Ask a child to say one sentence about the picture. For example, 'Some sharks swim in the sea.' 'The man digs in the sand.' 'I see a sunset.'
- Choose some words to blend and write them on the board; examples could be: *map, dig, pirate.*
- Some words will be straightforward to spell by listening for the sounds, but others will need some guidance.
- *Pirate*: tell the children that the ‹i› in this word makes a long /ie/ sound. Remind them of the saying, 'If the short vowel doesn't work, try the long vowel.'
- It may help the children to use the 'say it as it sounds' technique when spelling *pirate*. Encourage the children to pronounce the word as *pie-rat,* and tell them not to forget to put an ‹e› at the end.
- *Sea*: point out that the /ee/ sound in this word is spelt ‹ea›.
- Write the following sentence on the board.
  He went south and then north.
- Discuss it as you write, saying:
- Sentences start with a capital letter.
- Capital letters are always tall.
- Listen for the sounds in the words.
- Leave a space between each word.
- Don't forget the full stop.
- All the children copy the sentence. Those children who can write independently can try to write some more sentences on their own.
- At this stage, the children only know one way of writing each sound, so their spelling will not always be accurate, but their work will be readable. Spelling gradually improves through reading many books and learning the alternative letter-sound spellings.

Write over these 'caterpillar c' shapes.

37

Letter formation

- Joining the 'caterpillar c' letters can prove difficult for children.
- The children trace over the lines of 'caterpillar c' shapes to complete the sea picture.
- Remind the children to stop at the top of the wave and come back round for the ‹c› shape.

Further blending practice

- Write the following list of words on the board and blend them with the children:
  bringing, jester, messy, windmill, easy.
- Write the following sentences on the board, pointing out the tricky words and blending any unknown words with the children.
  1. Give your sister some lemonade.
  2. The bonfire made the ground all black.
  3. Do you live here?
  4. Some tadpoles live in this pond.

Alternatives: ‹ow›

Flash cards
• Revise some of the basic 42 sounds, plus ‹y› as /ee/ and /ie/, ‹a_e›, ‹e_e›, ‹i_e›, ‹o_e›, ‹u_e›, ‹ay›, ‹oy›, ‹ea›.

Alternatives: ‹ow› as /oa/ and /ou/
• The digraph ‹ow› can make two sounds: the /oa/ sound, as in *yellow*, and the /ou/ sound, as in *owl*.
• Remind the children of the rule, 'If one way doesn't work try the other,' which can help them to read words containing ‹ow›.
• Say the word *yellow* and ask the children what sound they can hear at the end of this word. They should say an /oa/ sound.
• Ask the children how an /oa/ sound is usually written. They should say ‹oa›.
• Write the word *yellow* on the board. Explain that the /oa/ sound can also be written ‹ow› and point to the ‹ow› at the end of the word *yellow*.
• Now say the word *owl* and ask the children what sound they can hear at the beginning of this word. They should say an /ou/ sound.
• Ask the children how an /ou/ sound is usually written. They should say ‹ou›.
• Write the word *owl* on the board. Explain that the /ou/ sound can also be written ‹ow› and point to the ‹ow› at the beginning of the word *owl*.
• Explain to the children that the digraph ‹ow› has two sounds: it can make an /oa/, as in *yellow*, or /ou/, as in *owl*.
• When the children are reading words with an ‹ow› digraph, they should first try one pronunciation of ‹ow› to see if it makes a word. If it does not make a word, they should try reading the word with the other pronunciation of ‹ow›.
• The children look at the blending words on their page. First, read the /ou/ sound words with the children. Point out the letters making the /ou/ sound in each word.
• The /ou/ words are:
   shout, south, mouse, flour,
   town, brown, owl, flower.

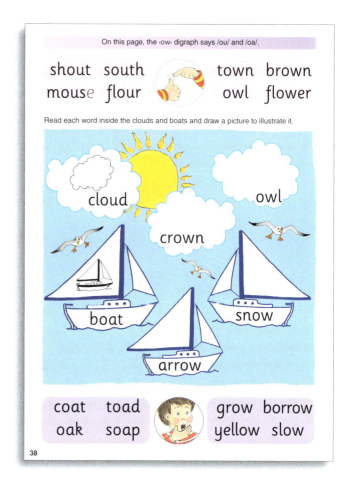

• Now read the /oa/ sound words with the children. Point out the letters making the /oa/ sound in each word.
• The /oa/ words are:
   coat, toad, oak, soap,
   grow, borrow, yellow, slow.

Read and draw: clouds and boats
• The children read the words in the clouds and boats and draw a picture to illustrate each one.
• The words are:
cloud, crown, owl (in clouds);
boat, arrow, snow (in boats).

Further blending practice
• Write the following list of words on the board and blend them with the children:
shallow, drown, sparrow, shower, rainbow.

Handwriting and Dictation

Flash cards
- Revise some of the basic 42 sounds, plus ‹y› as /ee/ and /ie/, ‹a_e›, ‹e_e›, ‹i_e›, ‹o_e›, ‹u_e›, ‹ay›, ‹oy›, ‹ea›.

Dictation words
- Dictate the following words:

run,	*bad,*
lip,	*just,*
melt,	*moth,*
sang,	*porch,*
rescue,	*magpie.*

- The children write these words on the lines in their *Phonics Pupil Books*.

The alphabet
- Look at the alphabet with the children.
- Say the alphabet, pointing to each letter as you say it and pausing between each group.

Handwriting
- The children revise writing the letters that start with a 'caterpillar c':
  ‹c›, ‹a›, ‹d›, ‹o›, ‹g›, ‹q›.

Writing activities
- Look at the first picture with the children and say the word, *moon*.
- The children listen for the sounds in the word: /m/, /oo/, /n/.
- The children write the word on the lines underneath the picture.
- There is a line for each sound in the word. A longer line indicates that a digraph is needed.
- The children look at the rest of the pictures. They say each word to themselves and identify all the sounds in each word.
- The pictures are: *moon, drum, queen*.
- When the children have finished writing, they can colour the pictures.

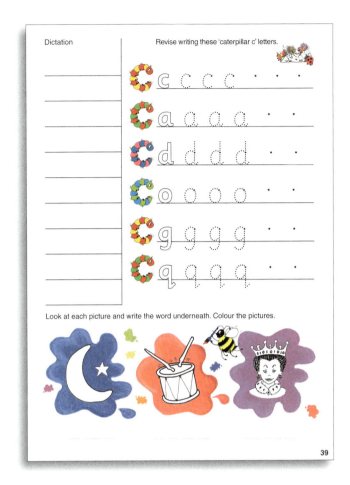

Further blending practice
- Write the following list of words on the board and blend them with the children:

  caterpillar,
  beaming,
  away,
  stocky,
  flea.

Reading sentences
- Write the following sentences on the board, pointing out the tricky words and blending any unknown words with the children.
  1. Give me those beaten eggs.
  2. Did you give your toys to her?
  3. Do sheep live in houses or on farms?
  4. We went on the bumper cars at the theme park.

Tricky Words

Flash cards

- Use the flash cards, or *Tricky Word Wall Flowers*, to revise the tricky words already taught, including *one, by, only, old, like, have, live* and *give*.

Tricky words

- Introduce the two new tricky words: *little* and *down*.
- The children look at the words in red flowers at the top of the page: *little* and *down*.
- Point out that *down* is not really tricky, because the children now know that ‹ow› can say /ou/.
- The children write inside the outline letters using a red pencil.

Word search

- The children read the tricky words written in the red and yellow flowers surrounding the grid.
- They search for each word in the grid and circle the word when they find it.

Look, copy, cover, write, check

- Look at the first word, *little*, with the children.
- Say the letter names (not the letter sounds) in that word. The children write over the dotted word *little*.
- Then the children cover up all instances of the word *little* on their page and try writing the word in the next column.
- Once the children have had one try at writing *little*, they check their spelling. Then they cover up all instances of the word *little* again, and have another go at writing the word in the final column.
- Repeat these steps with the word *down*.

Further blending practice

- Write the following list of words on the board and blend them with the children:
  frowning,
  blow,
  crowded,
  mown,
  how.

Reading sentences

- Write the following sentences on the board, pointing out the tricky words and blending any unknown words with the children.
1. The little boy ran down the hill.
2. We went up and down in the lift.
3. Show me that little book.
4. The little mole lives deep down underground.

Words and Sentences

Flash cards
- Revise some of the basic 42 sounds, plus ‹y› as /ee/ and /ie/, ‹a_e›, ‹e_e›, ‹i_e›, ‹o_e›, ‹u_e›, ‹ay›, ‹oy›, ‹ea›, ‹ow› as /oa/ and /ou/.

Words and sentences
- Look at the picture and discuss it with the children.
- Ask a child to say one sentence about the picture. For example, 'I can see a shark.' 'The shark is swimming.' 'The ship has sunk.'
- Choose some words to blend and write them on the board; examples could be: *shark, ship, wreck.*
- Some words will be straightforward to spell by listening for the sounds, but others will need some guidance.
- *Shark*: because *shark* has a long vowel sound, /ar/, only a ‹k› is needed to make the /ck/ sound at the end.
- *Wreck*: the word *wreck* has a silent ‹w› at the beginning. The /ck/ sound in *wreck* is spelt ‹ck› because *wreck* has the short vowel sound /e/.
- Write the following sentence on the board. *The strong shark swam in and around the ship.*
- Discuss it as you write, saying:
- Sentences start with a capital letter.
- Capital letters are always tall.
- Listen for the sounds in the words.
- Leave a space between each word.
- Don't forget the full stop.
- All the children copy the sentence.
- Those children who can write independently can try to write some more sentences on their own.
- At this stage, the children only know one way of writing each sound, so their spelling will not always be accurate, but their work will be readable. Spelling gradually improves through reading many books and learning the alternative letter-sound spellings.

Reading words
- The children read each word at the bottom of the page and join it to the matching picture.

Further blending practice
- Write the following list of words on the board and blend them with the children:
  - *allow,*
  - *below,*
  - *sunflower,*
  - *throw,*
  - *bowl.*

Reading sentences
- Write the following sentences on the board, pointing out the tricky words and blending any unknown words with the children.
1. The rude little clown was very funny.
2. Do you have a little sister?
3. The little frog jumps up and down.
4. There are some foxes outside.

Alternatives: ‹er›, ‹ir› and ‹ur›

Flash cards

- Revise some of the basic 42 sounds, plus ‹y› as /ee/ and /ie/, ‹a_e›, ‹e_e›, ‹i_e›, ‹o_e›, ‹u_e›, ‹ay›, ‹oy›, ‹ea›, ‹ow› as /oa/ and /ou/.

Alternatives: ‹er›, ‹ir› and ‹ur› as /er/

- Say the word *summer* and ask the children what sound they can hear at the end of this word.
- They should say an /er/ sound.
- Ask the children how an /er/ sound is usually written.
- They should say ‹er›.
- Write the word *summer* on the board and point to the ‹er› at the end.
- Explain to the children that the /er/ sound can also be written as ‹ir›, or ‹ur›.
- Now say the word *bird* and ask the children what sound they can hear in the middle of this word.
- They should say an /er/ sound.
- Write the word *bird* on the board.
- Explain that, in this word, the /er/ sound is spelt ‹ir› and point to the ‹ir› in the middle of the word *bird*.
- Now say the word *burn* and ask the children what sound they can hear in the middle of this word.
- Again, they should say an /er/ sound.
- Write the word *burn* on the board.
- Explain that, in this word, the /er/ sound is spelt ‹ur› and point to the ‹ur› in the middle of the word *burn*.

Read and draw

- The children read the /er/ words in the gingerbread men, birds and turkeys and draw a picture to illustrate each one.
- The words are:
    - *summer, winter* (in gingerbread men);
    - *skirt, shirt* (in birds);
    - *purple, purse* (in turkeys).

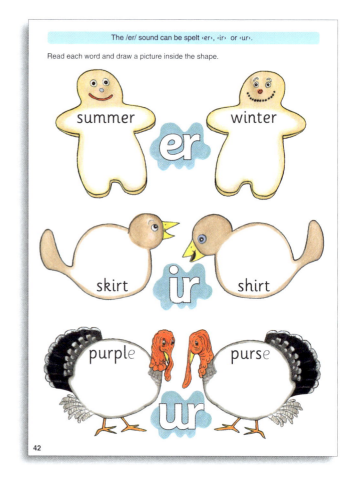

The /er/ sound can be spelt ‹er›, ‹ir› or ‹ur›.

Read each word and draw a picture inside the shape.

summer   winter

er

skirt   shirt

ir

purple   purse

ur

42

Further blending practice

- Write the following list of words on the board and blend them with the children:
    - *thirteen,*
    - *burst,*
    - *thirsty,*
    - *turnip,*
    - *first.*

Reading sentences

- Write the following sentences on the board, pointing out the tricky words and blending any unknown words with the children.
1. Your little skirt is much too short.
2. I had a surprise party on my birthday.
3. We had a barbecue and Dad burnt all the burgers.
4. My cat's fur is black and brown.

Handwriting and Dictation

Flash cards
· Revise some of the basic 42 sounds, plus ‹y› as /ee/ and /ie/, ‹a_e›, ‹e_e›, ‹i_e›, ‹o_e›, ‹u_e›, ‹ay›, ‹oy›, ‹ea›, ‹ow› as /oa/ and /ou/.

Dictation words
· Dictate the following words:

> *can,*
> *hen,*
> *pit,*
> *best,*
> *went,*
> *wing,*
> *chart,*
> *three,*
> *tried,*
> *toadstool.*

· The children write these words on the lines in their *Phonics Pupil Books*.

The alphabet
· Look at the alphabet with the children.
· Say the alphabet, pointing to each letter as you say it and pausing between each group.

Handwriting
· The children revise writing the tall letters: ‹b›, ‹d›, ‹h›, ‹k›, ‹l›, ‹t›.

Finish the alphabet
· If you think the children will be able to remember the alphabet, cover any visible copies of the alphabet around the classroom before the children start this activity.
· The children fill in the missing capital letters to complete the alphabet.
· They use a red pencil to write the letters A-E, a yellow pencil for the letters F-M, a green pencil for the letters N-S and a blue pencil for the letters T-Z.

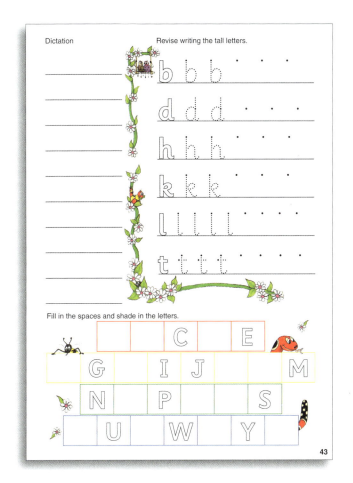

Further blending practice
· Write the following list of words on the board and blend them with the children:

> *powder,*
> *marrow,*
> *vowel,*
> *fellow,*
> *arrow.*

Reading sentences
· Write the following sentences on the board, pointing out the tricky words and blending any unknown words with the children.
1. Did you throw that pillow at me?
2. There is a spooky shadow by that window.
3. My grandad grows carrots and marrows.
4. That little dog howls all day long.

Tricky Words

Flash cards

- Use the flash cards, or *Tricky Word Wall Flowers*, to revise the tricky words already taught, including *one, by, only, old, like, have, live, give, little* and *down*.

Tricky words

- Introduce the three new tricky words: *what, when* and *why*.
- The children look at the words in red and green flowers at the top of the page.
- Explain that the ‹wh› at the beginning of each of these words makes a /w/ sound.
- The children could underline the ‹wh› at the beginning of each of these words in purple, to remind them that this is the 'tricky bit'.
- Point out that *what, when* and *why* are all words that we use to ask questions.
- The children write inside the words *what* and *when* using a red pencil and the word *why* using a green pencil.

Look, copy, cover, write, check

- Look at the first word, *what*, with the children.
- Say the letter names (not the letter sounds) in that word. The children write over the dotted word *what*.
- Then the children cover up all instances of the word *what* on their page and try writing the word in the next column.
- Once the children have had one try at writing *what*, they check their spelling. Then they cover up all instances of the word *what* again, and have another go at writing the word in the final column.
- Repeat these steps with the words *when* and *why*.

Word and picture matching

- The children read the words at the bottom of the page and look at the pictures in the leaves around the edge.
- The words are:
    lie, snail, tree, soap,
    nail, road, leek, pie.

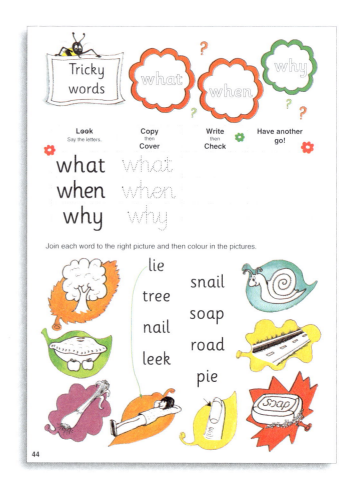

- The children join each word to the corresponding picture and then colour the pictures.

Further blending practice

- Write the following list of words on the board and blend them with the children:
    curly,
    stirring,
    Saturn,
    sir,
    hurting.

Reading sentences

- Write the following sentences on the board, pointing out the tricky words and blending any unknown words with the children.
  1. When did Dad lay the turf in the garden?
  2. There is a bird's nest in our fir tree.
  3. What is the first thing you remember?
  4. Why are there muddy footprints on the rug?

Words and Sentences

Flash cards
· Revise some of the basic 42 sounds, plus ‹y› as /ee/ and /ie/, ‹a_e›, ‹e_e›, ‹i_e›, ‹o_e›, ‹u_e›, ‹ay›, ‹oy›, ‹ea›, ‹ow› as /oa/ and /ou/, ‹ir› and ‹ur›.

Words and sentences
· Look at the picture and discuss it with the children.
· Ask a child to say one sentence about the picture. For example, 'I can see a car.' 'The boy is helping his Dad.' 'They are putting oil in the car.'
· Choose some words to blend and write them on the board; examples could be: *boy, Dad, oil, car*.
· Some words will be straightforward to spell by listening for the sounds, but others will need some guidance.
· *Boy*: remind the children that the /oi/ sound is usually spelt ‹oy› when it comes at the end of the word.
· Write the following sentence on the board.
    He helps to check the oil in the car.
· Discuss it as you write, saying:
· Sentences start with a capital letter.
· Capital letters are always tall.
· Listen for the sounds in the words.
· Leave a space between each word.
· Don't forget the full stop.
· All the children copy the sentence.
· Those children who can write independently can try to write some more sentences on their own.
· At this stage, the children only know one way of writing each sound, so their spelling will not always be accurate, but their work will be readable.
· Spelling gradually improves through reading many books and learning the alternative letter-sound spellings.

Reading words
· The children read each word at the bottom of the page and join it to the corresponding vehicle.

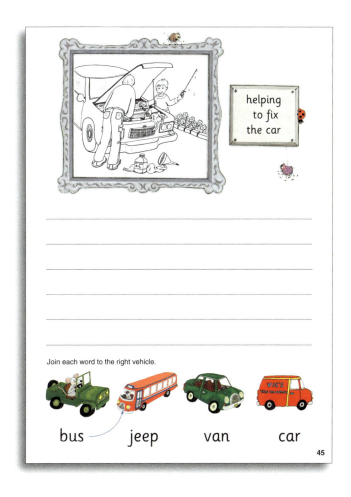

helping
to fix
the car

Join each word to the right vehicle.

bus   jeep   van   car

45

Further blending practice
· Write the following list of words on the board and blend them with the children:
    burglary,
    firmly,
    further,
    twirl,
    churn.

Reading sentences
· Write the following sentences on the board, pointing out the tricky words and blending any unknown words with the children.
1. When is the next train?
2. What is that blue stuff on his shirt?
3. Why do the leaves on the trees turn brown?
4. When is granny visiting?

Handwriting and Dictation

Flash cards
- Revise some of the basic 42 sounds, plus ‹y› as /ee/ and /ie/, ‹a_e›, ‹e_e›, ‹i_e›, ‹o_e›, ‹u_e›, ‹ay›, ‹oy›, ‹ea›, ‹ow› as /oa/ and /ou/, ‹ir› and ‹ur› as /er/.

Dictation words
- Dictate the following words:
  - *rub,*
  - *man,*
  - *get,*
  - *land,*
  - *test,*
  - *long,*
  - *mouth,*
  - *bench,*
  - *yard,*
  - *toothbrush.*
- The children write these words on the lines in their *Phonics Pupil Books*.

The alphabet
- Look at the alphabet with the children.
- Say the alphabet, pointing to each letter as you say it and pausing between each group.

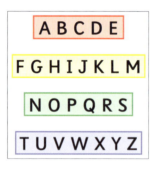

Handwriting
- The children revise writing the tail letters: ‹f›, ‹g›, ‹j›, ‹p›, ‹q›, ‹y›.

Finish the alphabet
- If you think the children will be able to remember the alphabet, cover any visible copies of the alphabet around the classroom before the children start this activity.
- The children fill in the missing capital letters to complete the alphabet.
- They can use a red pencil to write the letters A-E, a yellow pencil for the letters F-M, a green pencil for the letters N-S and a blue pencil for the letters T-Z.

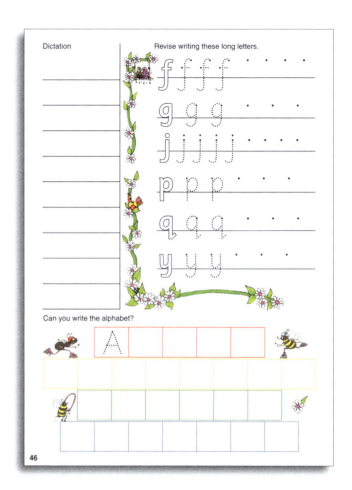

Further blending practice
- Write the following list of words on the board and blend them with the children:
  - *hamster,*
  - *Thursday,*
  - *continue,*
  - *sensible,*
  - *storybook.*

Reading sentences
- Write the following sentences on the board, pointing out the tricky words and blending any unknown words with the children.
  1. Why is the snow melting?
  2. He went down the lane by himself.
  3. What did you borrow from Pete?
  4. Why is my shadow so long?

Tricky Words

Flash cards
- Use the flash cards, or *Tricky Word Wall Flowers*, to revise the tricky words already taught.

Tricky words
- Introduce the three new tricky words: *where, who* and *which*. The children look at the words in green flowers at the top of the page.
- Explain that the ‹wh› at the beginning of the words *where* and *which* makes a /w/ sound, but the ‹wh› at the beginning of *who* makes a /h/ sound.
- The children could underline the ‹wh› at the beginning of each of these words in purple, to remind them that this is the 'tricky bit'.
- Point out that *where, who* and *which* are all words that we use to ask questions.
- The children write inside the outline letters using a green pencil.

Look, copy, cover, write, check
- Look at the first word, *where*, with the children.
- Say the letter names (not the letter sounds) in that word. The children write over the dotted word *where*.
- Then the children cover up all instances of the word *where* on their page and try writing the word in the next column.
- Once the children have had one try at writing *where*, they check their spelling. Then they cover up all instances of the word *where* again, and have another go at writing the word in the final column.
- Repeat these steps with the words *who* and *which*.

Reading activities
- The children read each sentence, and illustrate it in the picture frame above.
- The sentences are:
  I see the moon and stars.
  A boy is asleep in bed.
  A duck is swimming on the pond.
  The girl has a green dress.

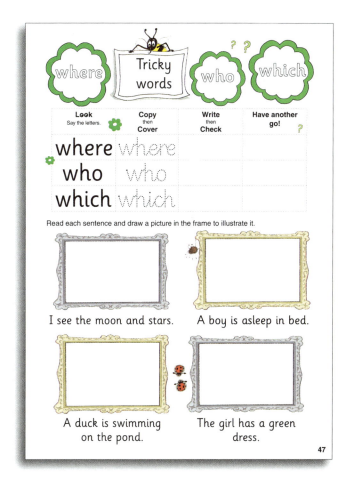

Further blending practice
- Write the following list of words on the board and blend them with the children:
  blanket,
  untrue,
  playground,
  yogurt,
  return.

Reading sentences
- Write the following sentences on the board, pointing out the tricky words and blending any unknown words with the children.
  1. Where shall we go today?
  2. Who will come with us?
  3. Who spilt all this brown paint on the mat?
  4. Which of these cupcakes do you like best?

Words and Sentences

Flash cards
- Revise some of the basic 42 sounds, plus ‹y› as /ee/ and /ie/, ‹a_e›, ‹e_e›, ‹i_e›, ‹o_e›, ‹u_e›, ‹ay›, ‹oy›, ‹ea›, ‹ow› as /oa/ and /ou/, ‹ir› and ‹ur›.

Words and sentences
- Look at the picture and discuss it with the children.
- Ask a child to say one sentence about the picture. For example, 'I can see a statue.' 'The man has a lamb.' 'The sun shines.'
- Choose some words to blend and write them on the board; examples could be: *statue, lamb, bird, sunshine*.
- Some words will be straightforward to spell by listening for the sounds, but others will need some guidance.
- *Bird*: remind the children that the /er/ sound in *bird* is spelt ‹ir›.
- *Lamb*: the word *lamb* has a silent ‹b› at the end.
- *Sunshine*: the /ie/ sound in the word *sunshine* is written with a ‹i_e› digraph.
- Write the following sentence on the board.
  > *The statue has a hat and coat.*
- Discuss it as you write, saying:
- Sentences start with a capital letter.
- Capital letters are always tall.
- Listen for the sounds in the words.
- Leave a space between each word.
- Don't forget the full stop.
- All the children copy the sentence. Those children who can write independently can try to write some more sentences on their own.
- At this stage, the children only know one way of writing each sound, so their spelling will not always be accurate, but their work will be readable.
- Spelling gradually improves through reading many books and learning the alternative letter-sound spellings.

Reading words
- The children read each word at the bottom of the page and join it to the matching picture.

Join each word to the right picture.

tie   lamb   bird   boot

48

Further blending practice
- Write the following list of words on the board and blend them with the children:
  > *creamy,*
  > *lower,*
  > *broomstick,*
  > *smirk,*
  > *dreaming.*

Reading sentences
- Write the following sentences on the board, pointing out the tricky words and blending any unknown words with the children.
  1. Who likes peanut butter sandwiches?
  2. Where are all the tennis balls?
  3. What is the quickest way to the pool?
  4. Which bird is bigger, a sparrow, or an ostrich?

Teaching with Phonics Pupil Book 3

In *Phonics Pupil Book 3*, the children continue to build upon the reading and writing skills learnt in *Phonics Pupil Books 1* and *2*. The exercises in *Phonics Pupil Book 3* give the children a greater understanding of the alternative letter-sound spellings and introduce them to the remaining tricky words. The children are also encouraged to write with increasing independence in *Phonics Pupil Book 3* and many of the activities are designed to improve the children's comprehension skills alongside their reading and writing skills. In *Phonics Pupil Book 3*, the teaching covered during each lesson follows a pattern and the following activities are covered on a regular basis.

Alternatives

In *Phonics Pupil Book 3*, the children are gradually encouraged to apply their knowledge of alternative letter-sound spellings to writing as well as reading. However, at this early stage, the children cannot be expected to use the correct alternative letter-sound spellings consistently in their work. The children are taught number of rules that relate to the letter-sound spellings. For example, they are taught that ‹i› is 'too shy' to come at the end of a word and is replaced by ‹y›. This means that when the /ai/ sound comes at the end of a word it is spelt ‹ay›. Rules like these can help the children to choose the correct letter-sound spellings when writing a word. The children are also introduced to the following alternative letter-sound spellings in *Phonics Pupil Book 3*.

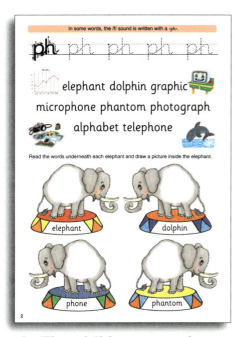

‹ph› making an /f/ sound, as in *phonic*
soft ‹c›, when ‹c› is followed by ‹e›, ‹i›, ‹y› it makes a /s/ sound
soft ‹g›, when ‹g› is followed by ‹e›, ‹i›, ‹y› it makes a /j/ sound
‹igh› making the /ie/ sound
‹ew› making the /ue/ sound
‹air›, ‹are› and ‹ear› making the /air/ sound, as in *fairy*

The following alternatives are revised in *Phonics Pupil Book 3*:

‹ai› and ‹ay› making the /ai/ sound
‹ee›, ‹ea› and ‹e_e› making the /ee/ sound
‹ie›, ‹y› and ‹i_e› making the /ie/ sound
‹oa›, ‹ow› and ‹o_e› making the /oa/ sound
‹ue› and ‹u_e› making the /ue/ sound

‹ou› and ‹ow› making the /ou/ sound
‹oi› and ‹oy› making the /oi/ sound
‹er›, ‹ir› and ‹ur› making the /er/ sound

Tricky words

In *Phonics Pupil Book 3*, dictation and tricky words are covered on the same page.

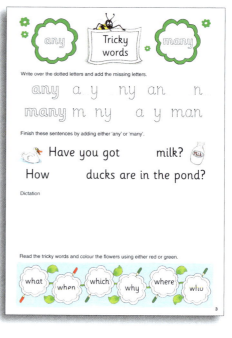

Tricky words

These pages introduce the children to more of the tricky words as well as helping them to revise the tricky words that have already been taught. For more information, see pages 30 to 33 of this book for the section on tricky words.

The following tricky words are introduced in *Phonics Pupil Book 3*:

any, many, more, before, other, were, because, want,
> (green words)

saw, put, could, should, would, right, two, four, goes, does, made, their,
> (pink words)

once, upon, always, also, of, eight, love, cover, after, every, mother, father.
> (brown words)

Dictation

In *Phonics Pupil Book 3* the children begin to write sentences from dictation. The dictation sentences, provided in the Daily Lesson Plans, give the children a chance to practise spelling tricky words as well as phonetically regular words. For more information about dictation, see page 25 of the introduction.

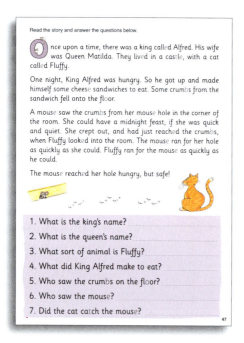

Comprehension

The comprehension pages in *Phonics Pupil Book 3* cover a range of activities, all of which aim to improve the children's blending abilities as well as their comprehension skills. There is a greater emphasis on comprehension in *Phonics Pupil Book 3*.

Words and sentences

In *Phonics Pupil Book 3*, the children are given the opportunity to write with an increasing amount of freedom. They are no longer provided with a model sentence to copy, or with a discussion picture to write about. Instead, they are provided with the title for their piece of writing and a blank picture box in which they can illustrate their writing.

• The teacher initiates a class discussion about the given topic, or about a theme of the teacher's own choosing.
• He or she then selects some key words from the discussion to write on the board, pointing out any alternative spelling patterns in these words.
• The children write freely and independently about the class discussion topic and illustrate their writing in the picture frame.

At this stage, the children's spelling will not always be accurate, but their work will be readable. Spelling gradually improves through reading many books and learning the alternative letter-sound spellings.

Teachers should feel free to set their own writing subject. The title of the writing exercise does appear on the children's pages, but the picture frame is empty and the lines are blank. It may be that the children would like to write about a recent holiday they have celebrated, or a story they have heard. If this is the case, teachers can set their own title and guide the children's writing accordingly.

The more able children can move on to the Green Level of *Jolly Phonics Readers* when they have learnt the tricky words up to and including *which* and once they have been introduced to the 'hop-over ‹e›' digraphs found in words like *shake*, *these*, *bike*, *rose* and *cube*. This knowledge is covered by the end of *Phonics Pupil Book 2*.

Alternatives: ‹ph›

Flash cards
• Revise some of the letter sounds introduced in *Phonics Pupil Books 1* and *2*.

Alternatives: ‹ph› as /f/
• Say the word *phone* and ask the children what sound they can hear at the beginning of this word. They should say a /f/ sound.
• Write the word *phone* on the board.
• Explain that, in some words, the /f/ sound is written ‹ph›. This is because these words originally come from the Greek language.
• Point to the ‹ph› at the beginning of the word *phone*.
• Tell the children that, when they come across a word with a ‹p› and an ‹h› next to each other, they need to say /f/ and not /p-h/ to read the word.
• The children look at the blending words on the page. Read the words with the children.
• The words are as follows:
> *elephant, dolphin, graphic,*
> *microphone, phantom, photograph,*
> *alphabet, telephone.*

Note 1: accent
• With some accents, the letter ‹a› in words like *graph* and *photograph* can make an /ar/ sound.

Letter formation
• The children write over the dotted ‹ph› digraphs at the top of the page.

Read and draw: elephants
• The children read the words underneath each elephant.
• They draw a picture inside the elephant to illustrate each word.
• The words are as follows:
> *elephant, dolphin,*
> *phone, phantom.*

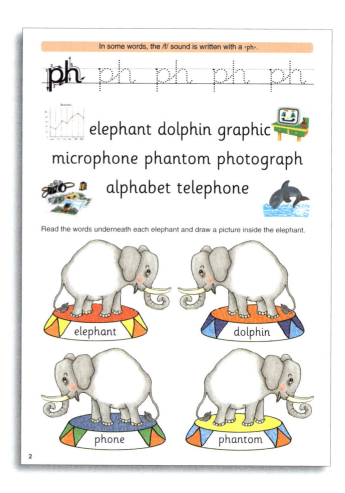

In some words, the /f/ sound is written with a ‹ph›.

ph ph ph ph ph

elephant dolphin graphic
microphone phantom photograph
alphabet telephone

Read the words underneath each elephant and draw a picture inside the elephant.

elephant   dolphin

phone   phantom

2

Further blending practice
• Write the following list of words on the board and blend them with the children:
> *phonic,*
> *buttercup,*
> *orphan,*
> *phrase,*
> *philosopher.*

Reading sentences
• Write the following sentences on the board, pointing out the tricky words and blending any unknown words with the children.
1. The elephants at the zoo had long trunks.
2. Who can say the alphabet?
3. Dolphins live in the sea.
4. Grandad spoke to me on the telephone.

Tricky Words and Dictation

Flash cards
- Use the flash cards, or *Tricky Word Wall Flowers*, to revise some of the tricky words taught so far.

Tricky words
- Introduce the two new tricky words: *any*, *many*.
- The children look at the words in green flowers at the top of the page: *any* and *many*.
- Point out that the word *many* is like the word *any*, but with an ‹m› at the beginning.
- The children write inside the words *any* and *many* using a green pencil.

Filling in the gaps
- The children trace inside the outline letters in the word *any*, saying the letter names as they do so.
- Then the children cover up all instances of the word *any* on their page and try to complete a line of this word, by tracing over the dotted letters and filling in the missing letters.
- The children repeat these steps for the word *many*.

Complete the sentences
- Read the first sentence, pausing at the gap:
  Have you got ___ milk?
- Ask the children whether they think they should write *any* or *many* in this gap.
- Read the sentence back to the children, including their chosen word, and ask them if they think the sentence makes sense with this word.
- The children write the correct word in the gap in their *Phonics Pupil Books*.
- The children read the next sentence by themselves and decide which of the tricky words completes the sentence.
- They write this tricky word on the line in the sentence.

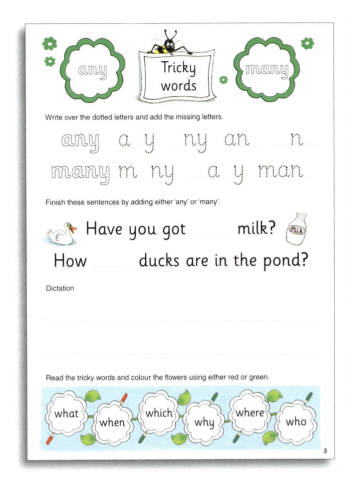

Dictation sentences
- Dictate the following sentences:
  We look to see if any fish are left.
  A shark has many sharp teeth.
- The children write these sentences on the lines in their *Phonics Pupil Books*.

Tricky word flowers
- The children look at the tricky words flowers at the bottom of their page.
- Read each tricky word with the children.
- The words are as follows: *what, when, which, why, where, who.*
- The children colour the flowers using either red or green.

Further blending practice
- Write the following list of words on the board and blend them with the children:
  muffin, dustbin, morning, frosty, cliff.

Short or Long Vowel?

Flash cards
- Revise some of the alternative letter sound spellings taught so far, including ‹ph›.

The vowel hand
- Remind the children that the vowel letters, ‹a›, ‹e›, ‹i›, ‹o›, ‹u›, can make a short sound or long sound.
- Usually, when these vowel letters are on their own, they make a short vowel sound.
- The children trace inside the outline letters for short vowels, saying each sound as they do so.
- Remind the children of the saying, 'When two vowels go walking, the first one does the talking.'
- Explain that when two vowels are together in a word, they usually make the long vowel sound of the first vowel letter. For example, the ‹ea› digraph in the word *sea* makes the long /e/ sound, /ee/.
- The children trace inside the outline letters for the vowel digraphs, saying the long vowels sounds as they do so.
- If the children know the short and long sound each vowel can make, they can use the rule, 'If one way doesn't make a word, try the other.' This is an extremely useful rule for reading.
- Teach the children to point to their fingertips when saying the short vowel sounds and to the base of each finger when saying the long vowel sounds, as in the picture on the children's page.
- Remind the children that the ‹ue› digraph sometimes makes a long /oo/ sound. Encourage them to say, 'If /u/ doesn't work, try /ue/ or /oo/.'

Short or long vowel?
- The children look at the first picture.
- Read the two words above this picture: *ran* and *rain*.
- These two words differ in their vowel sounds only; *ran* has a short vowel sound and *rain* has a long vowel sound.

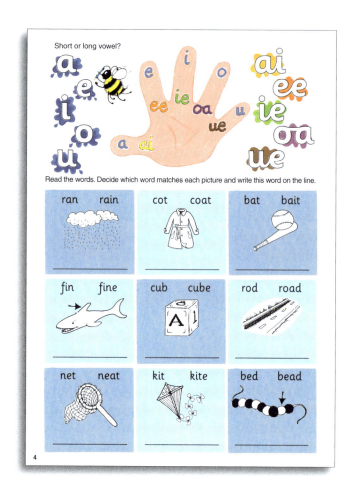

- Ask the children whether the picture illustrates the word *ran,* or the word *rain*?
- They should say *rain*.
- The children write the correct word on the line underneath the picture.
- The children repeat these steps for the rest of the pictures, reading the words to themselves and writing the correct words underneath each picture.
- The pictures are:
    rain, coat, bat,
    fin, cube, road,
    net, kite, bead.
- When the children have finished writing, they can colour the pictures.

Further blending practice
- Write the following list of words on the board and blend them with the children:
petticoat, crocodile, birdseed, curtain, seashell.

Comprehension

Flash cards
· Revise some of the alternative letter sound spellings taught so far, including ‹ph›.

Comprehension: the sea
· The children look at the empty sea scene on their page.
· They read the list of items underneath the scene and add each thing to their picture.
· The children should add the following:
1. six fish,
2. a big crab,
3. a flying seagull,
4. a starfish,
5. a shark with big teeth,
6. three red shells,
7. a boat,
8. a man in the boat
9. a yellow sun in the sky.

Further blending practice
· Write the following list of words on the board and blend them with the children:

seaside,
freezing,
crunchy,
slipping,
quicker,
chimpanzee,
trapeze,
quite,
envelope,
seaweed.

Add the following seaside things to the picture.

Add these seaside things:
1. six fish
2. a big crab
3. a flying seagull
4. a starfish
5. a shark with big teeth
6. three red shells
7. a boat
8. a man in the boat
9. a yellow sun in the sky

5

Reading sentences
· Write the following sentences on the board, pointing out the tricky words and blending any unknown words with the children.

1. The king and queen live in the royal tower.
2. How many yogurts are left?
3. The king has a silver crown.
4. The snail is very slow.
5. Is a dolphin a fish?
6. Mum and I had a picnic at the beach.
7. Are there any girls in the cricket club?
8. When can we try growing some beans?
9. We can read many phrases.
10. Can you throw the ball?

Alternatives: Soft ‹c›

Flash cards
- Revise some of the alternative letter sound spellings taught so far, including ‹ph›.

Alternatives: soft ‹c›
- Explain that if the letter ‹c› is followed by ‹e›, ‹i›, or ‹y›, it tends to make a /s/ sound. This is called the soft ‹c› sound.
- The children look at the soft ‹c› words at the top of their page.
- Point out the faint letter ‹e› at the end of some of the words.
- Tell the children that these ‹e› letters are faint because they make no sound.
- Read the words with the children.
- The words are as follows:
    excellent, ice, fence, face, circle,
    pencil, circus, cylinder, cycle, cygnet.

Read and match: circus tents
- The children look the list of words surrounded by circus tents.
- Point out that the first word, *ice-cream*, is written in dotted letters underneath the circus tent containing the ice-cream.
- The children write over the dotted word, *ice-cream*.
- Then they read the remaining words and write each word underneath the circus tent containing the corresponding picture.
- Once the children have finished writing, they can colour the pictures.
- The pictures (clockwise from *ice-cream*) are as follows:
    ice-cream, fence, circle, circus tent,
    cycle, pencil, cygnets, face.

Further blending practice
- Write the following list of words on the board and blend them with the children:
nice, concern, celery, excite, centipede.

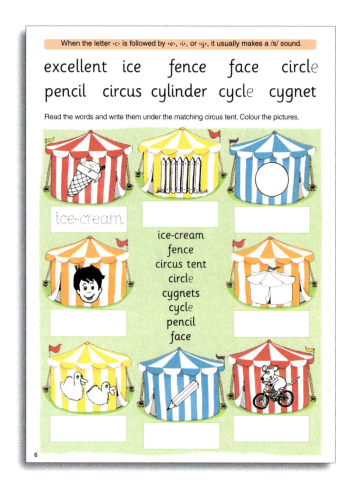

When the letter ‹c› is followed by ‹e›, ‹i›, or ‹y›, it usually makes a /s/ sound.

excellent   ice   fence   face   circle
pencil   circus   cylinder   cycle   cygnet

Read the words and write them under the matching circus tent. Colour the pictures.

ice-cream

ice-cream
fence
circus tent
circle
cygnets
cycle
pencil
face

Reading sentences
- Write the following sentences on the board, pointing out the tricky words and blending any unknown words with the children.
1. The mice ran away from the cat.
2. My uncle lives in the city.
3. I have been ill since Sunday.
4. Did you get the parcel I sent?
5. He is not good at running.
6. Can we go to the bookshop now?

Tricky Words and Dictation

Flash cards
- Use the flash cards, or *Tricky Word Wall Flowers*, to revise some of the tricky words taught so far, including *any* and *many*.

Tricky words
- Introduce the two new tricky words: *more* and *before*.
- The children look at the words in green flowers at the top of the page: *more* and *before*.
- Point out the ‹ore› at the end of both words makes an /or/ sound.
- The children could underline the ‹ore› at the end of each of these words in purple, to remind them that this is the 'tricky bit'.
- The children write inside the words *more* and *before* using a green pencil.

Filling in the gaps
- The children trace inside the outline letters in the word *more*, saying the letter names as they do so.
- Then the children cover up all instances of the word *more* on their page and try to complete a line of this word, by tracing over the dotted letters and filling in the missing letters.
- The children repeat these steps for the word *before*.

Complete the sentences
- Read the first sentence, pausing at the gap:
    I went swimming ___ lunch.
- Ask the children whether they think they should write *more* or *before* in this gap.
- Read the sentence back to the children, including their chosen word, and ask them if they think the sentence makes sense with this word. The children write the correct word in the gap in their *Phonics Pupil Books*.
- The children read the next sentence by themselves and decide which of the tricky words completes the sentence.
- They write this tricky word on the line in the sentence.

Dictation sentences
- Dictate the following sentences:
    I had some more crisps.
    We ran before the picnic.
- The children write these sentences on the lines in their *Phonics Pupil Books*.

Tricky word flowers
- The children look at the tricky words flowers at the bottom of their page.
- Read each tricky word with the children.
- The words are as follows: *which, why, where, who, any, many*.
- The children colour the flowers green.

Further blending practice
- Write the following list of words on the board and blend them with the children:
    December, balance, dice, cleaning, teapot.

Words and Sentences

Flash cards
· Revise some of the alternative letter sound spellings taught so far.

Words and sentences
· Write the title on the board, *This is me*.
· Read the title with the children.
· Ask a child to say one sentence about himself or herself. For example, 'My name is…' 'I am five years old.' 'I have a brown eyes.' 'I like running.'
· You may need to stop the child at the end of their sentence, as most children will try to carry on.
· Ask some other children to say a sentence about themselves. Encourage the children to say a different sentence each.

Writing
· The children copy the title, *This is me*, onto the top line.
· They write as much as they can about themselves on the remaining lines.

Picture
· The children draw a picture of themselves in the picture frame.

Note 1: spelling
· At this stage, the children's spelling will not always be accurate, but their work will be readable. Spelling gradually improves through reading many books and learning the alternative letter-sound spellings.

Note 2: title
· Teachers should feel free to set their own writing subject. The title of the writing exercise does appear on the children's pages, but the picture frame is empty and the lines are blank. It may be that the children would like to write about a recent holiday they have celebrated, or a story they have heard. If this is the case, teachers can set their own title and guide the children's writing accordingly.

Further blending practice
· Write the following list of words on the board and blend them with the children:

    reach,
    year,
    enjoys,
    stays,
    squeaking.

Reading sentences
· Write the following sentences on the board, pointing out the tricky words and blending any unknown words with the children.
1. Dad said that there are no more grapes.
2. The farmer raced to rescue his sheep.
3. May we have some more rice?
4. You must clean your face before you go to bed.

Comprehension

Flash cards
- Revise some of the alternative letter sound spellings taught so far, including ‹ph› and soft ‹c›.

Yes or no?
- Read the sentence underneath the first picture, *The cat is sleeping*.
- Ask the children to look at the picture above the sentence and decide whether this sentence is true or false.
- The children should say that the sentence is true. They write over the dotted word *yes* on the line.
- The children read each of the remaining sentences, looking at the picture to decide whether the sentence is true or false.
- If the sentence is true, the children write *yes* on the line and if the sentence is false, they write *no*.
- The sentences are:

The cat is sleeping.	(yes)
Rabbits are good at hopping.	(yes)
There are five red socks.	(no)
It is three o'clock.	(yes)
The dragon has ten eggs.	(no)
The magpie has a hat.	(no)

Further blending practice
- Write the following list of words on the board and blend them with the children:

  photocopy,
  rainbow,
  apply,
  butterfly,
  concern,
  cabin,
  phoneme,
  confidence,
  certificate,
  stir.

Reading sentences
- Write the following sentences on the board, pointing out the tricky words and blending any unknown words with the children.
  1. I spy some more insects under that tree.
  2. Who came first in the hopping race?
  3. How many mice are in the shed?
  4. May I have one more toffee?
  5. The spaceman went to the moon in a rocket.
  6. We must smarten up before our photograph.
  7. Can we play more games today?
  8. How many boys came to the party?
  9. Did you count all the coins?
  10. Read the book before you give it back.

Alternatives: Soft ‹g›

Flash cards

- Revise some of the alternative letter sound spellings taught so far, including ‹ph› and soft ‹c›.

Alternatives: soft ‹g›

- Explain that if the letter ‹g› is followed by ‹e›, ‹i›, or ‹y›, it tends to make a /j/ sound. This is called the soft ‹g› sound.
- The children look at the soft ‹g› words at the top of their page. Read the words with the children. The words are:

  oranges, large, vegetable, germ, giraffe, giant, ginger, magic, gypsy, gym, gymnast, dingy.

Vegetables

- Read the first soft ‹g› word, *oranges*, again.
- Point out that the ‹g› is making a /j/ sound because it is followed by an ‹e›.
- Point out the outline letters ‹ge› in the cauliflower.
- The children write the word *oranges* in the cauliflower.
- Then the children pick out all the other soft ‹g› words where the ‹g› is followed by an ‹e› and write these words in the cauliflower.
- Point out the outline letters ‹gi› in the potato.
- The children pick out all the soft ‹g› words where the ‹g› is followed by an ‹i› and write these words in the potato.
- Point out the outline letters ‹gy› in the carrot.
- The children pick out all the soft ‹g› words where the ‹g› is followed by an ‹y› and write these words in the carrot.
- In the word *ginger* the first soft ‹g› is followed by an ‹i› and the second is followed by an ‹e›, so the children need to write this word in both the cauliflower and the potato.
- Ask the children which word fits in two of the vegetables.

Read and draw

- The children read the soft ‹g› words and illustrate them in the vegetable frames.
- The words are as follows: *giraffe, gymnast.*

Further blending practice

- Write the following list of words on the board and blend them with the children:

  gentle,
  stage,
  space,
  price,
  pancake.

Reading sentences

- Write the following sentences on the board, pointing out the tricky words and blending any unknown words with the children.
  1. What do you call this vegetable?
  2. We had such fun at the magic show.
  3. All my pencils are broken.
  4. Are many girls going to camp?

Tricky Words and Dictation

Flash cards
- Use the flash cards, or *Tricky Word Wall Flowers*, to revise some of the tricky words taught so far, including *any, many, more* and *before*.

Tricky words
- Introduce the two new tricky words: *other* and *were*.
- The children look at the words in green flowers at the top of the page: *other* and *were*.
- Teach the children to use the 'say it as it sounds' technique, when spelling the word *other*.
- When writing *other*, the children should try to say it with an /o/ sound at the beginning, as though the word rhymes with *bother*.
- Point out that the ‹ere› at the end of the word *were* is the same as the ending of some other tricky words, such as, *here, there,* and *where*.
- The children write inside the words *other* and *were* using a green pen or pencil.

Filling in the gaps
- The children trace inside the outline letters in the word *other*, saying the letter names as they do so.
- Then the children cover up all instances of the word *other* on their page and try to complete a line of this word, by tracing over the dotted letters and filling in the missing letters.
- The children repeat these steps for the word *were*.

Complete the sentences
- Read the first sentence, pausing at the gap:
    We ___ skipping in the park.
- Ask the children whether they think they should write *other* or *were* in this gap.
- Read the sentence back to the children, including their chosen word, and ask them if they think the sentence makes sense with this word.
- The children write the correct word in the gap in their *Phonics Pupil Books*.

- The children read the next sentence by themselves and decide which of the tricky words completes the sentence.
- They write this tricky word on the line in the sentence.

Dictation sentences
- Dictate the following sentences:
    The other car was quicker.
    There were a hundred sheep in the barn.
- The children write these sentences on the lines in their *Phonics Pupil Books*.

Tricky word flowers
- The children look at the tricky words flowers at the bottom of their page.
- Read each tricky word with the children.
- The words are as follows: *where, who, any, many, more, before*.
- The children colour the flowers green.

145

Words and Sentences

Flash cards
• Revise some of the alternative letter sound spellings taught so far.

Words and sentences
• Write the title on the board, *My Family*.
• Read the title with the children.
• Ask a child to say one sentence about his or her family. For example, 'There are four people in my family' 'Everyone in my family has brown hair.' 'I have a little brother.'
• You may need to stop the child at the end of their sentence, as most children will try to carry on.
• Ask some other children to say a sentence about their family. Encourage the children to say a different sentence each.

Writing
• The children copy the title, *My Family*, onto the top line.
• They write as much as they can about their family on the remaining lines.

Picture
• The children draw a picture of their family in the picture frame.

Note 1: spelling
• At this stage, the children's spelling will not always be accurate, but their work will be readable. Spelling gradually improves through reading many books and learning the alternative letter-sound spellings.

Note 2: title
• Teachers should feel free to set their own writing subject. The title of the writing exercise does appear on the children's pages, but the picture frame is empty and the lines are blank. It may be that the children would like to write about a recent holiday they have celebrated, or a story they have heard. If this is the case, teachers can set their own title and guide the children's writing accordingly.

Further blending practice
• Write the following list of words on the board and blend them with the children:
> *wage,*
> *badger,*
> *bridges,*
> *mummy,*
> *daddy.*

Reading sentences
• Write the following sentences on the board, pointing out the tricky words and blending any unknown words with the children.
1. My other sister is nine years old.
2. I have a digital clock.
3. Were you at the fancy dress party?
4. The other children were at the park.

Alternatives: ‹ai›, ‹ay› and ‹a_e›

Flash cards
- Revise some of the alternative letter sound spellings taught so far, including ‹ph›, soft ‹c› and soft ‹g›.

Alternatives: the /ai/ sound
- Remind the children of the three main ways to write the /ai/ sound: ‹ai›, ‹ay› and ‹a_e›.
- Remind the children that the ‹ay› spelling usually comes at the end of a word.
- Tell them that this is because the letter ‹i› is too shy to go at the end of a word, so its cousin, 'toughy y' takes its place.
- The children look at the /ai/ words on their page.
- Point out that the ‹wh› at the beginning of the word *whale* makes a /w/ sound.
- Read these words with the children.
- The words are as follows:
  whale, paint, play, snake, train, tray, name, may, cake, tail, snail, hail.

‹ai›, ‹a_e› or ‹ay›?
- Read the first /ai/ word, *whale*, again.
- Ask the children whether the /ai/ sound is spelt ‹ai›, ‹a_e› or ‹ay› in this word.
- They should say ‹a_e›.
- Using a yellow pencil, the children circle the letters making the /ai/ sound in the word *whale*.
- Then they write over the dotted word *whale* in the large yellow ‹a_e› digraph on their page.
- The children read the remaining words and circle the letters making the /ai/ sound in each word.
- Then they write the words in the corresponding digraphs on their page.

Further blending practice
- Write the following list of words on the board and blend them with the children:
  grain, caveman, stray, make, spray.

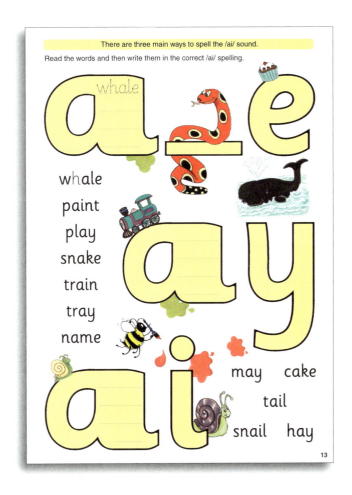

There are three main ways to spell the /ai/ sound.

Read the words and then write them in the correct /ai/ spelling.

whale
paint
play
snake
train
tray
name
may   cake
tail
snail   hay

Reading sentences
- Write the following sentences on the board, pointing out the tricky words and blending any unknown words with the children.
  1. We eat our cornflakes with milk.
  2. I made a mistake on the other page.
  3. Were you playing with my skates?
  4. The goldfish had many scales.
  5. Were the oranges nice?
  6. The other hamster is still in its cage.

Tricky Words and Dictation

Flash cards
- Use the flash cards, or *Tricky Word Wall Flowers*, to revise some of the tricky words taught so far, including *any, many, more, before, other* and *were*.

Tricky words
- Introduce the two new tricky words: *want* and *because*.
- The children look at the words in green flowers at the top of the page.
- Teach the children to use the 'say it as it sounds' technique, when spelling the word *want*.
- When writing *want*, the children should try to say it with an /a/ sound in the middle, as though the word rhymes with *pant*.
- For spelling the word *because*, it may help the children to learn this mnemonic:
  Big **e**lephants **c**atch **a**nts **u**nder **s**mall **e**lephants.
- Write the mnemonic on the board.
- Read the words to the children, pointing to the first letter of each word as you say it.
- Point out that if you write down the first letter of each word in this sentence, it spells *because*.
- The children write inside the words *want* and *because* using a green pencil.

Filling in the gaps
- The children trace inside the outline letters in the word *want*, saying the letter names as they do so.
- Then the children cover up all instances of the word *want* on their page and try to complete a line of this word, by tracing over the dotted letters and filling in the missing letters.
- The children repeat these steps for the word *because*.

Complete the sentences
- Read the first sentence, pausing at the gap:
  Do you ___ to help?
- Ask the children whether they think they should write *want* or *because* in this gap.
- They should write *want* in the gap.

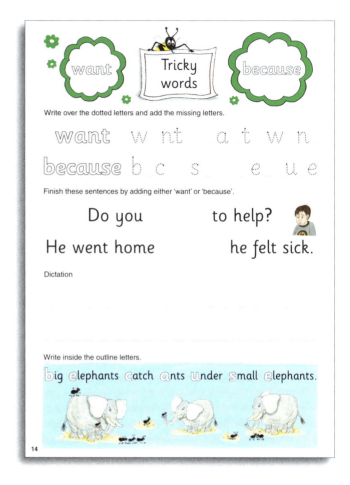

- The children read the next sentence by themselves and decide which of the tricky words completes the sentence. They write this tricky word on the line in the sentence.

Dictation sentences
- Dictate the following sentences:
  We want more good books.
  I need my coat because it is raining.
- The children write these sentences on the lines in their *Phonics Pupil Books*.

Mnemonics
- The children read the mnemonic:
  Big **e**lephants **c**atch **a**nts **u**nder **s**mall **e**lephants.
- Remind the children that if they write down the first letter of each word in this sentence, it spells *because*.
- On the children's page, the first letter of each word in this mnemonic is an outline letter.
- The children trace inside these letters to spell *because*.

Words and Sentences

Flash cards
• Revise some of the alternative letter sound spellings taught so far, including ‹ph›, soft ‹c› and soft ‹g›.

Words and sentences
• Write the title on the board, *My House*.
• Read the title with the children.
• Some children might not live in a house. This is a good opportunity to discuss the various different types of homes the children have.
• Ask a child to say one sentence about his or her home. For example, 'I live in a big apartment.' 'My house is quite small.' 'My house has a nice garden.'
• You may need to stop the child at the end of their sentence, as most children will try to carry on.
• Ask some other children to say a sentence about their home. Encourage the children to say a different sentence each.

Writing
• The children copy the title, *My House*, onto the top line.
• They write as much as they can about their home on the remaining lines.

Picture
• The children draw a picture of their home in the picture frame.

Note 1: spelling
• At this stage, the children's spelling will not always be accurate, but their work will be readable. Spelling gradually improves through reading many books and learning the alternative letter-sound spellings.

Note 2: title
• Teachers should feel free to set their own writing subject. The title of the writing exercise does appear on the children's pages, but the picture frame is empty and the lines are blank.

• It may be that the children would like to write about a recent holiday they have celebrated, or a story they have heard. If this is the case, teachers can set their own title and guide the children's writing accordingly.

Further blending practice
• Write the following list of words on the board and blend them with the children:
fragile, cage, waited, sprain, generally.

Reading sentences
• Write the following sentences on the board, pointing out the tricky words and blending any unknown words with the children.
1. Do you want the red paint or the green?
2. She fainted because the room was too hot.
3. Do you want to help me grate the carrots?
4. This salad dressing is too oily for me.

149

Alternatives: ‹ee›, ‹ea› and ‹e_e›

Flash cards
- Revise some of the alternative letter sound spellings taught so far, including ‹ph›, soft ‹c› and soft ‹g›.

Alternatives: the /ee/ sound
- Remind the children of the three main ways to write the /ee/ sound: ‹ee›, ‹ea› and ‹e_e›.
- Remind the children that the ‹e_e› spelling is not used very often.
- The children look at the /ee/ words on their page.
- Read these words with the children.
- The words are as follows:

  speed, sneeze, toffee, indeed,
  teacher, peanut, peach, seatbelt,
  eve, theme, these, Pete.

‹ee›, ‹e_e› or ‹ea›?
- Read the first /ee/ word, *feet*, and ask the children whether the /ee/ sound is spelt ‹ee›, ‹e_e› or ‹ea› in this word.
- They should say ‹ee›.
- Using an orange pencil, the children circle the letters making the /ee/ sound in the word *feet*.
- Then they write over the dotted word *feet* in the large orange ‹ee› digraph on their page.
- The children read the remaining words and circle the letters making the /ee/ sound in each word.
- Then they write the words in the corresponding digraphs on their page.

Further blending practice
- Write the following list of words on the board and blend them with the children:

  seaside,
  feeling,
  underneath,
  sheep,
  extremely.

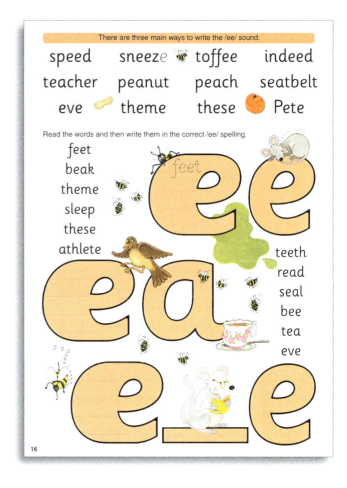

There are three main ways to write the /ee/ sound.

speed sneeze toffee indeed
teacher peanut peach seatbelt
eve theme these Pete

Read the words and then write them in the correct /ee/ spelling.

feet
beak
theme
sleep
these
athlete

feet

teeth
read
seal
bee
tea
eve

ee
ea
e_e

16

Reading sentences
- Write the following sentences on the board, pointing out the tricky words and blending any unknown words with the children.
  1. I got up because I had a bad dream.
  2. The circus performers swing on the trapeze.
  3. Do you want to stay for tea?
  4. The seagulls fly close to the beach.
  5. Are there more elephants than before?
  6. You must finish your lunch before you can have an ice-cream.

Tricky Words and Dictation

Flash cards
- Use the flash cards, or *Tricky Word Wall Flowers*, to revise some of the tricky words taught so far, including *any, many, more, before, other, were, want* and *because*.

Tricky words
- Introduce the two new tricky words: *put* and *saw*.
- The children look at the words in pink flowers at the top of the page: *put* and *saw*.
- Teach the children to use the 'say it as it sounds' technique, when spelling the word *put*. When writing *put*, the children should try to say it with an /u/ sound in the middle, as though the word rhymes with *shut*.
- The children write inside the words *put* and *saw* using a pink pencil.

Filling in the gaps
- The children trace inside the outline letters in the word *put*, saying the letter names as they do so.
- Then the children cover up all instances of the word *put* on their page and try to complete a line of this word, by tracing over the dotted letters and filling in the missing letters.
- The children repeat these steps for the word *saw*.

Complete the sentences
- Read the first sentence, pausing at the gap:
  I ___ my drum back in the toy box.
- Ask the children whether they think they should write *put* or *saw* in this gap.
- Read the sentence back to the children, including their chosen word, and ask them if they think the sentence makes sense with this word. The children write the correct word in the gap in their *Phonics Pupil Books*.
- The children read the next sentence by themselves and decide which of the tricky words completes the sentence.
- They write this tricky word on the line in the sentence.

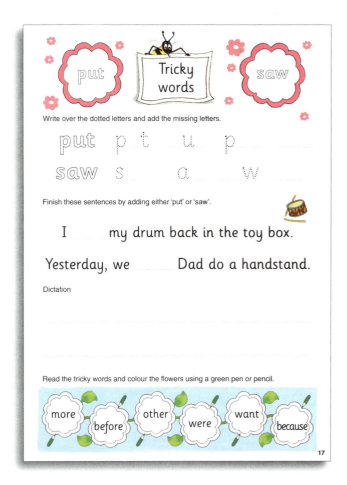

Dictation sentences
- Dictate the following sentences:
  Put the map in the car.
  We saw some frogs in the pond.
- The children write these sentences on the lines in their *Phonics Pupil Books*.

Tricky word flowers
- The children look at the tricky words flowers at the bottom of their page.
- Read each tricky word with the children.
- The words are as follows:
  more, before, other, were, want, because.
- The children colour the flowers green.

Further blending practice
- Write the following list of words on the board and blend them with the children:
  seesaw, pleasing, creepy, asleep, teabag.

Words and Sentences

Flash cards
• Revise some of the alternative letter sound spellings taught so far, including ‹ph›, soft ‹c› and soft ‹g›.

Words and sentences
• Write the title on the board, *My Best Dinner*.
• Read the title with the children.
• Ask a child to say one sentence about his or her favourite meal. For example, 'I like cheese sandwiches.' 'My favourite food is rice and peas.' 'I like to eat chicken curry for dinner.'
• You may need to stop the child at the end of their sentence, as most children will try to carry on.
• Ask some other children to say a sentence about the foods they like most. Encourage the children to say a different sentence each.

Writing
• The children copy the title, *My Best Dinner*, onto the top line.
• They write as much as they can about their favourite meal on the remaining lines.

Picture
• The children draw a picture of their favourite meal in the picture frame.

Note 1: spelling
• At this stage, the children's spelling will not always be accurate, but their work will be readable.

Note 2: title
• Teachers should feel free to set their own writing subject. The title of the writing exercise does appear on the children's pages, but the picture frame is empty and the lines are blank. It may be that the children would like to write about a recent holiday they have celebrated, or a story they have heard. If this is the case, teachers can set their own title and guide the children's writing accordingly.

Further blending practice
• Write the following list of words on the board and blend them with the children:
> *evening,*
> *teaspoons,*
> *street,*
> *athlete,*
> *reach.*

Reading sentences
• Write the following sentences on the board, pointing out the tricky words and blending any unknown words with the children.
1. I saw the man put the ladder away.
2. Please put the ice back in the freezer.
3. We saw that little girl win the race.
4. I can put this nice lace on her dress.

Comprehension

Flash cards

· Revise some of the alternative letter sound spellings taught so far, including ‹ph›, soft ‹c› and soft ‹g›.

Read and draw

· Read the first phrase to the children:
    a rabbit in a hutch.
· Point out the faint letter ‹t› in the word *hutch.*
· Tell the children that this letter ‹t› is faint because it makes no sound.
· The children illustrate this phrase in the picture frame above.
· The children read the remaining phrases and illustrate them in the picture frames.
· The phrases are:
    a rabbit in a hutch
    a big rainbow in the sky
    a black cat in red boots
    a bat in a tree
    the moon and some stars
    three snails in the rain

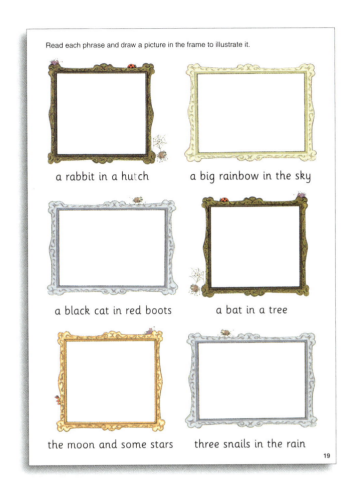

Read each phrase and draw a picture in the frame to illustrate it.

a rabbit in a hutch

a big rainbow in the sky

a black cat in red boots

a bat in a tree

the moon and some stars

three snails in the rain

19

Further blending practice

· Write the following list of words on the board and blend them with the children:
    sprain,
    mean,
    better,
    teeth,
    stealing,
    beehive,
    cleaner,
    steeper,
    yelp,
    stopper.

Reading sentences

· Write the following sentences on the board, pointing out the tricky words and blending any unknown words with the children.
    1. One kitten is black and the other is ginger.
    2. The elephants at the circus were very large.
    3. He wants to come to the baseball game.
    4. I need to go now because I am late.
    5. The goalkeeper has the ball.
    6. They played on the seesaw at the park.
    7. I saw her jump on the haystacks in the barn.
    8. We completed the jigsaw in no time at all.
    9. Put the clean socks in here.
    10. He put the peas by the sink.

Alternatives: ‹ie›, ‹y›, ‹i_e› and ‹igh›

Flash cards
- Revise some of the alternative letter sound spellings taught so far, including ‹ph›, soft ‹c› and soft ‹g›.

Alternatives: the /ie/ sound
- Say the word *sight* and ask the children what vowel sound they can hear in the middle of this word.
- They should say an /ie/ sound.
- Ask the children how an /ie/ sound is written.
- The children should say that /ie/ can be written as ‹ie›, ‹y› or ‹i_e›.
- Write the word *sight* on the board.
- Explain that the /ie/ sound can also be written ‹igh› and point to the ‹igh› in the middle of the word *sight*.
- The children look at the /ie/ words on their page.
- Read these words with the children, and point out the letters making the /ie/ sound in each word.
- The words are as follows:
    light, fly, like, pie, night, prize,
    lie, time, right, thigh, reply,
    my, die, kite, sky, tie.

‹ie›, ‹i_e›, ‹y› or ‹igh›?
- Read the first /ie/ word, *light*, again.
- Ask the children whether the /ie/ sound is spelt ‹ie›, ‹i_e›, ‹y› or ‹igh› in this word.
- They should say ‹igh›.
- Using a green pencil, the children circle the letters making the /ie/ sound in the word *light*.
- Then they write over the dotted word *light* in the large green ‹igh› digraph on their page.
- The children read the remaining words and circle the letters making the /ie/ sound in each word.
- Then they write the words in the corresponding digraphs on their page.

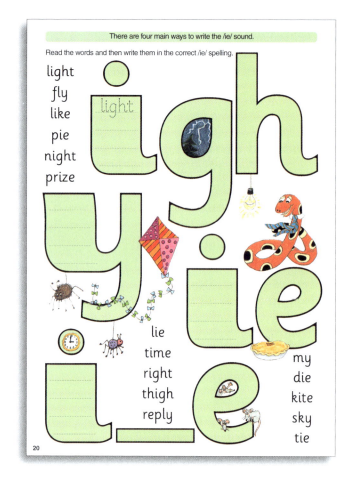

Further blending practice
- Write the following list of words on the board and blend them with the children:
    frighten,
    line,
    crying,
    sigh,
    prize.

Reading sentences
- Write the following sentences on the board, pointing out the tricky words and blending any unknown words with the children.
1. The butterfly flutters by my bike.
2. The sun shines so brightly.
3. The lighthouse stands on the cliff edge.
4. The moth flies too close to the flame.
5. She cannot eat nuts because she is allergic.
6. I want to have balloons at my party.

Tricky Words and Dictation

Flash cards
- Revise some of the tricky words taught so far.

Tricky words
- Introduce the three new tricky words: *could, should* and *would*. The children look at the words in pink flowers at the top of the page.
- Point out that the words *could, should* and *would* all have the same ‹ould› ending.
- Explain that in each of these words the ‹ould› makes an /oo-d/ sound (with the little /oo/).
- Point out that the sounds at the beginning of these words, /c/, /sh/ and /w/, are spelt in the usual way.
- The children could underline the ‹ould› at the end of each of these words in purple, to remind them that this is the 'tricky bit'.
- The children write inside the words *could, should* and *would* using a pink pencil.

Filling in the gaps
- The children trace inside the outline letters in the word *could*, saying the letter names as they do so. Then the children cover up all instances of the word *could* on their page and try to complete a column of this word, by tracing over the dotted letters and filling in the missing letters.
- The children repeat these steps for the words *should* and *would*.

Complete the sentences
- Read the first sentence, pausing at the gap:
  ___ you like some more tea?
- Ask the children whether they think they should write *could, should*, or *would* in this gap.
- Read the sentence back to the children, including their chosen word, and ask them if they think the sentence makes sense with this word. The children write the correct word in the gap in their *Phonics Pupil Books*.
- The children read the next two sentences by themselves and decide which of the tricky words completes the sentence. They write the correct tricky word on the line in each sentence.

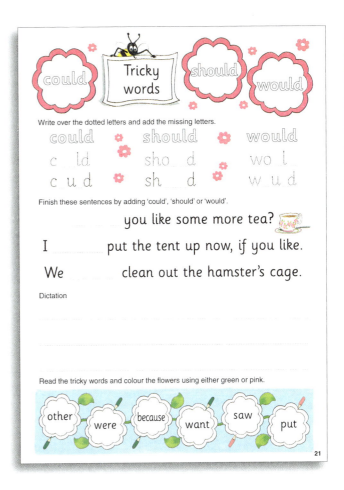

Dictation sentences
- Dictate the following sentences:
  We could sing a song next.
  It should be a good outing.
  It would be fun to go on the swings.
- The children write these sentences on the lines in their *Phonics Pupil Books*.

Tricky word flowers
- The children look at the tricky words flowers at the bottom of their page.
- Read each tricky word with the children.
- The words are as follows: *other, were, because, want, saw, put.*
- The children colour the flowers using a green or pink pencil.

Further blending practice
- Write the following list of words on the board and blend them with the children:
  intelligent, charges, emergency, excite, cool.

Words and Sentences

Flash cards
- Revise some of the alternative letter sound spellings taught so far, including ‹ph›, soft ‹c›, soft ‹g› and ‹igh›.

Words and sentences
- Write the title on the board, *The Animal I like Best*.
- Read the title with the children.
- Ask a child to say one sentence about his or her favourite animal. For example, 'I like fish best.' 'I like cats because they are fluffy.' 'I love dolphins.'
- You may need to stop the child at the end of their sentence, as most children will try to carry on.
- Ask some other children to say a sentence about the animal they like most. Encourage the children to say a different sentence each.

Writing
- The children copy the title, *The Animal I like Best*, onto the top line.
- They write as much as they can about their favourite animal on the remaining lines.

Picture
- The children draw a picture of their favourite animal in the picture frame.

Note 1: spelling
- At this stage, the children's spelling will not always be accurate, but their work will be readable.

Note 2: title
- Teachers should feel free to set their own writing subject. The title of the writing exercise does appear on the children's pages, but the picture frame is empty and the lines are blank. It may be that the children would like to write about a recent holiday they have celebrated, or a story they have heard. If this is the case, teachers can set their own title and guide the children's writing accordingly.

Further blending practice
- Write the following list of words on the board and blend them with the children:
  hippopotamus,
  giraffe,
  tiger,
  blackbird,
  raccoon.

Reading sentences
- Write the following sentences on the board, pointing out the tricky words and blending any unknown words with the children.
  1. We would like to ride our bikes outside.
  2. He should do his chores.
  3. Could you teach me how to make tea?
  4. They should get away from the angry bees.

Alternatives: ‹oa›, ‹ow› and ‹o_e›

Flash cards
· Revise some of the alternative letter sound spellings taught so far, including ‹ph›, soft ‹c›, soft ‹g› and ‹igh›.

Alternatives: the /oa/ sound
· Remind the children of the three main ways to write the /oa/ sound: ‹oa›, ‹ow› and ‹o_e›.
· Remind the children that the ‹ow› spelling usually comes at the end of a word.
· The children look at the /oa/ words on their page.
· Read these words with the children.
· The words are as follows:

> toast, coach, coast, raincoat,
> tadpole, those, home, joke,
> rainbow, elbow, snow, window.

‹oa›, ‹o_e› or ‹ow›?
· Read the first /oa/ word, *those*, and ask the children whether the /oa/ sound is spelt ‹oa›, ‹o_e› or ‹ow› in this word.
· They should say ‹o_e›.
· Using a purple pencil, the children circle the letters making the /oa/ sound in the word *those*.
· Then they write over the dotted word *those* in the large purple ‹o_e› digraph on their page.
· The children read the remaining words and circle the letters making the /oa/ sound in each word.
· Then they write the words in the corresponding digraphs on their page.

Further blending practice
· Write the following list of words on the board and blend them with the children:

> yellow,
> toaster,
> tightrope,
> window,
> flagpole.

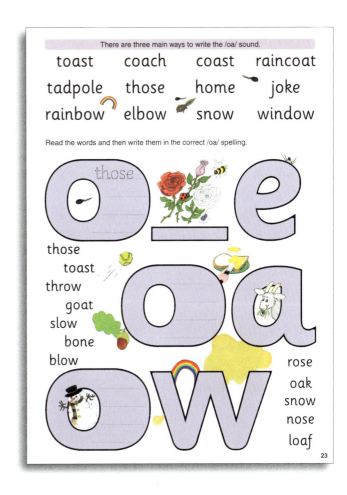

Reading sentences
· Write the following sentences on the board, pointing out the tricky words and blending any unknown words with the children.
1. Could we have some butter for our toast?
2. That girl should stop moaning.
3. The sea was very shallow at the beach.
4. I wish the snow would melt.
5. May we go home now?
6. The anteater has a very long nose.

Tricky Words and Dictation

Flash cards
- Use the flash cards, or *Tricky Word Wall Flowers*, to revise some of the tricky words taught so far, including *put, saw, could, should* and *would*.

Tricky words
- Introduce the four new tricky words: *right, two, four* and *goes*.
- The children look at the words in pink flowers at the top of the page: *right, two, four* and *goes*.
- Point out that *right* is not really tricky, because the children now know that ‹igh› can say /ie/.
- The children write inside the words *right, two, four* and *goes* using a pink pencil.

Filling in the gaps
- The children trace inside the outline letters in the word *right*, saying the letter names as they do so.
- Then the children cover up all instances of the word *right* on their page and try to complete a column of this word, by tracing over the dotted letters and filling in the missing letters.
- The children repeat these steps for the words *two, four* and *goes*.

Complete the sentences
- Read the first sentence, pausing at the gap:
  He got all the sums ___.
- Ask the children whether they think they should write *right, two, four* or *goes* in this gap.
- Read the sentence back to the children, including their chosen word, and ask them if they think the sentence makes sense with this word. The children write the correct word in the gap in their *Phonics Pupil Books*.
- The children read the remaining three sentences by themselves and decide which of the tricky words completes the sentence.
- They write the correct tricky word on the line in each sentence.

Dictation sentences
- Dictate the following sentences:
  He goes to the pool by bus.
  They must count them two by two.
  A dog has four legs.
  We went right then left.
- The children write these sentences on the lines in their *Phonics Pupil Books*.

Further blending practice
- Write the following list of words on the board and blend them with the children:
  telescope, choke, foaming, throws, toffee.
- Write the following sentences on the board, pointing out the tricky words and blending any unknown words with the children.
1. Two sheep and four goats were in the yard.
2. The swimming pool is on the right.
3. She goes bowling with her family.
4. The two tigers were quite frightening.

Words and Sentences

Flash cards
• Revise some of the alternative letter sound spellings taught so far, including ‹ph›, soft ‹c›, soft ‹g› and ‹igh›.

Words and sentences
• Write the title on the board, *My Best Day*.
• Read the title with the children.
• Ask a child to say one sentence about his or her best day. For example, 'We went to a party.' 'Dad took me to the beach.' 'I rode a horse.'
• You may need to stop the child at the end of their sentence, as most children will try to carry on.
• Ask some other children to say a sentence about a day they enjoyed. Encourage the children to say a different sentence each.

Writing
• The children copy the title, *My Best Day*, onto the top line.
• They write as much as they can about a day they enjoyed on the remaining lines.

Picture
• The children draw a picture illustrating their best day in the picture frame.

Note 1: spelling
• At this stage, the children's spelling will not always be accurate, but their work will be readable. Spelling gradually improves through reading many books and learning the alternative letter-sound spellings.

Note 2: title
• Teachers should feel free to set their own writing subject. The title of the writing exercise does appear on the children's pages, but the picture frame is empty and the lines are blank. It may be that the children would like to write about a recent holiday they have celebrated, or a story they have heard. If this is the case, teachers can set their own title and guide the children's writing accordingly.

Further blending practice
• Write the following list of words on the board and blend them with the children:
    bonfire,
    coast,
    stroked,
    owner,
    spoken.

Reading sentences
• Write the following sentences on the board, pointing out the tricky words and blending any unknown words with the children.
1. He goes home on the train.
2. My right foot is slightly bigger than my left.
3. The clock hands were at ten to four.
4. Those two cats ate all the shrimps.

Comprehension

Flash cards
- Revise some of the alternative letter sound spellings taught so far, including ‹ph›, soft ‹c›, soft ‹g› and ‹igh›.

Reading and comprehension
- The children look at the sentences and pictures on their page.
- Read the first sentence to the children, pausing at the gap:

    The tall oak ___ is green.
- Ask the children what word they think will fit in this gap. If they struggle to answer, tell them that the picture beside the sentence is a clue.
- The children should say that the missing word is *tree*. They write this word in the lines.
- There is a line for each sound in the missing word.
- A longer line indicates that a digraph is needed.
- Read the completed sentence back to the children:

    The tall oak *tree* is green.
- Ask the children if the tree in the picture is green. They should say that it is not.
- The children colour the picture of the tree green, so that it matches the sentence.
- The children read the remaining sentences to themselves.
- They fill in the gaps to complete each sentence and colour the pictures to match.
- The sentences are:

    The tall oak (tree) is green.
    My (tie) is long and has red and green stripes.
    My blue (coat) has a big collar.
    The little green (frog) jumped into the pond.
    The (moon) shines in the night.
    I found a (snail) in the garden.
    It had a yellow shell on its back.

Read the sentences and fill in the gaps. Colour the pictures to match each sentence.

The tall oak   is green.

My   is long and has red and green stripes.

My blue   has a big collar.

The little green   jumped into the pond.

The   shines in the night.

I found a   in the garden. It had a yellow shell on its back.

26

Further blending practice
- Write the following list of words on the board and blend them with the children:

    stoke,
    roasted,
    throwing,
    stone,
    follows.

Reading sentences
- Write the following sentences on the board, pointing out the tricky words and blending any unknown words with the children.
  1. Those four boys made that boat.
  2. Do not sit on the two broken seats.
  3. Which room is the right one?
  4. They should not boast so much.

Alternatives: ‹ue›, ‹ew› and ‹u_e›

Flash cards
- Revise some of the alternative letter sound spellings taught so far, including ‹ph›, soft ‹c›, soft ‹g› and ‹igh›.

Alternatives: the /ue/ sound
- Remind the children of the three main ways to write the /ue/ sound: ‹ue›, ‹ew› and ‹u_e›.
- Remind the children that the digraphs ‹ue›, ‹ew› and ‹u_e› can make a long /oo/ sound as well as a /ue/ sound.
- The children look at the /ue/ words on their page.
- Read these words with the children.
- The words are as follows:
     bluebell, rescue, true, statue,
     ruler, use, excuse, tune,
     news, chew, threw, stew.

‹ue›, ‹u_e› or ‹ew›?
- Read the first /ue/ word, *cube*, and ask the children whether the /ue/ sound is spelt ‹ue›, ‹u_e› or ‹ew› in this word.
- They should say ‹u_e›.
- Using a brown pencil, the children circle the letters making the /ue/ sound in the word *cube*.
- Then they write over the dotted word *cube* in the large brown ‹u_e› digraph on their page.
- The children read the remaining words and circle the letters making the /ue/ sound in each word.
- Then they write the words in the corresponding digraphs on their page.

Further blending practice
- Write the following list of words on the board and blend them with the children:
     Tuesday,
     June,
     newer,
     excuse,
     screws.

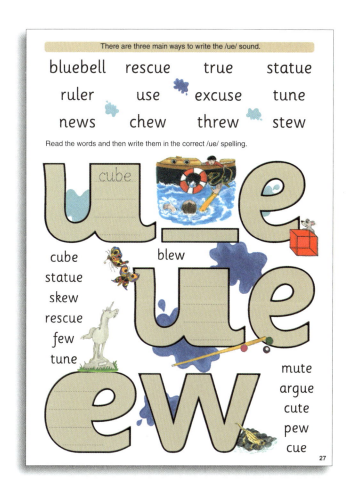

Reading sentences
- Write the following sentences on the board, pointing out the tricky words and blending any unknown words with the children.
  1. We should let the tea brew before drinking it.
  2. I saw so many bluebells in the wood.
  3. She drew four blue flowers in my book.
  4. They used all the ice cubes.
  5. Should the teapot go on this mat?
  6. Before mathematics, we have singing.

Tricky Words and Dictation

Flash cards

- Use the flash cards, or *Tricky Word Wall Flowers*, to revise some of the tricky words taught so far, including *put, saw, could, should, would, right, two, four* and *goes*.

Tricky words

- Introduce the three new tricky words: *does, made* and *their*.
- The children look at the words in pink flowers at the top of the page.
- Point out that the letters ‹oe› in the word *does* make an /u/ sound.
- Point out that *made* is not really tricky, because the children now know that ‹a_e› can say /ai/.
- The children write inside the words *does, made* and *their* using a pink pencil.

Filling in the gaps

- The children trace inside the outline letters in the word *does*, saying the letter names as they do so.
- Then the children cover up all instances of the word *does* on their page and try to complete a column of this word, by tracing over the dotted letters and filling in the missing letters.
- The children repeat these steps for the words *made* and *their*.

Complete the sentences

- Read the first sentence, pausing at the gap:
    We ___ some cakes yesterday.
- Ask the children whether they think they should write *does, made,* or *their* in this gap.
- Read the sentence back to the children, including their chosen word, and ask them if they think the sentence makes sense with this word. The children write the correct word in the gap in their *Phonics Pupil Books*.
- The children read the next two sentences by themselves and decide which of the tricky words completes the sentence.
- They write the correct tricky word on the line in each sentence.

Dictation sentences

- Dictate the following sentences:
    He does not swim with the rest.
    She made a big car with some boxes.
    They hang their coats on the pegs.
- The children write these sentences on the lines in their *Phonics Pupil Books*.

Tricky word flowers

- The children look at the tricky words flowers at the bottom of their page.
- Read each tricky word with the children.
- The words are as follows: *should, would, right, two, four, goes.*
- The children colour the flowers using a pink pencil.

Further blending practice

- Write the following list of words on the board and blend them with the children:
    plum, complete, Saturday, starting, brakes.

Words and Sentences

Flash cards
- Revise some of the alternative letter sound spellings taught so far, including ‹ph›, soft ‹c›, soft ‹g› and ‹igh›.

Words and sentences
- Write the title on the board, *My Game*.
- Read the title with the children.
- Ask a child to say one sentence about his or her favourite game. For example, 'I love cricket.' 'I like to play chess.' 'We play tag.'
- You may need to stop the child at the end of their sentence, as most children will try to carry on.
- Ask some other children to say a sentence about their favourite games. Encourage the children to say a different sentence each.

Writing
- The children copy the title, *My Game*, onto the top line.
- They write as much as they can about their game on the remaining lines. The children might like to write about the rules of their game, or about the people they play it with.

Picture
- The children draw a picture illustrating their game in the picture frame.

Note 1: spelling
- At this stage, the children's spelling will not always be accurate, but their work will be readable.

Note 2: title
- Teachers should feel free to set their own writing subject. The title of the writing exercise does appear on the children's pages, but the picture frame is empty and the lines are blank. It may be that the children would like to write about a recent holiday they have celebrated, or a story they have heard. If this is the case, teachers can set their own title and guide the children's writing accordingly.

My Game

Further blending practice
- Write the following list of words on the board and blend them with the children:
    homemade,
    computer,
    chewing,
    ruler,
    tuned.

Reading sentences
- Write the following sentences on the board, pointing out the tricky words and blending any unknown words with the children.
1. The clowns did not amuse him.
2. Does she like the pink paint?
3. Their sister made a new floral dress.
4. Does the river flow by their home?

Comprehension

Flash cards
- Revise some of the alternative letter sound spellings taught so far, including ‹ph›, soft ‹c›, soft ‹g› and ‹igh›.

Comprehension: at the zoo
- The children look at the picture of the zoo, in the bottom right hand corner of their page.
- Read the first question to the children:
    How many animals are in the tree?
- The children should say that there are three monkeys in the tree.
- They write *three* on the line next to the first question.
- The children read the remaining questions and write the answers on the lines.
- The questions (with answers in brackets) are:
    1. How many animals are in the tree?
        (three)
    2. Which animal has a trunk?
        (the elephant)
    3. What sort of animal is an ostrich?
        (it is a bird)
    4. Where is the crocodile swimming?
        (in the pool)
    5. Who has black and white stripes?
        (the zebras)
    6. How many giraffes are there?
        (two)

Note 1: spelling
- At this stage, the children's spelling will not always be accurate, but their work will be readable. Spelling gradually improves through reading many books and learning the alternative letter-sound spellings.

Anagrams
- The children look at the word *elephants* on their page. Point out that a number of other words can be made from the letters of the word *elephants*.
- Say the word *sheep* to the children.
- Point out that all the letters in the word *sheep* can be found in the word *elephants*.

At the zoo: answer the questions by looking at the zoo picture underneath.

1. How many animals are in the tree?

2. Which animal has a trunk?

3. What sort of animal is an ostrich?

4. Where is the crocodile swimming?

5. Who has black and white stripes?

6. How many giraffes are there?

Make as many words as you can from the letters in the word:

elephants

sheep

30

- The children write over the dotted word *sheep*.
- Then they make as many words as they can from the letters in the word *elephants*.
- If plastic or magnetic letters are available, they can be very useful for this activity.
- The children can move the plastic letters around to try and make words. When they find a word they can copy it into their books.
- Examples of words made from the letters in *elephants* are:
    sheep, sleep, please, sea, she, he, pant, heel, peel, pale, sale, seal, plan, nap, tap, lap, heap, leap, help, ants, snap, hen, then, than, lean, pen, pan, let, set, pet, net and *sent*, but there are many more.

Further blending practice
- Write the following list of words on the board and blend them with the children:
    cracking, blend, fewer, further, freezing.

Alternatives: ‹ou› and ‹ow›

Flash cards
•Revise some of the alternative letter sound spellings taught so far, including ‹ph›, soft ‹c›, soft ‹g› and ‹igh›.

Alternatives: the /ou/ sound
•Remind the children of the two main ways to write the /ou/ sound: ‹ou› and ‹ow›.
•The children look at the /ou/ words on their page.
•Read these words with the children.
•The words are as follows:
>*flour, about, count,*
>*mouse, found, sound,*
>*flower, shower, brown,*
>*downhill, vowel, clown.*

‹ou› or ‹ow›?
•Read the first /ou/ word, *mouse*, and ask the children whether the /ou/ sound is spelt ‹ou› or ‹ow› in this word.
•They should say ‹ou›.
•Using a pink pencil, the children circle the letters making the /ou/ sound in the word *mouse*.
•Then they write over the dotted word *mouse* in the large pink ‹ou› digraph on their page.
•The children read the remaining words and circle the letters making the /ou/ sound in each word.
•Then they write the words in the corresponding digraphs on their page.

Further blending practice
•Write the following list of words on the board and blend them with the children:
>*greenhouse,*
>*cowshed,*
>*however,*
>*growl,*
>*found.*

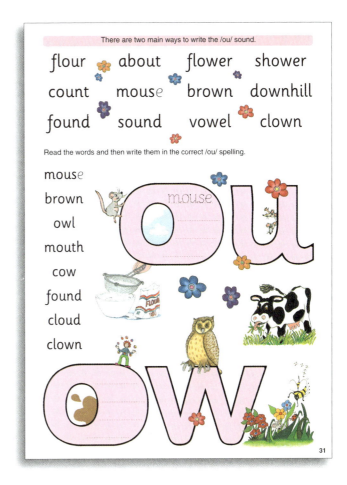

Reading sentences
•Write the following sentences on the board, pointing out the tricky words and blending any unknown words with the children.
1. Mum had a new blouse for her birthday.
2. There was a large crowd at the festival.
3. There are their hats and coats.
4. He does not want any more sandwiches.
5. We ate a thick stew at their house.
6. They made little statues from modelling clay.

Tricky Words and Dictation

Flash cards
- Revise some of the tricky words taught so far.

Tricky words
- Introduce the three new tricky words: *once, upon* and *always*.
- The children look at the words in brown flowers at the top of the page: *once, upon* and *always*.
- The children write inside the words *once, upon* and *always* using a brown pencil.

Filling in the gaps
- The children trace inside the outline letters in the word *once*, saying the letter names as they do so.
- Then the children cover up all instances of the word *once* on their page and try to complete a column of this word, by tracing over the dotted letters and filling in the missing letters.
- The children repeat these steps for the words *upon* and *always*.

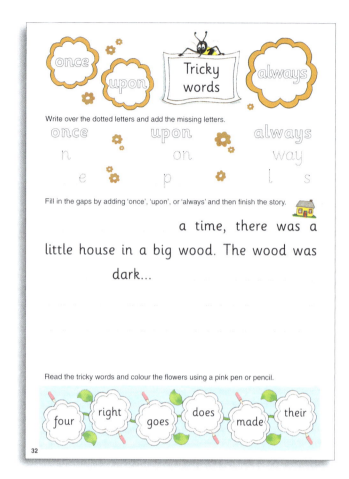

Complete the story
- This time, rather than completing sentences, the children have to fill in the gaps and complete a story.
- Read the first sentence to the children, pausing at the two gaps.

    ___ ___ a time, there was a little house in a big wood.

- Ask the children which of the three tricky words they have just learnt might come at the beginning of this sentence.
- Children's stories often begin with the phrase, 'Once upon a time...' and, with a bit of encouragement, the children should say *once* and *upon*.
- The children write *once* and *upon* in the first two gaps.
- Now read the first two sentences, including the two words filled in so far, and pause at the remaining gap.

    Once upon a time, there was a little house in a big wood. The wood was ___ dark.

- Ask the children whether they think the remaining tricky word, *always*, might fit in this gap. The children should agree that it does and write the word *always* in the final gap.
- The children read the two completed sentences again and finish the story on the remaining lines. They might like to continue their stories on some extra paper, which can then be stuck into their books.

Tricky word flowers
- The children look at the tricky words flowers at the bottom of their page.
- Read each tricky word with the children.
- The words are as follows:
  four, right, goes, does, made, their.
- The children colour the flowers using a pink pencil.

Words and Sentences

Flash cards
- Revise some of the alternative letter sound spellings taught so far, including ‹ph›, soft ‹c›, soft ‹g› and ‹igh›.

Words and sentences
- Read a story that the children know well and like.
- Write the title of the story on the board.
- Read the title with the children.
- Ask a child to say one sentence about the story. You may need to stop the child at the end of their sentence, as most children will try to carry on.
- Ask some other children to say a sentence about the story. Encourage the children to say a different sentence each.

Writing
- The children copy the title of the story onto the top line and re-tell the story on the remaining lines.

Picture
- The children draw a picture illustrating the story in the picture frame.

Note 1: spelling
- At this stage, the children's spelling will not always be accurate, but their work will be readable. Spelling gradually improves through reading many books and learning the alternative letter-sound spellings.

Note 2: title
- Teachers should feel free to set their own writing subject. The title of the writing exercise does appear on the children's pages, but the picture frame is empty and the lines are blank. It may be that the children would like to write about a recent holiday they have celebrated, or a story they have heard. If this is the case, teachers can set their own title and guide the children's writing accordingly.

Further blending practice
- Write the following list of words on the board and blend them with the children:

  crown,
  shouted,
  frowning,
  around,
  powder.

Reading sentences
- Write the following sentences on the board, pointing out the tricky words and blending any unknown words with the children.
  1. She is always bouncing up and down.
  2. They have only been to the park once.
  3. At night, I lay upon my bed.
  4. He always sings that song.

Comprehension

Flash cards
- Revise some of the alternative letter sound spellings taught so far, including ‹ph›, soft ‹c›, soft ‹g› and ‹igh›.

Comprehension: at the park
- The children look carefully at the picture of the park.
- Discuss the picture with the children.
- Read the first sentence to the children, pausing at the gap:

   The dog is carrying a ___.
- Point out the two words next to the sentence, *stick* and *stuck*.
- Ask the children whether the dog in the picture is carrying a *stick* or a *stuck*.
- The children should say a *stick*.
- The children circle the word *stick* and write this word in the gap to complete the sentence.
- The children read the remaining sentences to themselves and complete each sentence by writing the correct word in the gap.
- The completed sentences are:
   1. The dog is carrying a (stick).
   2. There is a cat in the (tree).
   3. The fox is looking at the (rabbit).
   4. The ducks (quack) on the pond.
   5. The boys have a bat and (ball).
   6. The bird is (singing).

Further blending practice
- Write the following list of words on the board and blend them with the children:

   without,
   sprouting,
   showery,
   about,
   salute,
   outing,
   mounted,
   coaches,
   sunflower,
   power.

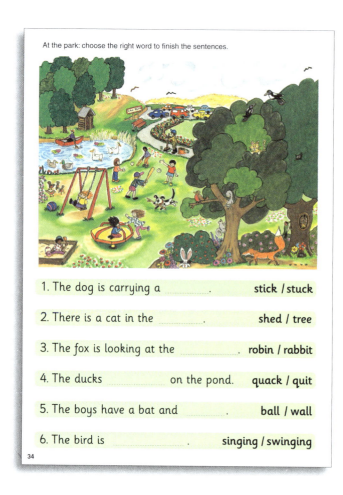

At the park: choose the right word to finish the sentences.

1. The dog is carrying a _____.	stick / stuck
2. There is a cat in the _____.	shed / tree
3. The fox is looking at the _____.	robin / rabbit
4. The ducks _____ on the pond.	quack / quit
5. The boys have a bat and _____.	ball / wall
6. The bird is _____.	singing / swinging

34

Reading sentences
- Write the following sentences on the board, pointing out the tricky words and blending any unknown words with the children.
   1. We always want more vegetables.
   2. We must sift the flour into a bowl.
   3. It is always hot when the sun is out.
   4. Mum and I went camping by the lake once.
   5. Those angry dogs always bark loudly.
   6. Once upon a time, there was a frog who turned into a prince.

Alternatives: ‹oi› and ‹oy›

Flash cards
- Revise some of the alternative letter sound spellings taught so far, including ‹ph›, soft ‹c›, soft ‹g› and ‹igh›.

Alternatives: the /oi/ sound
- Remind the children of the two main ways to write the /oi/ sound: ‹oi› and ‹oy›.
- Remind the children that the ‹oy› spelling usually comes at the end of a word. Tell them that this is because the letter ‹i› is too shy to go at the end of a word, so its cousin, 'toughy y' takes its place.
- The children look at the /oi/ words on their page.
- Read these words with the children.
- The words are as follows:

  royal, boy, annoy, enjoy, toys, joy, spoil, coin, oil, point, join, boil.

‹oi› or ‹oy›?
- Read the first /oi/ word, *point*, and ask the children whether the /o/ sound is spelt ‹oi› or ‹oy› in this word.
- They should say ‹oi›.
- Using a grey pencil, the children circle the letters making the /oi/ sound in the word *point*.
- Then they write over the dotted word *point* in the large grey ‹oi› digraph on their page.
- The children read the remaining words and circle the letters making the /oi/ sound in each word.
- Then they write the words in the corresponding digraphs on their page.

Further blending practice
- Write the following list of words on the board and blend them with the children:

  *spoilt,
  royalty,
  ointment,
  flowerpot,
  joystick.*

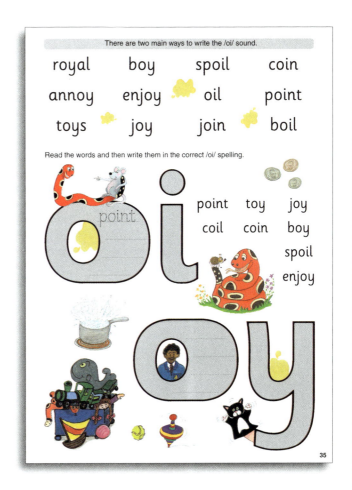

Reading sentences
- Write the following sentences on the board, pointing out the tricky words and blending any unknown words with the children.
  1. We should put tinfoil around this dish.
  2. They avoid the deep river.
  3. Have you ever eaten oysters?
  4. I put the sunflower seeds in the soil.
  5. You are one of the noisiest boys here.
  6. Her painting is spoilt now.

Tricky Words and Dictation

Flash cards
- Use the flash cards, or *Tricky Word Wall Flowers*, to revise some of the tricky words taught so far, including *once, upon* and *always*.

Tricky words
- Introduce the three new tricky words: *also, of* and *eight*.
- The children look at the words in brown flowers at the top of the page: *also, of* and *eight*.
- The children write inside the words *also, of* and *eight* using a brown pencil.

Filling in the gaps
- The children trace inside the outline letters in the word *also*, saying the letter names as they do so.
- Then the children cover up all instances of the word *also* on their page and try to complete a column of this word, by tracing over the dotted letters and filling in the missing letters.
- The children repeat these steps for the words *of* and *eight*.

Dictation sentences
- Dictate the following sentences:
  She also waits for the bus.
  They counted eight hundred ants.
  She put a pinch of nutmeg in the mix.
- The children write these sentences on the lines in their *Phonics Pupil Books*.

Complete the sentences
- Read the first sentence, pausing at the gap:
  There are lots ___ sheep on the farm.
- Ask the children whether they think they should write *also, of* or *eight* in this gap.
- Read the sentence back to the children, including their chosen word, and ask them if they think the sentence makes sense with this word.
- The children write the correct word in the gap in their *Phonics Pupil Books*.

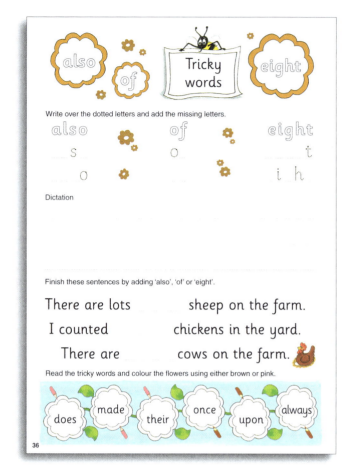

- The children read the next two sentences by themselves and decide which of the tricky words completes the sentence.
- They write the correct tricky word on the line in each sentence.

Tricky word flowers
- The children look at the tricky words flowers at the bottom of their page.
- Read each tricky word with the children.
- The words are:
  does, made, their, once, upon, always.
- The children colour the flowers using a pink or brown pencil.

Further blending practice
- Write the following list of words on the board and blend them with the children:
  enjoying, pointed, destroys, ahoy, employ.

Words and Sentences

Flash cards
• Revise some of the alternative letter sound spellings taught so far, including ⟨ph⟩, soft ⟨c⟩, soft ⟨g⟩ and ⟨igh⟩.

Words and sentences
• Write the title on the board, *My Best Story*.
• Read the title with the children.
• Pick one child and ask him or her for the title of their favourite story.
• Ask the child to describe, very briefly, what happens in the story.
• Ask some other children to say a sentence about their favourite stories. Encourage the children to say a different sentence each.

Writing
• The children write the title of their favourite story on the top line.
• They write as much as they can about their favourite stories on the remaining lines.

Picture
• The children draw a picture illustrating their favourite story in the picture frame.

Note 1: spelling
• At this stage, the children's spelling will not always be accurate, but their work will be readable. Spelling gradually improves through reading many books and learning the alternative letter-sound spellings.

Note 2: title
• Teachers should feel free to set their own writing subject. The title of the writing exercise does appear on the children's pages, but the picture frame is empty and the lines are blank. It may be that the children would like to write about a recent holiday they have celebrated, or a story they have heard. If this is the case, teachers can set their own title and guide the children's writing accordingly.

Further blending practice
• Write the following list of words on the board and blend them with the children:
    plays,
    twenty,
    squirrel,
    film,
    coy.

Reading sentences
• Write the following sentences on the board, pointing out the tricky words and blending any unknown words with the children.
    1. We go on holiday in eight days' time.
    2. There are lots of sticks on the ground.
    3. Are you afraid of the dark?
    4. We also play cricket in the summer.

Comprehension

Flash cards
- Revise some of the alternative letter sound spellings taught so far.

Comprehension: Moat Farm
- Read the story *Moat Farm* to the children.
- If you have enough copies of the *Jolly Phonics Reader, Moat Farm*, the children could read the story for themselves. Alternatively, you could write the story on the board for the children to read. The story is as follows:

Moat Farm
This is Moat Farm.
Farmer Green lives on Moat Farm.
Ben and Neb are sheepdogs.
Neb and Ben help on the farm.
This morning, Ben and Neb run up the hill...
...and help round up the sheep.
Farmer Green checks that the sheep are well.
Neb and Ben rest in the back of the truck.

- The children look at the comic strip version of *Moat Farm* on their page.
- Point out that there are a number of words missing from the story. Explain that the missing words are printed at the top of the page.
- Read the first sentence, pausing at the gap:
  This is Moat ___.
- Ask the children which of the words at the top of the page should go in this gap.
- They should say *Farm*. The children write this word in the gap, and cross it out at the top of the page.
- The children read the remaining sentences to themselves and fill in the gaps as follows:
  1. This is Moat (Farm).
  2. Farmer Green (lives) on Moat Farm.
  3. Ben and Neb are (sheepdogs).
  4. (Neb) and (Ben) help on the farm.
  5. This morning, Ben and Neb run up the (hill) and help round up...
  6. ...the (sheep).
  7. Farmer (Green) checks that the sheep are well.
  8. Neb and Ben rest in the back of the (truck).

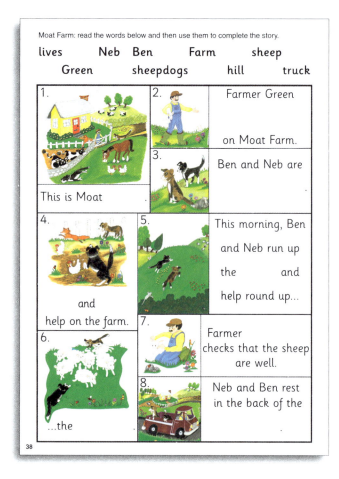

Moat Farm: read the words below and then use them to complete the story.

lives   Neb   Ben   Farm   sheep
Green   sheepdogs   hill   truck

Further blending practice
- Write the following list of words on the board and blend them with the children:
  tractor,
  farmhouse,
  fence,
  dungarees,
  helping.

Reading sentences
- Write the following sentences on the board, pointing out the tricky words and blending any unknown words with the children.
  1. Farmer Green has a flock of sheep.
  2. Ben has black fur, but Neb's fur is brown.
  3. Farmer Green also has eight cows.
  4. A fox tried to steal one of the chickens.

Alternatives: ‹er›, ‹ir› and ‹ur›

Flash cards
· Revise some of the alternative letter sound spellings taught so far, including ‹ph›, soft ‹c›, soft ‹g› and ‹igh›.

Alternatives: the /er/ sound
· Remind the children of the three main ways to write the /er/ sound: ‹er›, ‹ir› and ‹ur›.
· Point out that, when the /er/ sound comes at the end of a word, it is often spelt ‹er›.
· Point out that the /er/ sound in the days of the week, *Saturday* and *Thursday*, is spelt ‹ur›.
· The children look at the /er/ words on their page.
· Read these words with the children.
· The words are as follows:
> *helicopter, sister, numbers, cooker,*
> *girl, thirsty, third, bird,*
> *Saturday, purple, Thursday, hurt.*

‹er›, ‹ir› or ‹ur›?
· Read the first /er/ word, *dinner*, and ask the children whether the /er/ sound is spelt ‹er›, ‹ir› or ‹ur› in this word.
· They should say ‹er›.
· Using a blue pencil, the children circle the letters making the /er/ sound in the word *dinner*.
· Then they write over the dotted word *dinner* in the large blue ‹er› digraph on their page.
· The children read the remaining words and circle the letters making the /er/ sound in each word.
· Then they write the words in the corresponding digraphs on their page.

Further blending practice
· Write the following list of words on the board and blend them with the children:
> *sunburnt,*
> *thunder,*
> *thirteen,*
> *tweezers,*
> *burger.*

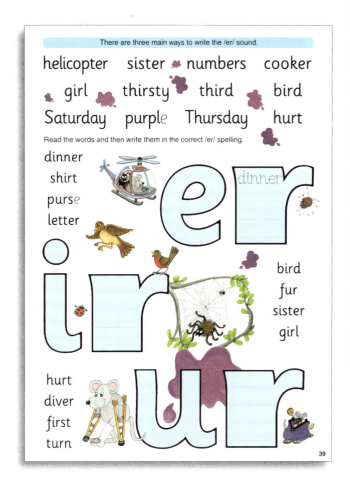

There are three main ways to write the /er/ sound.

helicopter   sister   numbers   cooker
girl   thirsty   third   bird
Saturday   purple   Thursday   hurt

Read the words and then write them in the correct /er/ spelling.

dinner
shirt
purse
letter

hurt
diver
first
turn

dinner

bird
fur
sister
girl

er
ir
ur

39

Reading sentences
· Write the following sentences on the board, pointing out the tricky words and blending any unknown words with the children.
1. On Thursday we will have supper together.
2. She is better at swimming than we are.
3. Some of those stones are quite dirty.
4. Your new shirt is also very smart.
5. All spiders have eight legs.
6. We would also like to join the club.

Tricky Words and Dictation

Flash cards
- Use the flash cards, or *Tricky Word Wall Flowers*, to revise some of the tricky words taught so far, including *also, of* and *eight*.

Tricky words
- Introduce the three new tricky words: *love, cover* and *after*.
- The children look at the words in brown flowers at the top of the page.
- Point out that the ‹o› in the words *love* and *cover* makes an /u/ sound.
- The children write inside the words *love, cover* and *after* using a brown pencil.

Filling in the gaps
- The children trace inside the outline letters in the word *love*, saying the letter names as they do so.
- Then the children cover up all instances of the word *love* on their page and try to complete a column of this word, by tracing over the dotted letters and filling in the missing letters.
- The children repeat these steps for the words *cover* and *after*.

Dictation sentences
- Dictate the following sentences:
  We love our dog.
  She has a pink cover on her bed.
  We went out after lunch.
- The children write these sentences on the lines in their *Phonics Pupil Books*.

Complete the sentences
- Read the first sentence, pausing at the gap:
  I ___ to go swimming.
- Ask the children whether they think they should write *love, cover,* or *after* in this gap.
- Read the sentence back to the children, including their chosen word, and ask them if they think the sentence makes sense with this word.
- The children write the correct word in the gap in their *Phonics Pupil Books*.

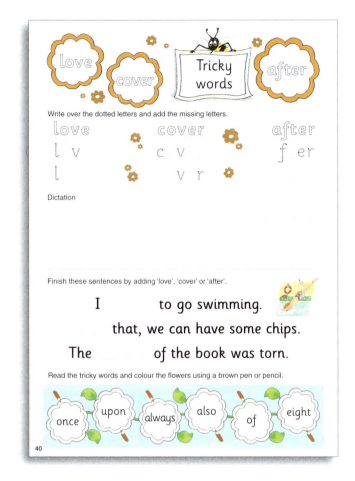

- The children read the next two sentences by themselves and decide which of the tricky words completes the sentence.
- They write the correct tricky word on the line in each sentence.

Tricky word flowers
- The children look at the tricky words flowers at the bottom of their page.
- Read each tricky word with the children.
- The words are as follows:
  once, upon, always, also, of, eight.
- The children colour the flowers using a brown pencil.

Further blending practice
- Write the following list of words on the board and blend them with the children:
  loyal, squirt, twirling, fur, returns.

Words and Sentences

Flash cards
· Revise some of the alternative letter sound spellings taught so far, including ‹ph›, soft ‹c›, soft ‹g› and ‹igh›.

Words and sentences
· Write the title on the board, *Inky's Day Out*.
· Read the title with the children.
· Discuss day trips with the children.
· Ask a child to say one sentence about a recent day out. For example, 'We went to the seaside.' 'Granny took me to the park.' 'I went on a boat.'
· Then ask the children where they think Inky and her friends might go on a day out.
· Encourage the children to say a different sentence each.

Writing
· The children write the title, *Inky's Day Out*, on the top line.
· They write their own story about Inky's day out on the remaining lines.

Picture
· The children illustrate their story about Inky in the picture frame.

Note 1: spelling
· At this stage, the children's spelling will not always be accurate, but their work will be readable. Spelling gradually improves through reading many books and learning the alternative letter-sound spellings.

Note 2: title
· Teachers should feel free to set their own writing subject. The title of the writing exercise does appear on the children's pages, but the picture frame is empty and the lines are blank. It may be that the children would like to write about a recent holiday they have celebrated, or a story they have heard. If this is the case, teachers can set their own title and guide the children's writing accordingly.

Further blending practice
· Write the following list of words on the board and blend them with the children:
> *nightingale,*
> *untied,*
> *myself,*
> *brighter,*
> *highest.*

Reading sentences
· Write the following sentences on the board, pointing out the tricky words and blending any unknown words with the children.
1. I love to make snowmen in winter.
2. Did you remember to cover the cakes?
3. She twirls and spins in her new skirt.
4. We can see the sharks after looking at the dolphins.

Comprehension

Flash cards
• Revise some of the alternative letter sound spellings taught so far, including ‹ph›, soft ‹c›, soft ‹g› and ‹igh›.

Crossword
• The children read each crossword clue.
• They write the answer to each clue, starting at the correct square.
• The clues (with answers in brackets) are:
  1. This will help you find your way.
     (map)
  2. This heats food for you to eat.
     (cooker)
  3. A small insect that lives in a nest underground.
     (ant)
  4. If you go camping, you may sleep in this.
     (tent)
  5. You wash with ___ and water.
     (soap)
  6. An animal that hisses.
     (snake)
  7. The time of year when it is cold.
     (winter)
  8. A chick hatches from this.
     (egg)
  9. This is on the end of your arm.
     (hand)
  10. A sort of stone.
      (rock)
  11. The sky is blue and the trees are ___.
      (green)
  12. At night it is ___.
      (dark)

Read the clues and write the answers in the crossword grid.

1. This will help you to find your way.
2. This heats food for you to eat.
3. This small insect lives in a nest underground.
4. If you go camping, you may sleep in this.
5. You wash with   and water.
6. This animal hisses.
7. The time of year when it is cold.
8. A chick hatches from this.
9. This is on the end of your arm.
10. A sort of stone.
11. The sky is blue and the trees are
12. At night it is

42

Reading sentences
• Write the following sentences on the board, pointing out the tricky words and blending any unknown words with the children.
  1. They cover the food with butter and herbs.
  2. I love my Mum and Dad very much.
  3. We could have a running race after skipping.
  4. Nine comes after eight, but before ten.
  5. Cover the pot with this cloth.
  6. I would love to come to your party.

Further blending practice
• Write the following list of words on the board and blend them with the children:
  one, two, three, four, five, six, seven, eight, nine, ten.

Handwriting and Comprehension

Flash cards
- Revise some of the alternative letter sound spellings taught so far, including ‹ph›, soft ‹c›, soft ‹g› and ‹igh›.

Handwriting: the alphabet
- The children revise writing the capital letters for the alphabet.
- Take down, or cover, any visible copies of the alphabet so that the children have to remember how the capital letters are written.
- The children write inside each lower-case outline letter and then write the corresponding capital letter next to it.
- They use a red pencil for the letters A–E, a yellow pencil for the letters F–M, a green pencil for the letters N–S and a blue pencil for the letters T–Z.

Comprehension
- The children read each sentence and complete the picture so that it matches the sentence.
- The first sentence is:
    The boy has a blue drum.
- The children colour the boy's drum blue.
- The second sentence is:
    There are six red fish.
- There are five red fish in the picture and one black and white fish. The children colour this fish red.

Further blending practice
- Write the following list of words on the board and blend them with the children:
    sharper,
    neater,
    urban,
    thirsty,
    casserole.

Write inside each lower-case letter and write the capital letter next to it.

A a b c d e
f g h i
j k l m
n o p q r s
t u v w
x y z

Read each sentence and then colour the picture to match.

The boy has a blue drum.   There are six red fish.

43

Reading sentences
- Write the following sentences on the board, pointing out the tricky words and blending any unknown words with the children.
  1. You must look before you cross the road.
  2. Shall we have another game of tennis?
  3. He only cried after he fell off the stool.
  4. The bed cover has purple polka dots.
  5. We should put the ball away after our game.
  6. Who does this phone belong to?

Alternatives: ‹air›, ‹ear› and ‹are›

Flash cards
- Revise some of the alternative letter sound spellings taught so far, including ‹ph›, soft ‹c›, soft ‹g› and ‹igh›.

Alternatives: the /air/ sound
- The /air/ sound, as in the word *fair*, is a new sound for the children.
- The children look at the /air/ words on their page.
- Read these words with the children.
- The words are as follows:

  fairy, stairs, chair, pair,
  bear, wear, tear, pear,
  scarecrow, hare, square, dare.

- Point out the letters making the /air/ sound in each word.
- Explain that the /air/ sound is usually spelt ‹air›, ‹ear›, or ‹are›.

‹air›, ‹ear› or ‹are›?
- The children look at the bears and salmon on their page.
- The children read each word in the salmon and circle the letters making the /air/ sound.
- The children look at the first bear. The bear has a picture of a pear on its back.
- The children find the salmon containing the word *pear* and join it to this bear.
- They do the same with the remaining bears.
- When the children have joined all the bears to the correct salmon, they colour the /air/ pictures inside the bears.

Further blending practice
- Write the following list of words on the board and blend them with the children:

  hairy,
  spare,
  wearing,
  rare,
  fairly.

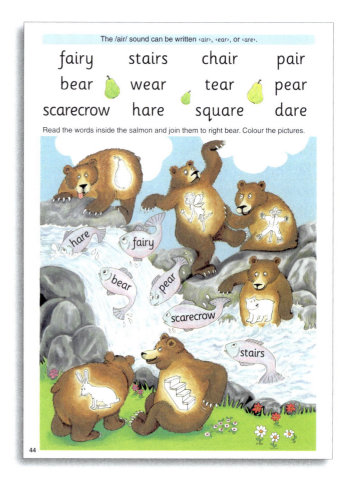

The /air/ sound can be written ‹air›, ‹ear›, or ‹are›.

fairy   stairs   chair   pair
bear   wear   tear   pear
scarecrow   hare   square   dare

Read the words inside the salmon and join them to right bear. Colour the pictures.

44

Reading sentences
- Write the following sentences on the board, pointing out the tricky words and blending any unknown words with the children.
1. I love this teddy bear most of all.
2. They went to the fair without their sister.
3. I was not scared by the phantom.
4. The hot-air balloon flew very high.
5. She has long brown hair.
6. We should share the puppets with those girls.

Tricky Words and Dictation

Flash cards
- Use the flash cards, or *Tricky Word Wall Flowers*, to revise some of the tricky words taught so far, including *once, upon, always, also, of, eight, love, cover* and *after*.

Tricky words
- Introduce the three new tricky words: *every, mother* and *father*.
- The children look at the words in brown flowers at the top of the page: *every, mother* and *father*.
- Encourage the children to use the 'say it as it sounds' technique when writing *mother* and *father*. They should say *mother* as though it rhymes with *bother*, and *father* as though it rhymes with *gather*.
- The children write inside the words *every, mother* and *father* using a brown pencil.

Filling in the gaps
- The children trace inside the outline letters in the word *every*, saying the letter names as they do so.
- Then the children cover up all instances of the word *every* on their page and try to complete a column of this word, by tracing over the dotted letters and filling in the missing letters.
- The children repeat these steps for the words *mother* and *father*.

Complete the sentences
- Read the first sentence to the children, pausing at the two gaps:
  My ___ and ___ are my parents.
- Ask the children which of the three tricky words they have just learnt might fit in the gaps in this sentence.
- They should write *mother* and *father* in the gaps.
- The children read the next sentence by themselves and decide which tricky word completes the sentence.
- They write the correct tricky word on the line.

Dictation sentences
- Dictate the following sentences:
  He gets a comic every week.
  She painted a card for her mother.
  Father took us to the park.
- The children write these sentences on the lines in their *Phonics Pupil Books*.

Tricky word flowers.
- The children look at the tricky words flowers at the bottom of their page.
- Read each tricky word with the children.
- The words are as follows:
  also, of, eight, love, cover, after.
- The children colour the flowers using a brown pencil.

Further blending practice
- Write the following list of words on the board and blend them with the children:
  flair, everyone, care, parent, prepare.

Words and Sentences

Flash cards
• Revise some of the alternative letter sound spellings taught so far, including ‹ph›, soft ‹c›, soft ‹g›, ‹igh› and the three ways of writing the /air/ sound.

Words and sentences
• Write the title on the board, *In the old tree lived...*
• Read the title with the children.
• Ask the children what kind of creature, or creatures, might live in the old tree.
• Encourage the children discuss what they think the creature looks like, or the kinds of things the creature might like to do.
• Try to develop the children's ideas into a story.
• If the children struggle to come up with ideas, the class could read the Jolly Reader *The Tree That Blinked*.

Writing
• The children write the title, *In the old tree lived...* on the top line.
• They write a story about the old tree and its inhabitants on the remaining lines.
• The children could write their own story, or the write story discussed by the class.

Picture
• The children illustrate their story in the picture frame.

Note 1: spelling
• At this stage, the children's spelling will not always be accurate, but their work will be readable. Spelling gradually improves through reading many books and learning the alternative letter-sound spellings.

Note 2: title
• Teachers should feel free to set their own writing subject. The title of the writing exercise does appear on the children's pages, but the picture frame is empty and the lines are blank.

In the old tree lived...

46

• It may be that the children would like to write about a recent holiday they have celebrated, or a story they have heard. If this is the case, teachers can set their own title and guide the children's writing accordingly.

Further blending practice
• Write the following list of words on the board and blend them with the children:
repair, beaten, stare, glare, tearing.
• Write the following sentences on the board, pointing out the tricky words and blending any unknown words with the children.
1. My father will pay my train fare.
2. You only say 'snap' when you have a pair.
3. Every day he sits in the same chair.
4. My mother is wearing her new beads.
5. In a square, every side is the same length.
6. My mother and father are playing chess.

Comprehension

Flash cards
• Revise some of the alternative letter sound spellings taught so far, including ‹ph›, soft ‹c›, soft ‹g›, ‹igh› and the three ways of writing the /air/ sound.

Story: The Midnight Feast
• The children look at the story, *The Midnight Feast*, on their page.
• Read the story with the children.
• The story is as follows:

The Midnight Feast

Once upon a time, there was a king called Alfred. His wife was Queen Matilda. They lived in a castle, with a cat called Fluffy. One night, King Alfred was hungry. So he got up and made himself some cheese sandwiches to eat. Some crumbs from the sandwich fell onto the floor.

A mouse saw the crumbs from her mouse hole in the corner of the room. She could have a midnight feast, if she was quick and quiet. She crept out, and had just reached the crumbs, when Fluffy looked into the room. The mouse ran for her hole as quickly as she could. Fluffy ran for the mouse as quickly as he could.

The mouse reached her hole hungry, but safe!

Comprehension: The Midnight Feast
• Read the first question to the children.
  What is the king's name?
• The children might not be able to remember the king's name.
• If the children are struggling, encourage them to look for the answer in the story in their books.
• The children write their answer on the line next to the first question.
• The children read the remaining questions to themselves, writing their answers on the lines.

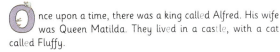

Read the story and answer the questions below.

Once upon a time, there was a king called Alfred. His wife was Queen Matilda. They lived in a castle, with a cat called Fluffy.

One night, King Alfred was hungry. So he got up and made himself some cheese sandwiches to eat. Some crumbs from the sandwich fell onto the floor.

A mouse saw the crumbs from her mouse hole in the corner of the room. She could have a midnight feast, if she was quick and quiet. She crept out, and had just reached the crumbs, when Fluffy looked into the room. The mouse ran for her hole as quickly as she could. Fluffy ran for the mouse as quickly as he could.

The mouse reached her hole hungry, but safe!

1. What is the king's name?
2. What is the queen's name?
3. What sort of animal is Fluffy?
4. What did King Alfred make to eat?
5. Who saw the crumbs on the floor?
6. Who saw the mouse?
7. Did the cat catch the mouse?

47

Further blending practice
• Write the following list of words on the board and blend them with the children:
  royalty,
  throne,
  golden,
  crumbly,
  quickly.

Reading sentences
• Write the following sentences on the board, pointing out the tricky words and blending any unknown words with the children.
1. Fluffy loves to chase mice.
2. Every mouse likes to eat cheese sandwiches.
3. Fluffy has ginger fur and a long tail.
4. Does the little mouse manage to escape?

Words and Sentences

Flash cards
- Revise some of the alternative letter sound spellings taught so far, including ‹ph›, soft ‹c›, soft ‹g›, ‹igh› and the three ways of writing the /air/ sound.

Words and sentences: celebrations
- Discuss a recent party or celebration with the children. For example, the class might discuss a carnival, a festival, a family celebration, or a birthday party they have been to recently.
- Read the first incomplete sentence on the children's page.

    We had a party for ___.
- Ask a child to say one sentence about why he or she was celebrating. For example, 'I got a new sister.' 'It was my birthday.'
- You may need to stop the child at the end of their sentence, as most children will try to carry on.
- Read the next incomplete sentence on the children's page.

    We ate some ___.
- Ask a different child to say a sentence about the special celebration food he or she ate. For example, 'We ate cake.' 'We ate carnival food.'
- The children complete the sentences on their page and write some sentences of their own on the remaining lines.
- The children illustrate each of their sentences in the picture frames.

Note 1: spelling
- At this stage, the children's spelling will not always be accurate, but their work will be readable.
- Spelling gradually improves through reading many books and learning the alternative letter-sound spellings.

Complete the sentences writing about a recent birthday, or a holiday celebration. Illustrate what you write in the frames.

We had a party for

We ate some

48

Further blending practice
- Write the following list of words on the board and blend them with the children:

    festival,
    feast,
    celebrate,
    enjoyment,
    carnival.

Reading sentences
- Write the following sentences on the board, pointing out the tricky words and blending any unknown words with the children.
1. We all lit lanterns at midnight.
2. We blew up one hundred yellow balloons.
3. The children were wearing lovely costumes.
4. There was drumming and singing at the carnival.

After the Phonics Pupil Books

For most children, the simple step-by-step teaching in the *Phonics Pupil Books 1, 2* and *3* will enable them to progress steadily, master the basic skills and read and write at an early age.

When the children have completed *Phonics Pupil Books 1, 2* and *3*, they should be able to do the following:

• Read and write the main 42 letter sounds,
• Recognise the alternative letter-sound spellings that have been introduced (when reading),
• Form letters correctly, using the tripod grip,
• Blend regular words that use the 42 letter sounds, for example, *sheep, teeth, raindrop, trip,*
• Blend words containing the alternative letter-sound spellings that have been introduced, for example, *happy, cage, kite, alphabet,*
• Write simple words, by listening for the sounds and writing the appropriate letters,
• Read the 72 tricky words and know how to spell many of them,
• Read the *Jolly Phonics Readers*, or equivalent decodable books, with some children progressing as far as the blue level of the *Jolly Phonics Readers*.

Most of the children in a class will be at, or approaching, this stage. However, in every class there will be a few children who find it difficult to memorise the letter sounds and who struggle to blend and segment words. These children tend to have a weak visual memory and poor auditory skills. However, this does not mean that they need different teaching from the more able children. In fact, they need the same teaching, but far more of it.

It is necessary to identify any struggling children at an early stage. It is a good idea to provide some extra teaching for these children if possible. Not all of the children who are struggling will be at the same stage; there will be a range of abilities. Some children will only need extra support for a few weeks before they begin to make steady progress. Other children may have more significant difficulties. Despite their differences, all the children should receive the same type of teaching. With regular blending and writing practice and by revising the letter sounds, teachers can ensure that the children master the five skills.

It is important to note that, if the children have a school holiday after completing *Phonics Pupil Book 3*, or indeed at any point during the year, they will need to spend some time revising the skills they have already learnt before moving on to the next step. This next step involves learning the more complex aspects of the written English language; these are taught in the *Grammar 1 Pupil and Teacher's Books*.

The Grammar 1 Pupil and Teacher's Books

The teaching in the *Grammar 1 Pupil Book* follows on from the teaching in the *Phonics Pupil Books 1*, *2* and *3*. The spelling exercises in the *Grammar 1 Pupil Book* help to reinforce the children's knowledge of the digraphs. These spelling exercises not only help those children who still struggle with the digraphs, but also encourage all the children towards more accurate writing and spelling.

The *Grammar 1 Pupil and Teacher's Books* also introduce the children to the rudiments of grammar. The children have already gained an understanding of basic sentence structure from the activities in the *Phonics Pupil Books* and the exercises in the *Grammar 1 Pupil Book* build upon this basic understanding by teaching the children about punctuation, alphabetical order, dictionary work and parts of speech.

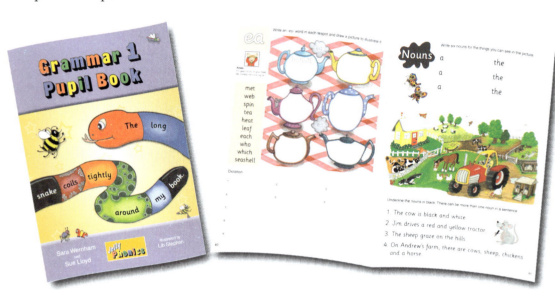